Audit and Accountancy Pitfalls

A Casebook for Practising Accountants, Lawyers and Insurers

Emile Woolf FCA
Moira Hindson FCA MAE MEWI

WILEY
A John Wiley and Sons, Ltd., Publication

This edition first published 2011

Registered office
John Wiley & Sons Ltd, The Atrium, Southern Gate, Chichester, West Sussex, PO19 8SQ, United Kingdom

For details of our global editorial offices, for customer services and for information about how to apply for permission to reuse the copyright material in this book please see our website at www.wiley.com.

Library of Congress Cataloging-in-Publication Data

Woolf, Emile.
Audit and accountancy pitfalls : a casebook for practising accountants, lawyers, and insurers/ Emile Woolf, Moira Hindson.
p. cm.
Includes index.
ISBN 978-0-470-68667-6
1. Accounting fraud. 2. Forensic accounting. 3. Auditing. I. Hindson, Moira. II. Title.
HF5636.W875 2010
657′.45–dc22
2010030443

ISBN: 978-0-470-68667-6

A catalogue record for this book is available from the British Library.

Typeset in 11/13pt Times by Aptara Inc., New Delhi, India
Printed in Great Britain by TJ International Ltd, Padstow, Cornwall.

Contents

Preface

As well as those involved directly in auditing and accountancy, the professionals who will find this book relevant to their work include solicitors and barristers involved with the professional negligence of accountants, as well as those working in the claims departments of leading brokers and underwriters who, in the majority of instances, are called upon to pay the piper.

Although the majority of cases referred to in this book are based on our direct experience in the field of forensic accountancy and expert witness work, a number of examples have been taken from insurers' case files that we have examined, as well as from the authors' Accountants' Digest 'Professional Liability of Practising Accountants' published by CCH and the Institute of Chartered Accountants in England and Wales (Copyright: Wolters Kluwer (UK) Ltd). We have also incorporated certain relevant passages from the latter publication, in respect of which we acknowledge the kind permission of the publishers.

Acknowledgements are also due to the partners and staff at Kingston Smith LLP who over the years have unstintingly provided us with their time and expertise. Perhaps the most important acknowledgement is to the unnamed accountants, lawyers and insurers whose woeful 'tales of the unexpected' have given us gainful employment for a quarter of a century, and whose lessons we are now happy to share.

Some of the terminology used in the text may be unfamiliar to readers and for this reason we append a glossary of terms following the final chapter.

1
Introduction

1.1 STAYING OUT OF TROUBLE

In this book, we do not explain the aptitudes demanded for a career in forensic accountancy. Nor do we provide a technical analysis of accounting and auditing requirements. In short, this book is not a text on how to become a forensic accountant, but instead it is about how to avoid *needing* a forensic accountant. Therefore, our purpose is practical and directly relevant to the work of accountants and auditors in public practice, the lawyers who act for them when trouble threatens and, of course, the insurers who underwrite their obligatory indemnity policies.

In compiling this text we have extracted the essential lessons that the circumstances hold for the generality of practising accountants. These lessons are distilled from hundreds of cases, in all of which accountants/auditors have found themselves in the legal or disciplinary firing line. For many years we have been personally involved in assessing the merits of claims brought against accountants for the benefit of the legal advisors of either defendants or claimants. Indeed, most of the cases that feature in this book, all of which are taken from 'real life', have been drawn from our own extensive case-book. All names used in these cases are, for obvious reasons, fictitious!

From the above it will be clear that this book is not a theoretical treatise. It is a first-hand account of the consequences, for accountants, of the myriad types of mistake that would have been eminently avoidable 'if only they had . . .' whatever! After a combined experience of some 40 years in the business of forensic accountancy the authors have several enduring messages to pass on to professional colleagues everywhere.

Although most of the litigation described in this book is UK-based, there are no territorial barriers to allegations of negligence where accountants are concerned. Financial statements are universally required to present an entity's financial results and position 'fairly' or to 'give a true and fair view'; and the methodology whereby auditors put themselves in a position to append their imprimatur is increasingly standardised and globally adopted.

This text is divided broadly by reference to subject matter. However, there are no neat boundaries to the areas in which accountants can find themselves in difficulty. For example, issues that we have included in Chapters 2 and 3 on auditors' negligence may equally arise in the disciplinary context (Chapter 6), and claims arising from fee disputes, dealing with chaotic clients and failure to maintain adequate file documentation will give rise to lessons under several headings. Similarly, allegations of negligence may arise when accountants undertake specialist share valuations and when auditors are instructed to value shares held by parties in dispute – in this book such instances will be found in Chapters 2 and 3 on auditors' negligence and Chapter 4 on accountants' negligence. The apparent overlap of subject matter should therefore be understood in this context.

1.2 THE FORENSIC ACCOUNTANT'S ROLE

Although this book is not about how to become a forensic accountant, it would not have been possible to write it if the authors had not spent so many years in the roles of forensic accountant and expert witness, principally in the area of accountants' negligence and disciplinary transgressions.

The book is aimed primarily at practising accountants, their legal representatives and insurers. Although it is bound to be of interest to forensic accountants and expert witnesses, that interest is incidental and this section of the introductory chapter merely sets the scene by describing the rigorous disciplines that the authors have been subject to in the course of their long involvement with accountants' litigation. It is this experience that informs the subject matter of the chapters that follow.

The term 'forensic' is derived from the Latin 'forum', or meeting place. The modern term has been coined to connote a relationship with the forum of the Courts or with legal matters generally. Thus, *forensic accountancy* means the use of accountancy knowledge to assist the Courts, or in seeking otherwise to resolve legal disputes.

It is obvious that the technicalities of accounting, auditing and other specialisms within the accountant's skill-set are not widely understood by non-accountants. If, therefore, in the context of a legal dispute, the conduct of an accountant is in issue, the parties, their legal advisers and, ultimately, the Court will require 'expert' evidence from one or more independent accountants. This is why forensic accountants are frequently called upon to act as 'expert witnesses'.

Not all accountants practise auditing, although most will, on qualifying as accountants, have gained (through their training, experience and examinations) an entitlement to undertake audits, subject to obtaining 'responsible individual' status. Since the auditing discipline clearly demands a comprehensive grasp of accounting and financial reporting standards, regulation and general professional practice, the term forensic accountancy should be taken to include expertise in the key sub-discipline of auditing.

1.3 MAINTAINING IMPARTIALITY

Although expert witnesses are usually appointed by one or other of the litigating parties, it is essential that such witnesses maintain a detached and independent stance at all stages of the litigation process. Expert witnesses may choose to measure success in terms of the number of cases in which the decision of the Courts has favoured their clients. For us, however, just as critical a measure has been the number of cases in which we have prevailed upon an indignant client (and his or her lawyers) to *desist* from pursuing litigation that lacks sufficient merit to withstand the spotlight of objective courtroom scrutiny.

The conduct of civil litigation is governed by the 1999 Civil Procedure Rules (CPR). These rules were introduced to ease pressure on the Courts by weeding out cases that would be more cost-effectively dealt with by recourse to alternative methods of dispute resolution such as arbitration, expert determination or, in particular, mediation.

1.4 THE DISCIPLINES OF EXPERT WITNESS WORK

Those giving expert evidence, although invariably bound to observe the standards and codes of conduct of their own professional bodies, are equally bound to adhere to those sections of the CPR that relate specifically to the role of experts, whether party-appointed or, in an increasing number of cases, appointed by the parties jointly or even by the Court.

Experts whose evidence, whether as presented in their formal reports or given orally under cross-examination, appears to the Court to be biased in favour of those instructing them, risk the disapprobation of the Court and of having their evidence totally discredited.

In the specific field of professional negligence the Courts are bound to rely, in the context of accounting, tax or audit work, on evidence submitted by the professional peers of those whose conduct is alleged to have fallen below the requisite 'standard'. The latter is an objective test applied by the Courts, although it relies in particular cases on the subjective assessment of experts in the relevant field. Such an assessment may, in key respects, differ substantively as between one expert and another – which is obvious, since if the respective parties' experts found themselves to be in complete agreement on the issues, there would be little scope for expensive litigation!

1.5 CONDUCT THAT IS 'REASONABLY COMPETENT'

The requisite standard referred to in the previous section is, of course, the standard of work that would have been undertaken by a *reasonably competent* accountant, auditor or tax adviser, as the case may be. If, for example, a company's audited balance sheet includes assets that are shown subsequently to have been materially overstated, the Court will wish to hear expert evidence on whether a *reasonably* competent (not the *most* competent auditor in the land) would, in the ordinary course of the audit, have performed tests that had a reasonable expectation of detecting that overstatement.

The expert accountant or auditor engaged to provide an opinion on a fellow professional's work brings to bear not only technical expertise on the specific issues, but also a wealth of experience gained in comparable cases, and is thus able to inject a crucial measure of objectivity into often fraught proceedings. Claimants are understandably indignant at having lost money, while their auditors may be instinctively over-defensive, even deeply offended, at the very idea of being sued. Yet the most cost-effectively sensible resolution, which will often have the backing of the auditor's insurers, is usually for the claimant to seek compensation for the consequences of perceived wrongs through the process of a negotiated settlement. The impartial input of an independent expert can be the catalyst for achieving this aim.

1.6 THE DISCIPLINARY ARENA

The majority of practising accountants, like members of most respected professions, are required to comply with codes of conduct developed and periodically updated by their professional bodies to keep pace with changing circumstances. The Code of Ethics published by the ICAEW in 2006 is one example. These codes are laid down either as guidance on best practice or as mandatory rules with which all members must comply. These strictures are supported by disciplinary sanctions that are applied in instances of proven non-compliance.

The emphasis in the non-mandatory guidance is on the need for members to conduct themselves in such a manner that their professional integrity is seen to be maintained and not impugned, and will relate to such matters as keeping the client informed of the scale of charges being incurred, responding to correspondence within a reasonable timescale or putting in place an appropriate complaints procedure.

More serious issues are addressed in the codes of mandatory conduct and concern, for example, matters such as the following: competence with which the accountant's work has been performed; the need to avoid conflicts of interest when, say, acting for both parties to a transaction; preserving independence when acting in an auditing capacity and ensuring that such independence is *perceived* to be in place; undertaking work in a 'reserved area' in which the accountant demonstrably lacks proven competence; and, more generally, not performing any action that might bring the accountant, the firm, the professional body or the profession of accountancy into disrepute as a consequence.

For the disciplinary machinery to be set in motion, a formal complaint needs to be registered with the professional body, and there are designated procedures for assessing the weight and the seriousness with which complaints should be taken. Since adverse findings in a disciplinary forum may prove to be a preamble to litigation, accountants and their insurers clearly need to view any such complaints with the utmost seriousness. Complaints considered by the professional body to be frivolous, mischievous or otherwise unworthy of further consideration will be given short shrift. Others, which clearly demonstrate that there is a case to be answered, will be dealt with in accordance with a disciplinary process that is thorough but often hugely time-consuming for the accountant and his or her firm. Complaints that concern matters with a prominent public profile, either because of the sums of money involved or because of sensitivities due to the high profile of the parties/entities involved, or because of widespread interests such as in a public offering of shares, will normally be dealt with in the more public arena of the Joint Disciplinary Scheme or the Accountants and Actuaries Discipline Board.

Although the conduct of disciplinary procedures is less formal than in a Court of law, there are obvious parallels in the way evidence is heard, and the tribunal hearing a particular case may well include a lawyer and a lay member. This is clearly another area in which the services of suitably experienced expert witnesses will be critical.

1.7 LITIGATION IN THE CURRENT CLIMATE

The current economic crisis, which began in 2008, is global in its sweep, and yet there is no consensus on the apportionment of culpability to each of its contributing elements. Several such elements have been publicly cited, including: inept governance; 'light-touch' regulation; negligent audits; procyclical financial reporting standards that exacerbate distortion; outdated computer modelling by rating agencies; and the bonus culture that has blinded banks to the precariousness of their own crumbling balance sheets.

What is certain, however, is that this lethal cocktail of self-serving deception has led to the loss of vast amounts of money, in respect of which restitution will continue to be sought via civil Courts in many countries, but most notably in the UK and USA.

Shareholders in financial institutions whose holdings have effectively been destroyed by 'rescue' rights issues, shot-gun 'mergers' with other investment houses or banks or, more simply, by the discovery that an apparently healthy, *audited*, balance sheet is in reality crippled with worthless assets, may well feel encouraged to test the conduct of the management and the auditors in the objective forum of the Courts.

Even if the factors contributing to the 2008/9 credit crisis are set aside, it is an historic fact that an inverse relationship exists between the severity of any economic downturn and a rise in disputes requiring recourse to law. When times are tough overdrafts are called in, staff are laid off, suppliers are more demanding, and businesses that in their own commercial terms are unquestionably viable are suddenly faced with having to call in the receivers.

Whenever money is lost, compensation is sought; and professional advisers, notably accountants and auditors, are consistently perceived as having deep insurance-backed pockets. The question of *merit* is often relegated to the status of an afterthought.

Many claimants, desperate for recovery of at least some of their losses, will adopt a scatter-gun strategy in a legal framework that still incorporates joint and several liability, in anticipation that professional defendants (and their insurers) will prefer to settle a claim rather than face the risks, trauma and expense of a full trial.

We live in such times.

To assist readers in forming a coherent grasp of the multi-faceted subject matter, at the conclusion of each chapter we restate the key lessons to be gleaned from the pitfalls described in that chapter's cases.

2

Auditors' Failure to Detect Theft, Embezzlement and Financial Crime

2.1 SUMMARY OF TYPES OF FRAUD

The following list provides a summary of some different types of fraud:

- Theft of cash through:
  - *Skimming*: removal of cash from an entity before it enters the accounting system. The most common skimming techniques are:
    - failing to record sales;
    - understating sales;
    - theft of incoming cheques.
  - *Larceny*: stealing funds belonging to an entity.
  - *Fraudulent disbursements*: These frauds include:
    - preparation of fraudulent cheques for personal benefit;
    - diversion of cheques intended for a third party for personal benefit;
    - fraudulent refunds and void entries on a cash register;
    - submission of fraudulent invoices to cause an entity to buy non-existent, overpriced or unnecessary goods or services, for example, the creation of shell companies, overbilling by apparently legitimate vendors or use of company funds to meet personal expenditure.
- Sales/debtors ledger frauds, which provide a mechanism for the theft of cash and usually involving:
  - teeming and lading (see glossary of terms);
  - setting up fictitious accounts in the sales/debtors ledger to disguise fictitious sales;
  - recording false credit entries as discounts, returns or write-offs.
- Stock frauds, which involve the misappropriation of stock for personal use, stealing stock or scrap, or charging funds misappropriated to stock.

- Theft or unauthorised personal use of fixed assets is a common type of fraud, particularly if the assets are easily removable from the entity's premises.

2.2 INTRODUCTION

The discovery of any long-running corporate fraud invariably triggers questions concerning the failure of auditors to detect it. Even when the auditors themselves bring the fraud to light, they will be challenged on why they did not do so in the course of earlier audits.

Were they asleep on their watch? How could they have attached their 'true and fair' imprimatur to accounts that failed to disclose the fact that serious fraud had depleted corporate assets and profits?

When, in the USA in the mid-1970s, the massive Equity Funding fraud became public, a frequently heard refrain was offered by apologists for the auditing profession to the effect that routine auditing procedures are simply not designed to detect fraud. As Raymond Dirks and Leonard Gross, authors of *The Great Wall Street Scandal* (McGraw Hill, 1974, p. 272), put it: '*If routine auditing procedures cannot detect 64,000 phony insurance policies, $25 million in counterfeit bonds, and $100 million in missing assets, what is the purpose of audits?*'

Over 35 years later this question remains relevant and continues to be asked whenever serious fraud is discovered. It is of course correct that auditors instructed to focus specifically on fraud detection would have to adapt their work programmes and their skills to this rather different, and somewhat narrower, target. But that fact will not serve as a defence to a negligence action in circumstances when *normal* audit procedures should have detected material misstatements in the accounts as a consequence of a fraud that raided the corporate coffers.

Auditors are always perceived by outsiders as the primary independent safeguard against fraudulent abuse by management or employees, a role that saddles them with a tremendous burden of expectation. Moreover, they are a soft target because their professional indemnity insurers will invariably prefer to negotiate a settlement rather than risk the hazards of the litigation lottery – sometimes without due regard to merit.

Insurers' statistics show that claims against auditors for 'failure to detect defalcations' exceed those arising from all other audit work – in terms of both incidence and monetary amount. It is therefore obvious that attempts, however reasonable they may seem, wholly to disclaim such a responsibility have little practical effect.

2.3 AUDITORS' RESPONSIBILITY FOR FRAUD DETECTION

The principle here (supported by the Courts in past cases) is that the origins of auditing, as we now know it, are inseparably linked with the function of fraud detection. Although there would appear to be no positive *prevention* duties (it is hoped that the audit presence, per se, has that effect), the detection function has always, in the public mind, been associated with the audit. Although this detection function has gradually become subordinated to the principal aim of confirming (or otherwise) the truth and fairness of financial statements and their compliance with statutory requirements – hence endowing them with a degree of credibility they otherwise would lack – it is incorrect to deduce from this that the former role has been completely superseded by the latter: concern with the existence and consequences of fraud within the client organisation remains within the auditor's sphere of responsibility in every practical sense.

It is a mistake to regard the two objectives in question (fraud detection and 'true and fair' reporting) as mutually exclusive; indeed, the chief virtue of an engagement letter is that it formulates a reliable and realistic synthesis between both of them. A well-drafted engagement letter would include a term to the effect that: 'we shall endeavour to plan our audit so that we have a reasonable expectation of detecting material misstatements in the financial statements or accounting records resulting from irregularities or fraud'.

It is therefore imperative that, although not explicitly focusing on fraud detection, auditors maintain a sharp professional scepticism at all times and design procedures that will give them a *reasonable opportunity* to detect any material misstatements that may exist, regardless of how caused – including fraud.

It should of course be remembered that litigation always involves the question of burden of proof, including proof of loss and causation. In cases of negligence involving third parties, not only must financial loss be involved, but also it must be attributable to the negligence of the defendant accountant. In cases involving the claimant's contributory negligence damages would be reduced accordingly. In other words, the Courts do not encourage third parties who have suffered loss to view auditors as convenient scapegoats, perhaps based on the presumption of insurance cover, even if there is a prima facie case of negligence. The further consideration of attributable loss must be proved to the Courts' satisfaction.

Defendant auditors are understandably aggrieved when claims against them arise from issues that fall within the responsibility of others, such as directors of client companies. Yet the law is far from clear on the extent to which contributory negligence has relevance to cases brought in contract rather than tort, and the Courts will not necessarily take into account the negligence of directors in failing to impose effective internal controls when auditors are sued for failing to detect frauds by employees.

2.4 LIMITING LIABILITY

The law permits auditors to set a contractual limit (or 'cap') on their liability, based on the extent to which they have caused loss to the company. Such a cap must have regard to considerations of what is 'just, fair and reasonable' and must be approved by the company's members. This statutory provision may be considered to be a step in the direction of proportional liability, rather than joint and several liability under which any culpable party may be targeted for recovery of the full losses suffered.

Auditors themselves could address this issue by adopting incorporation with limited liability, but this is hardly the whole answer. A proactive approach, that would pay long-term dividends, would be for auditors of public interest (and hence high-risk) entities, before accepting appointment or reappointment, to insist that the client's directors be insured for at least as much cover as the directors would expect the auditor to carry.

2.5 PERSPECTIVES ON FRAUD – RESPECTIVE RESPONSIBILITIES OF MANAGEMENT AND AUDITORS

Attempts have been made over many years to clarify the respective responsibilities of management and auditors, including the requirement for financial reports to incorporate clear statements of such responsibilities. Since the outcome of so many cases rests on the question of how blame should be apportioned, it may be helpful to provide an objective view of the current perception of where responsibility lies:

- *Management responsibility*. The prevention of fraud, error and comparable irregularities lies firmly within the province of management supervision and other internal controls. Management cannot validly rely on the audit function as a substitute for internal controls, and to attempt this would be an unwarranted abrogation of one of management's most important responsibilities.

- *Management letters.* Auditors, acting in an advisory capacity (a distinction that the engagement letter should make clear), may offer recommendations for the enhancement of management controls based on their and their staff's observations in the course of an audit. This is usually provided in the management letter. It is obligatory to communicate such matters either in writing or at a meeting with the client, followed by a letter.
- *Essential and non-essential matters.* In making any such recommendations, auditors are strongly advised to distinguish (and to evidence such distinction in the audit files) between (i) those that they regard as essential from their point of view and (ii) those offered gratuitously under the previous point, which the client is at liberty to implement or not as the directors see fit. Once auditors are aware of weaknesses, however, they are expected to perform procedures that take those weaknesses into account. Simply reporting them to management cannot be regarded as the end of the story.
- *Disregard by management.* Recommendations regarded by the auditor as essential would relate to controls without which internally originated evidence would lack adequate support, such as evidence that goods purchased have been received before suppliers' invoices are passed for payment. Such matters might, in the face of persistent disregard by management of their importance, result in a qualified audit report, especially if no other means are available to verify the authenticity and completeness of liabilities.
- *Investigation by management.* The occurrence of irregularities such as defalcations (and errors) represents a failure of internal control and, as such, its detection is again the responsibility of management. Management, being responsible for the establishment of controls in the first place, is logically responsible for the detection of lapses in control, investigating their causes (such as their inherent ineffectiveness or the failure of subordinates to apply them) and instituting improvements designed to ensure their non-recurrence.
- *Effect on financial statements.* The prime audit duty of reporting within the terms of the Companies Act cannot, however, be fulfilled without a proper consideration of the possible effect of the irregularities in question on the truth and fairness of the financial statements being audited. In this regard the responsibilities of auditors and management overlap.

- *Measuring materiality.* The irregularities in question may be either individually or cumulatively material in relation to the view presented by financial statements. For the purpose of determining whether this might be so, it is necessary for auditors to have a general materiality measure available. Without this it is not possible for audit work to be said to have been satisfactorily completed or, by the same token, a reliable opinion given.
- *Satisfying the engagement letter.* The auditor is expected to undertake to plan the audit so as to have a reasonable expectation of detecting material misstatements in the financial statements resulting from fraud. The use of the word 'material' creates a specific and complementary duty to consider how, in each circumstance, materiality should be assessed for the purposes of substantive testing, and reflected in ensuing audit procedures. The use of materiality criteria also protects the auditor from unreasonable claims based on non-discovery of minor defalcations below the auditor's materiality threshold.

2.6 DISCLOSURE OF MANAGEMENT FRAUD

The Courts and other government regulators have made it clear that when auditors discover or suspect serious management fraud they should regard its disclosure as a duty to be exercised 'in the public interest', and that any such disclosure by auditors would, if made in good faith to the appropriate authority, entitle them to immunity from any subsequent action in respect of breach of duty of confidentiality or other legal obligation.

In this regard the auditing standard on 'fraud and the auditor' goes somewhat further than any earlier advice and deals specifically with the question of disclosure of fraud (actual or suspected) to third parties in the public interest, and the protection that the law would provide if such disclosure is properly made. It also gives guidance on the criteria to be used when considering whether disclosure is justified in the public interest, including:

- the extent to which the fraud is likely to result in material gain or loss for any person or to affect a large number of persons;
- the extent to which non-disclosure of the fraud may enable it to be repeated with impunity;
- the gravity of the matter;
- whether there is a general management ethos in the entity of flouting the law or regulations;
- the weight of evidence that a fraud has actually been committed.

The drastic step of reporting suspicions of management fraud to a third party regulator is by no means the only option available to auditors in circumstances where they believe that internally-sounded warnings would fall on deaf ears. A more effective instrument may in some cases lie in the auditors' right to resign, since this will require them to issue a statement of resignation circumstances if they consider these should be brought to a shareholders' or creditors' attention. They also have the right to require the directors to convene an extraordinary general meeting of the company, for the sole purpose of airing the auditors' concerns.

The auditors' statement must be filed at Companies House and must be circulated to everyone entitled to receive copies of the company's accounts. The auditors can require a similar statement to be circulated prior to the meeting at which their terms of office would have expired. Any director who fails to take all reasonable steps to ensure that the requisitioned extraordinary general meeting is convened is guilty of an offence.

Therefore, even in the case of a closely-held company, auditors can, if circumstances warrant it, deploy the armoury provided to them under company law to make life exceedingly difficult for dishonest senior executives. This is quite apart from the possibilities afforded by the professional duty to provide any nominated successor with all information considered relevant to their decision whether or not to act.

When solicitors realise that they have made a mistake that may give rise to loss or damage, they immediately disinstruct themselves and inform the client that a different firm may need to be engaged. Auditors are also in a potentially conflicting situation whenever they discover fraudulent conduct by an employee that may have been going on in earlier periods and which, had it been discovered earlier, might have saved the client company material sums and might also have materially affected the accounts for those periods.

When such distasteful realities are first brought to light, the client's natural reaction is shock followed by a desire to know the full extent of the damage. And who better to undertake this exercise than the auditors? Yet, understandably, such an assignment is often the precursor to a serious claim against the auditors who, having now explained the fraud's mechanics and its full dimensions, are less able to justify the failure of their own procedures to detect it in its infancy. Auditors seldom recover their fees for preparing 'fraud reports' in such circumstances!

2.7 MONITORING THE CLIENT'S REGULATORY CONDUCT

Accountants and auditors can easily become implicated if they fail to detect, consider or disclose the consequences for the client company's accounts of the transgressions of the company itself via the acts or omissions of its principal officers.

The context in which the relevant auditing standard applies is the legal framework within which the entity conducts its business and where non-compliance may reasonably be expected to have a fundamental effect on the present or future operations of the entity. Under this standard it is necessary for the auditor to carry out the following:

- obtain a general understanding of the legal and regulatory framework applicable to the particular entity and industry;
- inspect correspondence with any relevant licensing or regulatory authorities;
- enquire specifically of the directors whether they are on notice of any such possible instances of non-compliance;
- obtain formal written confirmation from the directors that they have made the auditors aware of any possible non-compliance of which they themselves are aware, together with the actual or contingent consequences which may arise therefrom.

Controversially, the standard requires auditors to familiarise themselves with the legal framework in which the client entity operates and to examine correspondence between the entity and any relevant regulatory authorities. This onerous duty goes further than merely seeking representations from directors regarding known or suspected regulatory transgressions, and there is therefore the implication that auditors' reporting responsibilities are widened by the standard.

The following extract is taken from a public address given by one leading underwriter on the subject of 'Insurance of environmental risks':

> When preparing Annual Reports accountants should obviously include all liabilities; yet horrendous potential exposure to pollution liabilities appears not to have been addressed in the past. Companies which appear solvent could very well be insolvent if such matters had been investigated. Any annual report which totally ignores the effect that pollution and its liabilities could have on the balance sheet could produce massive claims against accountants for professional negligence.

Of particular concern to auditors, including those acting for clients in a wider capacity, are, for example:

- pollution and environmental transgressions by the client;
- consumer protection legislation;
- maintenance of proper accounting records;
- VAT legislation breaches;
- PAYE and NI liability of subcontractors or freelance workers;
- health and safety at work;
- fire regulations;
- all client money regulations;
- capital adequacy regulations for financial services providers;
- vehicle licensing regulations;
- licensing laws for hotels, pubs and restaurants.

The cases outlined in the rest of this chapter carry their own, individual warning message, but they have a single common feature: in each case the auditors failed to meet the requisite standard of giving themselves a 'reasonable opportunity' to detect the fraud or other irregularity.

2.8 FRAUD BY EMPLOYEES

Despite the idea in the minds of many auditors that detection of employee fraud does not fall within their area of responsibility, claims under this heading are the highest in the auditing category. Furthermore, since these claims are brought in contract the claimant has no difficulty in establishing legal proximity.

The number of fraudulent gambits in this claims category that culprits exploit is too numerous to describe here, but based on the authors' own case files as independent expert witnesses, they can typically include such things as the following:

- The clerk who cashed his own cheques with his employer but did not bank them, covering the shortfall by 'teeming and lading' remittances from debtors.
- The misappropriation of funds by
  - theft of cash sales; or
  - inserting dummy names on payrolls.
- The requesting of signatures from directors on blank cheques claiming that they are intended for HM Revenue & Customs (HMRC) for PAYE and/or VAT, stating that 'I have not worked out the amounts yet!'.

(Note that throughout this book, the term HMRC is used as a general term to cover all references to the tax authorities, both before and after HM Customs and Excise were merged with HM Inland Revenue in April 2005.)

- The company secretary who, after being made a cheque signatory, paid his personal bills with company cheques and entered the payments against the directors' loan accounts. They all shared the same creditors, such as Amex, Visa and Telecom, not to mention the same wine merchant, travel agent and petrol filling station – thus by spreading his own payments evenly between four directors' loan accounts, the chances of detection were much reduced.
- The charity treasurer who controlled all accounting functions 'to economise on payroll costs', but more than made up for it by creating fictitious petty cash expenses, employing nonexistent casual staff, emptying most collection boxes before their official unsealing, and selling programme advertising space and pocketing most of the proceeds, recording the loss as 'discount'.
- The accounts clerk and her husband who were totally trusted by the directors and relied upon by the auditors for producing the accounts. The auditor issued a warning letter to the directors regarding excessive dependence on the clerk, but no paid cheques were examined in the course of successive audits. The clerk perpetrated a sustained fraud over five years by using company funds to meet her personal debts.

Where were the auditors? What did they do – or not do? Such questions always arise following discovery of fraud. It is therefore essential that engagement terms are set out clearly and agreed in advance. There is never a need for auditors to accept a *general* responsibility for fraud detection. If a fraud is so material, however, that its non-discovery affects the truth and fairness of the published accounts it would be difficult for the auditors to deny any responsibility.

A. Failure to carry out basic procedures

There is a tendency for auditors to reach their conclusions chiefly by reference to analytical procedures and directors' representations, and by reviewing accounts from a risk-related standpoint. Yet, as the cases described below demonstrate, certain basic procedures remain indispensable.

Case A.1

The audit client was a subsidiary of a large UK plc conglomerate producing components for the English East Midlands motor manufacturing industry. Despite having a turnover in excess of £45 million the audit of the subsidiary was left to a small team of six.

The national audit firm adopted a 'high level' audit approach that relied almost exclusively on IT and systems reviews of the client's accounting processes. No detailed examination of the underlying records took place. Although continuing to rely on the results of the systems reviews in the second and subsequent years of their audit, the auditors failed to update these and consequently relied on controls that were in fact no longer in place.

Over a period of at least five years Mrs Beatrice Lovewell, the company's financial director, systematically filled key positions in the accounts department with members of her own family or her in-laws, and managed to defraud the company of at least £2.4 million, probably a good deal more.

Her methods, initially carefully concealed but increasingly brazen as the uselessness of the audit became apparent, included:

- paying herself and/or her creditors using company cheques and entering false payees on the counterfoils, and then making the relevant 'corrections' by highly creative use of the company's journal;
- using the company's 'private' cash book to clear her substantial personal expenses incurred with the use of a company Amex card, including first class transatlantic flights, Fifth Avenue shopping and 'weekend break' hotel bills;
- misappropriating large amounts of cash sales from the trade counter and then using the journal to 'rectify' matters, usually by debiting 'discounts allowed';
- making unauthorised 'loans' to herself and other members of her accounts department 'family', which were reversed by journal before the year-end and re-reversed shortly thereafter;
- paying bogus wages and crudely amending the pink copies of the BACS sheets with white-out fluid and a typewriter.

The auditors' ability to defend themselves against allegations of negligence was somewhat compromised by the fact that most of Mrs Lovewell's 'weekend breaks' were spent amorously with the audit manager and, bizarrely, the case files include certain lascivious exchanges, sent by postcard, some of which were tucked into the back of the cash book – presumably because that was considered the last place the audit team would look!

Had the auditors departed even briefly from their policy of studiously avoiding any contact with company records, and merely *opened* the so-called 'private cash book' at any page, they would have detected the fraud immediately – so blatant was the evidence. The private cash book, originally designed solely to record directors' emoluments, had no fewer than 58 separate columns, most of them including fraudulent entries of one variety or another.

Mrs Lovewell even cocked a deliberately supercilious snook at the auditors by passing a single £75 million journal entry (crediting sales, debiting discounts) and triumphantly reversed it after the audit!

The matter was eventually settled through mediation at an undisclosed sum, subject to a confidentiality agreement.

Lessons to be noted

- In this case the client managed to negotiate a spectacularly low fee for the audit of its Midlands subsidiary, and budgetary constraints dictated the audit approach from the outset. Auditors should not allow such constraints to restrict the scope of necessary audit work. Failing to perform an effective audit cannot be justified on the basis that the fee budget does not allow for it. This has been a particular problem with larger firms, who may negotiate low fees for subsidiary audits in anticipation of covering any losses with more lucrative charges for other services.
- In this instance the audit firm was less concerned with the results and financial position of the subsidiary than might otherwise have been the case, because the subsidiary, in accounting terms, fell below the level of what might legitimately be regarded as 'group materiality'. The listed parent company was a conglomerate with holdings in a wide range of entities in several related industries, from IT to utilities. It should, however, be remembered that the auditors of every company, irrespective of its size in relation to the group, have an obligation under company law to express an opinion on its financial statements, and this work must meet exactly the same auditing standards as apply elsewhere.

- When relying on a review of IT or other internal control system with a view to limiting the scope of substantive testing, the controls must be checked for each year of the engagement to ensure that they are still applicable and can be relied upon. The original audit file conclusion, on which subsequent audits were based, was that the audit risk was 'low' and client internal controls were 'highly effective'!
- Patently, the company's management disregarded their own responsibilities to institute a modicum of internal control by ensuring that reciprocal accounting functions did not overlap. For example, employees who open the post should not be responsible for banking cash received; nor should anyone responsible for keeping the cash book up to date also participate in recording receipts and payments in sales and purchases ledgers.
- In this instance, however, Mrs Lovewell had so successfully managed to ingratiate herself with the directors (one of whom was a main board director) that the integrity of her work was never subject to query, still less independent review. She had filled all the key positions in the accounts department with friends and relations, including her husband, none of which was hidden. Even if senior management remains impervious to the obvious risks of such a state of affairs, the auditors are bound to view the set up with far greater circumspection and enhance their testing accordingly.

Case A.2

A further example of the necessity for the most basic procedures not to be overlooked concerns a high street general insurance broker whose dishonest bookkeeper was caught out when a newly installed computer system detected that she had failed to transmit certain premiums received from clients to the relevant insurance companies, leaving the clients uninsured.

Further investigation uncovered a host of irregularities and misappropriations that had been going on for years. The simplest yet most pervasive of these was perpetrated in the following manner:

1. The bookkeeper accurately recorded premiums receipts from clients in the manual cash book.
2. The manual cash book was then cast (i.e. added up) and an understated daily total was recorded, and this sum was then banked.

3. The bookkeeper relied on 'pipeline' delays between receipt of premiums and their onward transmission to insurers to facilitate such teeming and lading as was necessary for her purposes.

Lesson to be noted

- The auditors performed every test their auditing system prescribed, except checking the casts in the manual cash book. If they had done so, the fraud would have been discovered at the outset. Even the most basic checks can at times provide evidence of wrongdoing.

Case A.3

The claimant company was a distributor of sports goods based in Leeds. Pepper & Smart had acted as company auditors since 1992. The December 2005 accounts, which showed a trading loss, were both prepared and audited by Pepper & Smart, whose report was qualified due to doubts regarding the company's ability to continue to trade as a going concern and its dependence on the company's directors for financial support.

Although the directors were aware of the company's financial problems, they were of the opinion that these were temporary and that a return to normal levels of profitability would follow. Ten months later, however, despite having achieved turnover and gross margins comparable with the previous period, the directors were forced to cease trading through pressure from the bank.

Investigations showed that substantial stocks of sports equipment had been systematically stolen from the company's warehouse by two trusted employees working in collusion over an 18-month period. For the purpose of preparing the 2005 accounts the auditors had relied on the company's book stock records. Although there had been a physical stocktaking at the year-end, which the auditors did not attend, the inventories listed merely corroborated the book stock records.

The directors' investigations showed that both the book stocks and physical inventory lists had been deliberately inflated by the employees concerned in order to mask their thefts. Had the 2005 accounts reflected the losses due to theft, the result would have been a loss of approximately £160,000.

The police were notified and confessions obtained, followed by arrests. Stocks with a value of £65,000 were recovered from a garage used by the employees as a base from which they sold the stolen goods for cash, usually to one of the company's own retail customers at less than their original cost. Although collusion with the customer was suspected, further charges were not pressed. The employces had squandered the cash and there was no realistic prospect of any worthwhile recovery from their personal assets. Liabilities to the bank were settled by the directors, who had given personal guarantees.

The liquidator commenced proceedings against Pepper & Smart, the claim alleging that the 2005 accounts had been negligently prepared and audited by them. In particular it was alleged that if the auditors had attended the physical stocktaking they would have discovered the substantial stock shortages caused by the thefts.

Had the directors been aware of the true position the company could have ceased trading without incurring further losses; alternatively, remedial steps might have been taken immediately and the company saved from further loss.

In their defence Pepper & Smart maintained that they were entitled to rely on stock figures supplied by the directors and that, by approving and signing the accounts, for which they were responsible in law, the directors had confirmed the correctness of all amounts included therein. They furthermore maintained that responsibility for the detection of a carefully executed fraud, involving collusion by two senior executives, did not lie within the accepted scope of the audit.

The expert assisting Counsel for Pepper & Smart, however, identified the failure to attend the stock count as a significant omission, because formal auditing guidance has for many years highlighted the importance of this procedure.

In the particular circumstances of this fraud it might have been the only means of discovering the fraud. Its omission left Pepper & Smart with little prospect of such discovery.

The expert's report also noted that standard analytical procedures should have prompted Pepper & Smart to query the company's seriously deteriorating liquid position against an apparent background of only small losses in 2005 and improving profitability in the post balance sheet period prior to audit completion.

On the basis of legal and expert accountant's advice, the claim was settled at an amount representing the estimated cost of goods stolen during the ten months between the December 2005 stocktaking and the date on which the company was forced to cease trading. Costs of both sides were met by underwriters.

Lessons to be noted

- Attendance at a client's stocktaking is a particularly valuable audit procedure in cases where there is no other independent corroboration of book stock records. Periodic physical checks during the year, at which the auditor is present, will obviously provide assurance regarding the quantities in stock and its physical condition. In this case, however, it seems that no interim checks were arranged.
- The number of clients with December year-ends creates logistical problems for auditors' stocktaking attendance. Careful planning is therefore essential and, with adequate advance notice, some clients may be prepared to accommodate the auditor's requests for the timing of the count, particularly where there is little stock movement. In other cases it will be feasible for auditors to conduct a test count on a more convenient, but nevertheless proximate, date and reconcile the quantities back to the year-end by adjusting for known subsequent movements.
- As noted by their expert, Pepper & Smart might have detected the stock deficiency when reviewing the accounts they had prepared. The continuous purchases of stock required to replenish that which had in fact been stolen (although still included) produced accounts showing the stock level and the overdraft mounting simultaneously to alarming levels. The continuation of this pattern in the post balance sheet period should have put the auditors on enquiry.

It was fortunate that the claimant was prepared to settle on the basis of losses due to theft plus legal expenses. A further claim by the shareholders could easily have been made, based on the consequential losses of their investment in the company.

Case A.4

In this case, the nature of the client company's business required that substantial amounts of cash be kept on the premises in order to pay for casual labour and other disbursements such as payments to lorry drivers for deliveries.

The cashier covered up a deficiency of several thousand pounds, representing sums that he had misappropriated, by cashing three company cheques totalling over £24,000 immediately prior to the auditor's cash count, but he did not enter them in the cash book or petty cash book until later.

The count took place in early January in respect of a 31 December year-end, the company's offices having been closed over the Christmas period. The books showed a year-end cash balance of £25,786.02.

The auditors enquired about the remaining shortfall and the cashier thereupon produced a voucher for the same amount, subdivided between £1,244.50 for wages and £541.52 for expenses, purporting to represent items incurred just prior to the year-end but not yet entered in the books. The voucher in fact related to expenses incurred earlier in the year, and had already been inspected once by the auditors during a different audit test, but they failed to spot the duplication.

Following the cashier's resignation six months later, investigations showed that his misappropriations had totalled over £117,000, and the client sought to recover this from the auditors.

Advice given by Counsel acknowledged that although an auditor is not required to approach the books with fraud specifically in mind,

> with reasonable diligence the auditors should have been put on notice that something was suspect in the petty cash book, and that the amount of cash held at any time (coupled with the fact that controls were weak) should in any event have prompted a comprehensive audit. Had this occurred the further investigations would have revealed the true position.

Based on the advice of Counsel and an independent expert's report, the proceedings were settled at 75% of the sum claimed, the difference representing a discount for contributory negligence on the part of management.

Lessons to be noted

- Even relatively immaterial irregularities can accumulate to considerable amounts if not arrested at source, and can lead to worrying claims against auditors.
- The defence that the company's management is primarily responsible for the system of internal control, and hence that the audit should not be relied upon for this purpose, would be of little avail if, as part of their normal routine procedures, the auditors endeavour

to vouch the relevant entries and reconcile the resulting balance with the amount physically counted; and when (as was the case here) such steps are performed negligently.

- It should have been patently clear to the auditors that the set-up was highly susceptible to fraudulent abuse, the cashier effectively having carte blanche operational custody over very substantial amounts of cash. Accountability was virtually nonexistent. In such circumstances auditors have a duty to inform management that the imposition of independent internal controls is a priority and that failure will in future result in a qualified audit opinion arising from the auditors' inability to confirm that the actual cash balance represents the amount that should have been present.

Case A.5

The auditors acted for a clothes manufacturing company owning a chain of shops in the South East and Midlands of England. In 2005 a substantial majority shareholding was acquired by outside interests. An independent investigation subsequently caused the main shareholder to withhold further financial support. The bankers appointed a receiver, and liquidation followed. The shares are obviously worthless. Underwriters insuring the audit firm were advised to reserve £2 million following criticism of the company's stock valuation method prior to the acquisition.

It was the company's practice to mark up stock values to reflect

- additional outworkers' charges for finishing garments; and
- costs of distribution to retail outlets.

No allowance was made for slow-moving or obsolete stock because management always insisted that it would be able to sell everything. The published accounting policies nevertheless adopted the standard formula that stocks were valued at the lower of cost and net realisable value.

The auditors' method for arriving at net realisable value was to deduct a specific percentage from the selling price of the stock items and then obtain assurances from the directors that the realisable value was no less than the sum thus arrived at. They did not apply any reliable sampling method for checking post balance sheet proceeds against balance sheet values.

The receivers, appointed by the company's bankers, alleged the following: stocks and work-in-progress were grossly overvalued in the most recent pre-acquisition accounts; creditors of over £100,000 were entirely omitted; and work with invoice value of £160,000 was billed as sales before the year-end although not completed until more than two months later.

The auditors had accepted a computer printout of stock figures after brief assurances from the managing director. They maintained that the purchase invoices excluded from the accounts were deliberately suppressed by the director.

Proceedings against the auditors were commenced by the bank under which a claim was made for the sum that the bank failed to recover from the liquidator or the directors under their personal guarantees. The bank claimed to have relied on the accounts to its detriment. The underwriters were advised to reserve £600,000, which was the limit of the firm's indemnity cover.

Lessons to be noted

- It is permissible for auditors to rely upon management representations as a form of evidence, but all too frequently this is regarded as a 'soft option' in circumstances when auditing methodology should be used to verify the assets in question. In this case the specific percentage adopted as the mark-up between made-up cost of clothing and their selling price should have been subjected to rigorous testing, albeit on a sampling basis, by reference to actual sales in the post balance sheet period. Only in this way is it possible for auditors to ensure that the raw material cost, the cost of factory labour, outworkers' charges and inward delivery costs are comfortably recovered in the sales prices achieved. Far too much was simply left to assurances from directors.
- Although any action brought against auditors by a third-party lender would have to satisfy contemporary standards of proximity, and hence that the auditors owe the company's bankers an actionable duty of care, in this case it would have been difficult for the auditors to use this argument as a main line of defence, bearing in mind that
  - The auditors as a matter of routine sent copies of the quarterly management accounts (which they had reviewed) as well as the draft final accounts, directly to the bank, thereby demonstrating their awareness of the bank's reliance on the company's accounts

for the purposes of monitoring the status of its loans to the company.
  - The directors, who of course had primary responsibility for the accuracy of the accounts, had joined the bank as co-claimants in respect of the personal guarantees that they had been obliged to honour. The auditors acknowledged that they were aware that the bank's security included the directors' guarantees.
- It is a fact that at the end of each season, clothing manufacturers are left with a quantity of unsold stock that over the course of time will either be sold at whatever price can be achieved or simply scrapped. The auditors appear to have ignored the reality of slow-moving items. Again, they should have tested on a sample basis the directors' assertion that 'everything is sold' by age-testing selected items included in closing stock.
- There are a number of ways in which it is possible to contrive an understatement of creditors, the most usual being the suppression of invoices received from suppliers – in this case for cloth or dockets received from outworkers. Auditors respond to this risk by the use of analytical techniques designed to ensure the consistency from one year to the next of gross profit percentages and ratios of stock to turnover and stock to purchases. It is also necessary for auditors to examine post balance sheet payments to creditors and note the dates when the items in question were first invoiced. When concerns about the completeness of creditors persist, auditors should undertake a circularisation of the company's usual suppliers requesting confirmation of the year-end account balance.
- Had the auditors matched on a test basis a sample of sales invoices with the delivery notes to customers or retail branches, they would have had an opportunity to detect instances in which sales had been inflated by the inclusion of clothing items that had not yet been completed. Although this is a standard audit test, it was in fact not performed.

B. Failure to recognise a client's excessive reliance on a trusted employee

Although the directors are responsible for introducing and maintaining adequate systems of internal control, thereby safeguarding company assets and protecting the interests of outside creditors and shareholders, auditors have a duty to review such controls and to test their efficacy in practice. Unless this is done there is no objective basis for auditors' reliance on those controls, and hence no basis for assuming that the company's records accurately reflect the transactions undertaken during the period and the company's financial position.

In many cases, directors' reliance on key members of staff grows with their length of service and may reach the point where it leads to laxity. Excessive reliance is a form of laziness – and manifests in, for example, leaving blank signed cheques with the in-house accountant for completion and payment at a later point in time, or simply leaving the accountant with far too many functions under his or her personal control. Ideally any system of control worthy of the name will incorporate a division of responsibility that serves as a self-checking mechanism automatically to ensure the accuracy and integrity of the accounting records.

Whoever is responsible for dealing with and banking remittances from customers should have no involvement with the sales ledger or, ideally, making entries in the cash book. Conversely, whoever prepares the payments cycle of the company, including the submission of cheques to the directors for signature, should play no part in either entering those payments in the cash book or making postings to the creditors' ledger.

The cases that follow illustrate graphically the hazards of leaving too much responsibility in the hands of the loyal, trustworthy and long-serving employee.

Case B.1

As is common with many small companies, no ideal form of internal control existed in this instance. Quite simply, the company had too few employees to allow for the checking of one person's work by another in the ordinary course of the latter's duties.

The company created a leading brand in the South of England in the field of signwriting. Although the business expanded dramatically when it secured a large contract from a single customer, its total establishment never exceeded 25 employees.

Mrs Alicia Donald was in sole control of the accounting records, including petty cash and salary records. Dating back to the company's inception, she was also responsible for the administration of PAYE and VAT. It was her practice simply to present the records to the auditors for the purpose of preparing each year's financial statements.

Mrs Donald maintained no nominal ledger, nor did she prepare any control accounts to establish the accuracy of the purchases and sales ledgers. The petty cash book was not analysed and did not record receipts. No comprehensive stock records were maintained.

Following the engagement of a new accountant to cope with the company's expansion, he discovered that Mrs Donald had been stealing money from the company for at least five years and probably longer and was able to conceal her theft by various processes of false accounting. The discovery itself occurred when the new accountant wrote to the bank asking for the return of a large number of the company's paid cheques in order to fill in gaps in the records. Mrs Donald intercepted the post but the accountant persisted and eventually caught her going through the parcel of returned cheques before giving it to him. He took the cheques from her and it became immediately apparent that many of them had in fact been made payable to her, her husband or their personal creditors rather than the ostensible payee shown on the cheque stubs.

Over her many years of loyal service to the company a relationship of complete and unquestioning trust had built up between Mrs Donald and the directors. Indeed, she and her husband were treated for all practical purposes as members of their families, were invited to their children's parties and other seasonal festivities. When the demands of meeting customers' orders necessitated many hours of overtime late into the evenings, Mrs Donald was always there with coffee and sandwiches. The discovery that she had been embezzling company funds for so many years left the directors aghast with disbelief.

All too many frauds betray a breach of the level of trust that builds up over the years, and which the employee in question relies upon to obviate the need for the most basic internal controls, even for a small company.

The following is a summary of Mrs Donald's practices:

- Whenever cheques were needed to pay suppliers or HMRC, she would present the directors with some pretext for requesting cheques to be signed in blank, no other details having been entered. She would wait until they were about to leave the office and say, for example, that she was still working on the amounts due and the prioritisation of who should be paid in that particular batch. She would then make the cheques payable to herself, her husband or some of the range of their personal creditors.

- Where payments ostensibly to suppliers had in fact been misappropriated, creating a debit balance in the purchases ledger, she generated false invoices to balance the account.
- She entered cheques in the cash book as having been required for petty cash, again using them for fraudulent purposes. Conversely, cheques shown in the cash book as having been paid to suppliers were in fact made out to cash, which was then stolen.
- The total sums passing through the petty cash system were very substantial and totally disproportionate for a company of this size. Yet there was no imprest system whereby the petty cash float could be reconciled with payments made by reference to authorised vouchers. Mrs Donald was therefore able to misappropriate prodigious amounts of cash with the use of false expenditure headings.

One outcome of this case, apart from Mrs Donald receiving a five-year custodial sentence, is that the company mounted a substantial claim in negligence against its auditors and the resulting settlement covered the major proportion of the losses identified by police and other forensic investigations subsequent to the fraud's discovery.

The fact that the audit files, by reference to prevailing standards, were woefully deficient in so many ways, proved to be a major obstacle in any defence the auditors might have been able to mount, most notably and obviously the contributory negligence of the owner/directors and their failure to install even the most rudimentary controls. The working papers were more in the nature of accountancy schedules, and included no evidence of audit planning, no audit programmes and no record of any procedures actually undertaken. Nor was there any evidence of a review, analytical or otherwise, being undertaken on the financial statements. There were schedules of sensible audit queries relating to, say, payments not entered in the cash book, having been raised, but the recorded responses of the more senior auditors included 'What a joke!', 'Don't ask!' and 'Crap'.

Despite the deficiencies in the audit files, they included sufficient evidence to indicate that further enquiry, which would undoubtedly have led to the discovery of the fraud, was warranted. The audit queries referred to above should have raised genuine concerns regarding the authenticity of many payments. Furthermore the auditors were aware that no nominal ledger existed and hence that no self-balancing records could be created for the support and control of double-entry bookkeeping. The auditors' response to this problem was simply to create their own nominal ledger entries for the sole purpose of preparing statutory accounts for filing.

The following was evident to the auditors: the cash book, written up by Mrs Donald, was totalled in pencil; it showed several gaps in the cheque sequence; it included many cheques entered out of numerical sequence, some up to nine months later; and it had several pages torn out. They would also have been aware that the weekly cash cheque drawn to pay wages was always increased by irregular amounts and the excess shown as petty cash.

Lessons to be noted

- It is arguable that the work done by the auditors was substandard to such a degree that this case study contains few practical relevant lessons. Its value, however, lies in exposing the small company syndrome of trust in a loyal employee: absence of even basic controls and accounting checks; readily accessible cash; failure of the directors to undertake basic supervision; and the fact that such deficiencies are widespread in small companies. The real failure, however, was that the auditors did not respond in a professional manner to what they found at the company. The mutual trust and familiarity between the directors and Mrs Donald had its lethal counterpart in the cosy relationship that had developed over the years between the audit partner and owners of the company. The basic audit queries, inherently appropriate, were clearly not taken seriously.
- When auditors encounter circumstances in which the small company syndrome is apparent they should not respond by automatically making good the deficiencies themselves. That is not their job and even though they may find it necessary to assist the client with some accounts finalisation work, they should not lose sight of the implications for potential fraud of the very deficiencies that they are busily seeking to remedy with their accounting hats on.
- Auditors may believe that a certain level of audit authentication is implicit in the act of performing accounting functions. Why, after all, audit your own work? How can it be cost effective to do so? This is the kind of thinking that allowed this company's auditors to acquiesce in a grossly unsatisfactory state of affairs without regard to the independent stance that they should have been taking.

- No matter how much accounting work is left undone by the client there are certain audit procedures that should always be considered obligatory, notably circularisation of debtors and creditors where the records are not self-balancing and hence inherently unreliable. It is also imperative that auditors need to attend physical stock-taking when no reliable stock records exist. Finally, a programme of random sampling of transactions must always be performed whereby book entries can be related to documents generated by third parties.

As a postscript, readers may be intrigued to learn that the new accountant, when he had put paid to Mrs Donald's nefarious activities, also proceeded to exploit the weaknesses in the accounting system that remained after he had instituted some basic reforms, such as a nominal ledger. He was far more effective than Mrs Donald, in terms of both the amounts embezzled and his cover-up methodology! But that's another story.

Case B.2

This case involves an action in negligence brought by a company in the wholesale photographic equipment business against its auditors. The case is of additional interest in that it arose following a formal complaint made by the directors of the company to the Institute of Chartered Accountants in England and Wales. The complaint underwent process by both the Investigation Committee of the Institute and its Disciplinary Tribunal, following which the Tribunal concluded that the respondents had failed to comply with the relevant auditing standards and ordered that they should be reprimanded and fined.

The case demonstrates that a successful complaint brought in this way is often the precursor to a successful court action, given that the court is unlikely to depart from the Tribunal's conclusions on the standard of audit work, despite the fact that different criteria apply in that forum compared with those in the disciplinary arena.

The fact that many of this company's customers, notably journalists, film directors and animation artists, appeared to prefer to settle their accounts in cash, made it easier for the in-house accountant to misappropriate significant sums without detection. Mr Damien Lilley was responsible for virtually the whole of the company's accounting records and his duties embraced every area of its activities. His responsibilities included the following:

- receiving and agreeing monies handed over from van drivers;
- banking of all cash and cheques received from customers;
- sending out customer statements and reminder letters;
- producing lists of overdue customer accounts for review by the directors;
- maintaining the petty cash system and internal branch monies.

This case is something of a classic in the genre of two-edged swords. In their defence to both the Disciplinary Tribunal and in their filed defence to the claim, the audit firm cited the rudimentary nature of the accounting records, the lack of internal controls and the failure to undertake periodic bank reconciliations as reasons for having to rely on representations made by management to the effect that supervisory controls by the directors served as an effective substitute. Again, the auditors were missing the point. Indeed, their files show that they categorised the audit risk level as 'low' for the very reason that Mr Lilley and the managing director worked closely together and that a relationship of mutual trust subsisted.

An auditor seeking to establish an appropriate independent assessment of the work would instead have reflected the lack of any effective controls in the audit plan. This would, inter alia, focus on entries in the sales ledger, given the comprehensive sway held by Mr Lilley over the five key functions listed above. The appropriate audit work would have included checking the following: on a sample basis that cash and cheques received from credit account customers had been promptly banked and posted to the relevant account in the ledger; that sales invoices had been correctly posted to the relevant accounts in the sales ledger; and that outstanding balances in that ledger represented valid collectable debts due from customers, and were capable of reconciliation to source documents and post balance sheet cash receipts and returns from a debtor circularisation.

Given that an unusually high proportion of the company's customers settled their sales transactions in cash, much of which was misappropriated by Mr Lilley, it was necessary for him to 'plug the gap' in the cash sales control account, in which van drivers' dockets had been recorded, by applying cheques received from credit customers. The 'gap' was thereby shifted to the sales ledger and its size grew in step with each and every such misappropriation. The process of applying remittances received from customers in the ordinary course of business to accounts showing an overdue position is known as *teeming and lading*. In the sense that it is matching fresh monies against existing shortfalls fraudulently created, teeming and lading may be thought of as a mini-Ponzi-type fraud.

Had the auditors' assessment of risk been categorised as 'medium' or 'high', as would clearly have been appropriate, their own audit approach would have obliged them to check a sample of the following:

- postings to the cash sales control account from source documents such as till rolls or van drivers listings;
- paying-in slips for cash bankings to the relevant bank statements;
- paying-in slips showing cheques from customers to individual customer accounts in the sales ledger;
- outstanding balances due from customers to post balance sheet remittances received;
- authenticating closing balances in the sales ledger by reference to a sample of confirmations received in response to a debtor circularisation.

Lessons to be noted

- In this case the auditors misunderstood the key inverse relationship between audit risk and audit work. By allocating a 'low' risk assessment – on the basis of a false premise that management, by virtue of its proximate involvement with the accounting function, and Mr Lilley in particular, was in effect exerting supervisory controls over Mr Lilley's activities – the level of audit work undertaken was bound to be insufficient.
- In their defence the auditors claimed that their procedures to confirm the reliability of the debtors figure in the records consisted of a verification of the posting of invoices in total to the sales ledger, and the agreement of bankings for the year to the sales ledger control account. In this way the defendants proved merely that the *total* funds received from customers, according to the sales ledger, agreed with the *total* amount of funds banked. This procedure was no more than an arithmetical exercise and it included no possibility of revealing that amounts that *should* have been banked (and posted to the sales ledger) had in fact been misappropriated.

- The auditors adopted a monetary materiality threshold for the purposes of their audit planning, but failed to recognise that such a materiality limit would be inappropriate when reviewing the financial statements prior to issuing an audit opinion. The reason for this is that, at the planning stage, it is not possible to know what the final accounts will show. Not only did the auditors adopt a planning materiality that was unduly high because of their negligent risk assessment, but they failed to consider the impact of potential errors and misstatements on the profit and net assets position as reflected in the financial statements to which their audit opinion related.

This was the basis of the finding by the Disciplinary Tribunal that the auditors had failed to comply with the relevant standard on planning work that would have given them a reasonable expectation of detecting material misstatements, whether caused by fraud or error. Their own approach to risk assessment, which they categorised as 'low', absolved them from undertaking any transaction testing whatsoever.

Case B.3

The defrauded entity was a highly successful film production company, specialising in documentaries for mainstream television channels. Its auditors, who had acted in that capacity for over ten years, were instructed to recruit a chief accountant to take over the financial control and record-keeping functions of this rapidly expanding company. The auditors in turn instructed their own 'captive' recruitment firm to undertake this exercise and a suitable candidate, Tracy Curwen, was identified. She was interviewed by the recruitment agency and put forward to the directors as a person fulfilling the requirements of the advertised post in accordance with the firm's standard procedures. Although she provided a complete CV of her past employment record, no references were sought from any previous employer.

The three directors were heavily engaged with the creative and marketing challenges of the business and left the whole of the financial administration to Ms Curwen. None of the directors had any management or accounting background and the field was clear for Ms Curwen to defraud her employer of very substantial sums, in excess of £2 million over a three-year period, in a relatively unsophisticated manner, chiefly by setting up her own company that then invoiced the employer company for fictitious services and supplies. Neither the directors nor the auditors were aware that she and her boyfriend owned the fraudulent vehicle whose name appeared against hundreds of payments in the cash book. Her fraudulent actions were eventually discovered when, in response to persistent questioning by the auditors regarding missing information, she capitulated and confessed.

As often happens in such cases, claims brought against auditors in negligence focus on losses suffered during the entire period between the first audit following the commencement of the fraud and its eventual discovery. Instead of being congratulated on their diligent investigation, they are castigated for not picking up the defalcations some years earlier.

An independent review of the audit files did indeed identify a number of failings. The key to most audits lies in the area of risk assessment. Where risk is categorised as 'high' the level of audit scrutiny is raised in terms of sample sizes, and the reverse applies when risk is considered 'low'. Firms usually have a range of subcategories such as 'negligible' and 'medium'. In this case the auditors employed a sampling scheme that was based on low risk, despite the fact that there was virtually no internal control within Ms Curwen's department. She dictated duties to the other members of staff and was herself able to make entries in the records, pay cheques or make direct bank transfers without her activities being subject to supervision or review.

Other factors should have alerted the auditors including: board minutes that regularly reported cash flow problems and sensitive correspondence with the company's bankers; severe delays in obtaining information from Ms Curwen; complaints from suppliers regarding late payment; an alarming increase in the level of Crown debts such as PAYE and VAT due to late payment; and an inexplicable difference in reported profit margins in the management accounts and annual financial statements respectively.

The auditors patently breached professional standards by omitting to issue management letters to the directors in which their concerns should have been clearly set out. Nor, according to their files, did they undertake any post balance sheet reviews of events that might have cast light on uncertainties existing at the balance sheet date.

Had they ascertained the cheque signatory limits agreed between the company and its bankers they might have been alerted to the remarkable frequency of payments made at precisely the limit of Ms Curwen's sole signatory powers. Indeed, on each occasion that her signatory limit was raised, the size of each of the fraudulent payments rose in step.

The section of the audit programme on payments instructed audit staff to examine the cash book in order to identify 'large and unusual items' for further authentication against supporting documents. The cash book contained an abundance of payments to Ms Curwen's company but, as noted, these were all at or below the limit of her sole signatory authority, which fell below the level of materiality used by the auditors, based in turn on their low-risk classification. The audit programme was flawed in requiring the audit staff to look through the cash book for items that were both large *and* unusual, because the relatively small amount of each of the fraudulent payments automatically disqualified them from selection.

Had the instruction been to search for items that were either large *or* unusual the auditors would have been obliged to note the huge number of round sum payments (ranging from £1,000 to £15,000, depending on Ms Curwen's current signature limit) being made to a purported supplier of goods and services, because it is standard audit procedure to treat round sum amounts as potentially suspect.

The claim was settled through mediation at 50% of the company's losses, the directors' contributory negligence being a significant factor in the negotiations.

Lessons to be noted

The many lessons to be derived from this case are implicit in the above description, but a number of additional observations are appropriate:

- The claim against the auditors included the allegation that negligently they failed to check Ms Curwen's credentials as a qualified accountant (which she was not) or to seek references from previous employers listed on her CV. Auditors are often asked to assist in seeking suitable employees to fill a finance or accounting function. Although this is a service that they are competent to undertake with regard to technical expertise and professional suitability, it would not normally be part of their remit to authenticate claimed qualifications or to seek references. The problem in this case was that the precise terms of the auditors' responsibility were never set down in writing or otherwise clarified with the client and this left them open to charges of negligence.
- Pre-determined, standard audit programmes need to be critically reviewed periodically to identify the potential for fraudulent or

erroneous transactions to slip through the net undetected. Audit tests cannot reasonably be expected to identify every such transaction, but auditing standards have always imposed a responsibility to ensure that any such items stand a reasonable chance of being selected. Even though the routine vouching of payments in the cash book might not have picked up any of the payments to Ms Curwen's company, the instruction to review the cash book as a whole should, if followed intelligently, have caused the auditors to notice the high frequency of payments to a single supplier, all in round-sum amounts containing three zeros.

- A competent audit would have assessed the control environment in which Ms Curwen held sway and on any objective appraisal, particularly in the light of other indications of adverse financial circumstances, a high-risk classification would have been appropriate. This would have completely altered the required audit approach. Instead of simply applying a mathematical formula to figures in the draft accounts to arrive at a suitable materiality level for audit tests, the auditors would have been obliged to adopt a 'bottom up' approach that would have included an assessment of the degree to which Ms Curwen was subject to management supervision and the potential consequences of its total absence.

As noted above, the obvious contributory negligence on the part of the directors served to achieve a settlement of the legal action at an amount substantially less than claimed. The irony is that the very features of the directors' own negligence were the same features that should have established in the minds of the auditors the high-risk nature of the client organisation.

Case B.4

The defrauded entity in this case was a world class ballet company operating from offices in West London staffed primarily with volunteer ballet school graduates looking to enhance their credentials within the world of classical ballet. In the summer of 2009 the company's finance director – who purported to be a specialist in charity and not-for-profit finance, particularly with respect to artistic institutions, and who received a salary in excess of £75,000 – resigned. He subsequently left on 31 August 2009, the company's year-end.

Shortly after his departure other members of the accounts department discovered that he had been embezzling funds in the time-honoured fashion of issuing cheques and BACS transfers payable to his personal creditors, mainly for expenditure relating to the refurbishment of his house. Initial investigations suggested that he had misappropriated approximately £250,000 in the last two years of his employment, but a further detailed review revealed that the fraud extended over virtually the whole five-year term of his employment and amounted to some £660,000 in total.

Although controls were in place to reduce the likelihood of such a fraud occurring, the finance director was able to use his position of authority to circumvent them. In the case of cheque payments he forged the signature of one of the other authorised signatories and in the case of BACS payments he simply instructed the accounts manager, who had custody of the required password, to make payments to an account number that he supplied.

The finance director had concealed the fraudulent payments in the accounting records, not by allocating them over a number of profit and loss expense headings, as usual in such cases, but by posting them as debit items to the accruals account in the nominal ledger and offsetting them against the opening balance on the account, which he deliberately neglected to reverse in the normal way. At the year-end he simply posted further accruals as necessary to ensure that the balance on the account was consistent with the list of accruals provided to the auditors.

He also ensured that the various debit and credit journal entries on the accruals account were so numerous and convoluted that the auditors would have little realistic chance of following their trail, and would in all probability content themselves with establishing that the balance on the account at the year-end agreed to the list of accruals they had been given, which could be verified to appropriate third-party documentation.

In order to conceal the effect of his fraudulent activity on the company's financial position, the finance director manipulated budgets and other management information to create the false impression that the company's cash reserves, which by August 2009 were almost entirely exhausted, remained intact.

As a consequence of being provided with false information by the finance director, the Board of Directors committed the company to expenditure on tours and performances that, had they known the actual, dismal, financial position, they would otherwise have avoided. Thus the company's cash position was depleted not only by the fraudulent payments to the finance director's creditors, but also by the fact that, for several years, the company's legitimate expenditure far exceeded its income from ticket sales, donations and an Arts Council grant.

In view of the negative publicity generated by the discovery of the fraud, the concern expressed by the Arts Council and other funders regarding the effectiveness of its accounts function and internal control procedures, and its current parlous financial position, the ability of the company to continue to operate as a going concern has inevitably been called into question.

The company has initiated legal proceedings against the auditors for their failure to discover the fraud during the course of their audit of the 2008 accounts and in earlier years.

Lessons to be noted

- A mere glance at the accruals account in the nominal ledger would have been sufficient to alert a reasonably experienced auditor to the fact that some strange accounting practices had been going on during the year and would have put such an auditor on enquiry as to the reason for these entries. In this case, however, the auditors appear to have been daunted by the very number and apparent complexity of the entries in the account and were no doubt relieved to note that the final balance agreed nicely with the list of accruals they had been provided with and which they could now happily verify to invoices and other supporting documentation.
- In practice, however, this type of audit fieldwork is usually delegated to relatively inexperienced members of the audit team who simply fail to recognise the significance of what they are seeing on the computer screen. The risk is that they will assume that the numerous debit and credit entries are part and parcel of the company's normal monthly accounting practices and, with one eye on their no doubt tight time budget for completing the aspect of the accounts that they have been allocated to audit, they perceive no good reason to dwell on entries that appear to reverse themselves from one month to the next, given that the final balance on the account is 'correct' by reference to the lead schedules prepared by the client.
- In this case, the relatively junior audit team were the only members of the audit firm that knew how to operate the company's

accounting software system and who therefore had sight of the accounting records. The partner's only visit to the premises occurred once the audit was complete for the purposes of discussing the accounts with Board. Hence he never actually laid eyes on the accounting records themselves.

- Audit finalisation could not have been achieved before the adequacy of ongoing financial headroom has been tested against the ballet company's bookings for home and overseas tours and the cost of mounting these events. Had the auditors done this thoroughly they would have reviewed the company's diary for future bookings over the next two to three years and compared the budget estimate with actual costs of comparable presentations in previous years. Given that Arts Council funding is not an open cheque, the auditors should have considered the adequacy of budget estimates of funding sources.
- There was a fatal hiatus between the knowledge of the audit partner and that of the junior team he sent to conduct the fieldwork. The fact that the audit partner was besotted by classical ballet did not aid his objectivity; when visiting the client, 90% of the time was spent discussing the splendour of the latest stagings, in respect of which he was much encouraged by the fraudulent finance director. The key lesson is to ensure that the highly technical audit juniors have horizons of competence that also extend to accounting plausibility.

C. General failure to recognise internal control weaknesses

It is not sufficient merely to recognise internal control weaknesses. Audit procedures that properly reflect the weaknesses that have been identified must be properly planned, controlled and documented. There is no such thing as a perfect system of internal control. Determined fraudsters, with or without the collusion of one or more other members of staff, will generally devise a method of stealing money or goods from their employers.

It is therefore impossible for directors ever to guarantee that the systems in place are foolproof, and it is important for the auditors to satisfy themselves that any weaknesses in the system are properly identified, evaluated in terms of risk and materiality, and taken fully into account when planning the ensuing audit work. At the conclusion of the audit they have a responsibility to draw significant weaknesses to the attention of the directors, explaining the potential consequences of failing to introduce such remedies as may be appropriate in the company's circumstances.

Case C.1

This case involved an accounts clerk working for a large machinery manufacturer in North East England who confessed to the police that he had defrauded his employers of almost £2.3 million over nine years. The reason for his confession was that a decline in the company's sales had made it more difficult for him to cover up his misappropriations. He explained that these had been conducted in the following ways:

- The company had separate payrolls for the main workforce and for apprentices attached to a government sponsored scheme. The accounts clerk sent out a separate cheque to the scheme administrators to cover the apprentices' wage, but also included this sum in the main weekly payroll cheque. The surplus cash thus arising on the latter (representing the apprentices' wages) should have been re-banked, but was instead pocketed by the clerk, who covered his position with remittances from debtors. Although settled, these accounts were shown in the books as outstanding, but were then covered by subsequent remittances – a classic teeming and lading fraud.
- The clerk would cash his own personal cheques with the company, but when banking cheques, would extract his own. Again he relied on debtor remittances to cover the position.
- Proceeds of cash sales for small parts would from time to time be handed to him for banking. He pocketed the cash and yet again used debtors' cheques to regularise matters.

At each year-end, and prior to the auditors' visit, the clerk ensured that only recently outstanding debts were shown in the debtor accounts. No fewer than nine audits were conducted without anything untoward being discovered. Enquiries regarding the conduct of the audit revealed the following:

- Circularisation of debtors was unsystematic and confined to a very small sample, usually those outstanding for long periods. Since the clerk always ensured that accounts used for his teeming and lading were shown to be more or less up-to-date, the audit test brought nothing to light. The auditors did raise periodic queries concerning long outstanding items, but claimed they always received satisfactory replies from the clerk.

- It is obvious that controls were weak at all material times, and yet the audit firm took no steps to alert management to such weaknesses, nor did they make recommendations for improvement. The audit files showed no evidence of tests being extended due to internal control deficiencies.
- Customers' names never appeared on the bank paying-in slip counterfoils. If these had been entered and a cross-check made against the ledgers, the defalcations would have come to light.
- At all times, the audit firm was unaware of the payroll procedures governing apprentices' wages. Had they compared payrolls, cash books and bank statements, they would probably have noted the extra amount regularly cashed on the main payroll and its re-banking by means of debtor cheque rather than in cash.

Lessons to be noted

- Sales ledger controls that are palpably weak should always trigger specific audit tests such as comprehensive circularisation of debtors on a positive basis. The sample must include a wide range of customer accounts, including those with nil balances and others recently outstanding, if valid conclusions are to be drawn.
- Transaction tests should cover the whole period under review and post balance sheet tests should note the extent to which settled accounts move back into substantial arrears after date.
- Control weaknesses should of course be brought to the attention of the Board and recommendations made for improvement. All such weaknesses should be correspondingly reflected in the audit tests conducted in the areas thereby affected.
- An elementary control – which is well within the scope of even a small enterprise and should have been recommended by the auditors in this case – is to insist upon post being opened by an employee unconnected with the sales ledgers. All incoming remittances should be listed in a memorandum 'cash diary', the total of which should be compared daily with the paying-in slip totals. This simple procedure ensures that all sums received by post are banked without delay, virtually excluding the possibility of teeming and lading.

Case C.2

The audit client in this case was a medium-sized building contractor that specialised in the construction of factory premises to customers' technical specifications. The company's standard terms and conditions required a substantial advance payment of up to one-third of the contract price and stage payments at agreed billing intervals thereafter, depending on the progress achieved and the projected length of the contract.

Responsibility for initiating interim invoices lay with the company's sales manager, based on his assessment of the work completed and, in the case of large contracts, architects' certificates. It was discovered, however, that on certain smaller jobs interim invoices were issued for only a fraction of the value of work completed, or were not issued at all. In at least two instances genuine invoices were issued to customers but the relevant copies were suppressed so that they were not recorded in the sales ledger.

The fraud came to light when a foreman complained to a director that neither he nor his team had been awarded bonuses due to them for early completion of a large factory extension, whereas the records showed that the invoiced sums fell below the value of work that qualified for the company's bonus system. Following discovery of the irregularities the manager confessed to having 'done deals' with certain customers whereby he was paid sums directly in return for low invoicing.

Proceedings against the company's auditors were commenced, based on the quantum of estimated losses suffered due to the manager's fraudulent acts. The value of the claim was £155,350, after taking account of £20,000 restitution made by him following discovery.

The claim alleged that normal audit procedures would have taken account of the company's control weaknesses and that tests on individual contracts would have revealed the disparities between costs and invoice value.

The auditors' defence denied such a responsibility for fraud detection and noted that their standard audit programme had identified no suspicious circumstances. However, they had issued a management letter two years prior to the fraud's discovery in which they had specifically identified the risks associated with the sales manager's pervasive role in that he

- initiated contractual arrangements with customers; and
- had responsibility for issuing invoices, which should have occurred independently in the accounts department.

His dual role as both sales and project manager made it possible for him to undervalue work completed for invoicing purposes. With this knowledge the auditors should have devised tests to bring to light any abuses related to the manager's position. Examination of the audit files showed that their awareness of the weaknesses was not reflected in their audit work, and this failure did not meet current standards of audit risk assessment. It was also reported that the defendant's audit programme had been developed eight years previously and no significant updating had occurred.

Lessons to be noted

- This case demonstrates the importance of adopting an internally consistent approach to audit assignments: once alerted to a weakness that can be exploited by a dishonest employee, auditors are required to reflect this awareness in their audit planning and approach. In this instance, having drawn their client's attention to the weakness, the auditors effectively ignored it in their conduct of the assignment. Although they performed standard tests on sales invoices against cash received from customers as reflected in the ledgers, they undertook no tests on the completeness of the sales population that might have detected the suppressed invoices. Nor did they examine a selection of individual contract accounts for plausibility – a test that might have revealed unexplained losses on certain contracts.
- This case also demonstrates the manner in which UK common law effectively allows auditors to be regarded as a substitute for proper management control. Simply put, the manager's fraud reflected the directors' own failure to impose basic controls; yet they were able to recover their losses from the auditors by suing them in the company's name. Although the damages were reduced by reference to contributory negligence, this was achieved by tactical negotiation on the part of insurers' solicitors rather than by right since the law of contributory negligence cannot be relied upon in cases such as this, brought in contract.

Case C.3

A partner, Anthony Dribble, in the West Midland's firm of Shute & Co acted as 'honorary auditor' to a Charitable Society in a local town and each year prepared a receipts and payments account from the Society's records. It was discovered in 2003 that the Treasurer, Nathan Hazell, had been embezzling money from Society funds. He was prosecuted, pleaded guilty to offences totalling £151,000, and was imprisoned for nine months.

Being a sole signatory to one of the Society's two bank accounts, Mr Hazell was able to draw cheques for cash for personal purposes. It seems that just prior to each year-end he repaid the amount taken but immediately thereafter drew it out again by cashing cheques.

Mr Dribble, who prepared and 'certified' the accounts each year, adopted the following form of words:

> Auditor's Report: The Charity, in common with many others of similar size, derives a substantial proportion of its income from voluntary donations which cannot be fully controlled until they are entered in the accounting records and are not therefore susceptible to independent audit verification.
>
> Subject to the foregoing, I have examined the books and records of the Society and certify that the above Income and Expenditure Account is in accordance therewith.

Mr Dribble considered that the assignment was confined to preparation of the accounts from the records, but it was alleged against him that, as honorary auditors, Shute & Co were under a duty to perform audit work, and counsel's advice stated that because of their own reference to themselves as auditors in succeeding reports it would be difficult for them to maintain otherwise.

Because Mr Dribble had been concerned that donations might not have been fully recorded and accounted for, he arranged a meeting with a Committee member and Mr Hazell. Shute & Co's defence was made more difficult by Mr Dribble's failure to follow up two matters that he raised at this meeting:

- He discovered that the balance remaining in one of the Society's special funds was considerably less than the records disclosed. This was in fact caused by transfers by Mr Hazell from the special fund to the Society's main bank account to cover cash he had extracted.

- He noticed and pointed out that several thousand pounds' expenditure on fund-raising activities had been entered twice in the books: Mr Hazell claimed at the meeting that this had been done in error.

Following the meeting, Mr Dribble wrote to Mr Hazell summarising the matters they had discussed and stated that unless improvements in the system were made along the lines suggested by him at the meeting he would not be prepared to continue to renew his appointment annually. He did not send the Committee a copy; and nor did Mr Hazell.

Mr Dribble conceded that had he examined post balance sheet transactions he would have noted a substantial number of cash cheques being drawn, and this might have alerted him to the fact that these were being used to repay Mr Hazell the funds he had previously stolen and had reimbursed to the company prior to the year-end. Despite the obvious contributory negligence on the Committee's part in giving Mr Hazell so much unsupervised power, Counsel believed that this is a common occurrence with charities that are charged by donors to minimise costs and economise on staff overheads. Hence his view that Shute & Co were vulnerable, particularly since there was a clear acceptance of some form of audit role. The claim was settled by underwriters at an amount close to that claimed.

Lessons to be noted

- This is a situation that can arise when firms act in an honorary capacity for charity clients with limited resources. Recommendations to institute basic internal controls are frequently met by a protestation that the costs of so doing would outweigh the risks of 'leaving everything to the tried and trusted treasurer'. There is obvious merit in this view, but if an accountant perceives that there is a real risk of misappropriation he or she should decline to accept any audit role and ensure that any audit connotation is explicitly removed from the terms of engagement and the form of words used in any report issued.
- In this case there was no letter of engagement setting out a clear and mutually acceptable understanding of the nature of the assignment. Particularly in non-statutory engagements, Courts generally take the view that it is incumbent upon the professional party in the arrangement to ensure that there is no misunderstanding regarding

the assignment's scope and definition. In this case the Society had a constitution that required the appointment of an 'Honorary Auditor', but the constitution had not been re-examined for over 50 years.

- The form of words adopted by Mr Dribble was a relic of a period some 30 years earlier when auditors qualified their reports in the accounts of virtually every small entity. Indeed, this became so rife that the standard wording adopted lost all significance. In this case it simply shows that Mr Dribble had never seriously reviewed the form of words in the reports being issued by his firm. References to 'audit' and 'auditor' compounded the difficulty, despite the fact that the drafting of the certificate made no reference to any audit conclusions. Even the negative comment that voluntary donations are not susceptible to audit implies an assumption of some audit responsibility.
- The fact that the work was of an honorary nature (which generally means that it is performed for a nominal charge rather than the full-time costs of its execution) makes no difference to liability for negligence. The entitlement of the Society and its members to rely on the work for any reasonable purpose itself imposes a duty of care.
- The contributory negligence element, especially in claims brought in contract, may make little difference in practice, and the Committee members claimed with some justification that it was reasonable for them and the Society's members to have relied on the work of the honorary auditor to provide comfort that its assets were protected. The certificate made no reference to any untoward findings beyond the veiled caveat concerning difficulty in auditing voluntary donations.
- Mr Dribble was obviously aware of Mr Hazell's unrestricted control over the Society's bank account, which should have alerted him at the very least to the need to convey his misgivings directly to the Committee.
- The deficiency in the special fund and the duplication in recorded expenditure, both matters of which Mr Dribble was aware, should have led to additional enquiries and tests until resolution was accomplished. A high proportion of claims of this type involve failure to resolve doubts arising from circumstances indicative of irregularity.

D. Inappropriate delegation of key audit tests

Audit work undertaken unintelligently, without a proper understanding of its purpose or place in the overall audit plan, is highly dangerous. The tedium that it instils in the participants causes them to overlook clues to irregularities that are staring them in the face. This loss of vigilance demeans the audit function and renders it worse than useless. Going through the motions mechanically and thoughtlessly robs the audit of its key purpose in maintaining a sceptical attitude to what is presented.

The most obvious instance in which this syndrome appears is when tasks are given to members of the team who lack the knowledge and experience to recognise when something is amiss. Balancing the audit team is sometimes difficult, particularly with 31 December year-ends that stretch the capacity of the firm to a degree that work is given to inexperienced juniors who have not had the advantage of a thorough briefing on the importance of what they are doing. Similarly, where the audit work requires a technical appreciation of some aspect of the client's work, such as recognising the nature of equipment being included in the stock count, it is essential that whoever performs the task is properly qualified to do so.

Case D.1

The entity involved in this action was a well-known national charity with a network of offices controlled through nine regional centres. Even the most dedicated charity managers take some holiday leave, and it was during such a sojourn that a deputy detected a discrepancy in the charity's inter-region returns that led to the discovery of a substantial fraud that had been going on for more than six years. The fraudster was an accountant who, in time-honoured fashion, indulged in the practice of writing cheques to himself or his personal creditors.

Although the sums involved in the fraud were substantial by most standards, they were not sufficiently material to threaten the viability of the charity. The amount abstracted in any one year fell below the materiality threshold adopted by the auditors for planning purposes.

Like the circumstances highlighted in earlier cases, the auditors fell victim to their own findings as recorded on file. Although they adopted an entirely legitimate 'rotational' approach to on-site visits to regional centres for the purposes of checking a sample of transactions or simply reviewing controls, it transpired that an audit team in fact spent one day at the very centre where the fraud was being committed, and that they performed a series of standard audit tests while they were present.

One such test required them to select a sample of nine cash book payments for verification to supporting invoices.

Sampling theory allows auditors to reach an appropriate conclusion on a population of items under scrutiny if, and only if, the following criteria apply:

- the sample size is statistically valid;
- the sample is representative of the population being tested; and
- the sample examined throws up no 'errors' as pre-defined in the sampling plan. For example, if the required invoice was simply unavailable for any reason, that would count as an error for this purpose.

In the event that errors are encountered, a valid audit conclusion can be reached only by expanding the sample size and reviewing the findings to ascertain whether the errors discovered in the original sample have been sufficiently diluted by the absence of errors in the larger sample. If a negative answer again results it may be necessary for the auditors to issue a qualified opinion on the area of the accounts to which the transactions relate.

Irrespective of whether the relatively small sample of nine items was appropriate, the audit team's selection included four payments that were in fact fraudulent. These are summarised as follows:

- Despite being recorded in the cash book as a payment to 'BT', the cheque was described on the audit schedule as 'petty cash reimbursement'. This would suggest that telephone charges had been paid in cash and that the cheque was intended to reimburse the petty cash float. It transpired that the actual cheque had been made payable to the financial controller personally. The problem for the auditors was that no query was raised by them in connection with a transaction that was quite obviously suspect.
- The audit schedule showed that two cheques were unsupported by relevant invoices on the day of the visit. It noted, however, that they were 'found and received' some five days after the day of the visit. It transpired that the requested invoices were fabricated by the accountant and subsequently sent to the audit firm by post. The fabricated invoices bore a close resemblance to supplier's genuine invoices and subtle differences in colour and font were noticeable only when genuine and false invoices were compared side by side. The auditors

should not have treated the absence of invoices required on the day as a normal occurrence to be remedied later. It was an obvious instance in which a larger sample should have been requested to ensure that there were no others similarly missing at the time of their visit.

- The final payment that should have been classified as unsatisfactory from an evidential point of view was made by cheque and recorded in the cash book as a payment to BT in respect of telephone charges. The related invoice, which was not from BT, was accepted by the auditors as evidence of the authenticity of the payment despite the fact that it had not been initialled as required and had no cheque number written on it – indeed, the audit schedule stated as much, and described the payment as 'purchase of satellite dish'. The invoice in fact made it clear that the payment related to 'Toshiba Satellite Pentium' and the computer in question was subsequently recovered by the police from the accountant's home following discovery of the fraud.

Lessons to be noted

The final payment in the above list (for 'purchase of satellite dish') should have triggered a series of key questions:

- Why was there a reference to 'BT – telephone charges' in the cash book when the payment had nothing to do with such charges?
- Why would a national charity be spending money in one of its regions on a satellite dish (the auditors' description of what was in fact a computer)?
- Was the satellite dish available for inspection, and had it been treated as a fixed asset in the nominal ledger?

This case illustrates a hazard regularly encountered. The cross-checking of payments in a cash book to supporting documents generated by third parties is a relatively straightforward operation in physical terms. For this reason, almost by default, it is delegated to the most junior member of the audit team, as happened in this case. It should, however, have been obvious to those planning the audit that the authentication of payments was one of the most critical aspects. Therefore, the audit needed to be undertaken by a member of the team with sufficient experience to recognise transactions that were inherently suspicious, and with the understanding of sampling theory to appreciate that even one 'error' in the sample would have the effect of invalidating audit conclusions without undertaking more work.

E. Failure to follow up suspicious circumstances

The authors recall an instance in which two junior members of the audit team became stupefied with boredom, as a result of having to vouch thousands of copy sales invoices to the sales day book. In the course of this monumental waste of resources they actually came across an entry in the day book for a sale that had no counterpart invoice on the file. On reporting this to the chief accountant, he thanked them for their diligence, typed out a fresh copy sales invoice and handed it to them. They promptly punched holes, placed it in its proper place on the file, bashed it with the inked audit stamp and carried on vouching!

The circumstances were not necessarily 'suspicious', but could conceivably have represented a deliberate inflation on the turnover figure. Instead of checking that the relevant customer account had been charged and payment subsequently received, the dopey duo were concerned only with form, not substance: a piece of paper was missing from the file, and once it was replaced they were quite happy to continue with their mindless activity.

The fault lay not with them, of course, but elsewhere. The purpose of ensuring that every invoice is included in turnover, and conversely that turnover is not overstated, was never explained to them.

Sometimes it is tempting to take the easy option and simply assume that everything is 'okay'. Most fraudsters rely on this incipient inertia when dealing with audit queries by providing answers that, to the alert mind, do not stack up.

Case E.1

This case involved a company that operated a golf hotel complex. The company maintained a separate bank account for lodging deposits received from customers in advance. In the course of their audit, the auditors noted and queried a discrepancy between the record of deposits received and the sums banked according to bank statements. The directors declined to commission a full investigation by the auditors, but requested their employee (unfortunately the same employee responsible for the misappropriation that caused the discrepancy) to perform the necessary investigation work.

The firm then completed their audit, but obtained from the directors a general letter of acknowledgement that although audit procedures might sometimes disclose irregularities and defalcations, responsibility for operating internal controls to prevent the occurrence of such matters rests with the directors.

Early the following year the auditors received a letter in which they were asked, without explanation, to resign. Following investigation work performed by succeeding auditors it appears that defalcations totalling £570,000 had occurred over a four-year period.

Despite the aforementioned directors' signed acknowledgement, the original auditors were put on enquiry by the discrepancy between deposits recorded and banked respectively, and their own file notes stand as clear testimony to their awareness of same, including their acknowledgement that it was potentially indicative of misappropriation.

This discovery should have alerted them to the following:

- the need for a satisfactory resolution to the discrepancy that they had brought to light;
- the possibility that other similar discrepancies might exist in sections of the records not selected for scrutiny; and
- the potential effect of such occurrences on the accounts on which they were reporting.

The subsequent settlement, at the full amount claimed, included interest lost on the sums misappropriated and substantial fees paid to succeeding auditors in respect of their work on the earlier defalcations.

Lesson to be noted

The directors' signed acknowledgement of responsibility for fraud prevention through internal control systems amounted to little more than is included in most standard letters setting out terms of engagement. Such standard wording may prove to be ineffective as a disclaimer if

- auditors have (as in this case) already been alerted to suspicious circumstances requiring resolution in the course of performing their routine audit duties – particularly since their own file notes made clear the potentially fraudulent implications of the discovered discrepancy; and
- the potential effect of such matters on the truth and fairness of the accounts subject to audit is material, the auditor's statutory reporting duties obviously taking precedence over any terms that the parties, or either of them, purport to interpose.

Case E.2

The client company is in the construction industry. In early 1999 it acquired a subsidiary that enjoyed recurring Ministry of Defence (MoD) contracts for dockyard work. The parent company auditors were appointed to audit the subsidiary's accounts for the year-ended 31 December 1999. In the course of the audit they queried certain unexplained cash payments to the MoD, ostensibly for materials, and were advised by the company secretary that the MoD supplies department held extensive stores at the dockyard, and were prepared to release urgently required materials to the contractors provided they were subsequently replaced or paid for.

The secretary explained that at the end of each month materials not replaced were paid for in cash, because no formal sales ledger account had been set up. The auditors noted, however, that the MoD invoices were issued on Challenge carbon notebook paper rather than official Ministry stationery. Although their suspicions persisted the auditors accepted the explanation on the grounds that the sums were not material in relation to the contract as a whole, and they included the matter on their 'points forward' schedule for the following year's audit.

The explanations provided by the company secretary masked a fraud that escalated rapidly over the next two years. Internal delays associated with the company's computerisation programme meant that the 2000 audit did not commence until October 2001, the intention being that the 2001 audit would follow on in early 2002, when the systems problems had been resolved.

The fraud, which involved collusion between the company secretary, two contract engineers and two MoD warehouse staff, consisted of requisitions and orders being formally approved by the secretary, and handed to the storemen at the MoD dockyard. They would then arrange for the deliveries, but concealed them by faking their stock records. The cash settlements were arranged by the secretary, who simply added the amount required to the already substantial monthly imprest for site agents' disbursements and casual labour. The extra cash was then misappropriated and split five ways.

Initially the requisitions represented materials genuinely required on the contract site, but as the fraud escalated the storemen widened their 'customer' base and made the deliveries themselves. The fraud was discovered only when the MoD delivery vehicle temporarily blocked a private driveway, causing a complaint. The MoD Transport Director queried the presence of one of their vehicles in that location, and began to watch the driver more closely, noting other deliveries to unauthorised addresses.

When later pressed about his actions the driver confessed to the entire scam and named his co-conspirators, also disclosing that more than £400,000 had been misappropriated in this way over the previous 12 months. All five participants are currently serving prison sentences.

The subsidiary company then commenced an action against its auditors alleging negligence in failing to

- follow up their discovery of unusual cash payments; and
- draw the matter to the attention of the directors.

Experts reported to insurers that only 5% of the sum lost had been stolen in periods for which no audit had been concluded. Although the auditors had been remiss in dismissing a potentially serious query on grounds of non-materiality, it was recommended that the claim should be strenuously resisted, particularly since the directors had themselves allowed substantial payments to be made in cash without any effective controls.

The claimants legal advisers reached a similar conclusion, and an offer of £207,000 in full settlement was accepted.

Lessons to be noted

- The circumstances of this case highlight the dangers of adhering slavishly to conventional notions of materiality. Although it is accepted that the extent of the fraud in the initial period was well below the auditor's materiality threshold, they should have
  - pursued their enquires until they discovered the facts of what was actually happening;
  - considered the *potential* impact of any abuses or systems weakness; and
  - reported their *findings* and recommendations directly to the Board in a formal management letter, as required by Auditing Standards, rather than leaving the matter with the company secretary who, unbeknown to them, was party to the fraud.
- The suspicious circumstances included
  - payments for site materials in cash; and
  - the related invoices carrying no official Ministry imprint.

The rule for auditors is that suspicious circumstances, regardless of the materiality of the sums involved, should always be probed until resolved. Had the auditors adopted such a course it is possible that this very substantial fraud might have been terminated in its infancy.

This is a classic illustration of de facto discovery by auditors of fraud perpetrated by employees, but preferring the easy option of believing explanations that they should have recognised to be spurious. It happens far more often than one might expect.

Case E.3

The client company, an international haulage contractor, operated its own transport department and also engaged the services of third party hauliers when its own vehicles were fully utilised. The transport department was under the day-to-day control of two senior managers with long service records. They were responsible for programming the loads and allocating jobs to company vehicles or subcontracting them to independent hauliers, after obtaining satisfactory references and price quotations.

It was noted by the Transport Director that one such company appeared to be using vehicles bearing a different name and livery, but was advised by the managers that the vehicle owners were invoicing through a separate company 'for tax reasons'. Over the ensuing three-and-a-half years the amount of transport business placed with this particular haulier expanded to the point that it became the company's largest supplier of transport services.

Following the introduction of new legislation affecting road transport vehicles, the client decided to upgrade and expand the company's own fleet. Part of the strategy was to acquire one of its existing haulage suppliers, and the accounts of those selected were obtained from Companies House. They were then passed to the company's auditors for an initial assessment.

When examining the accounts of the major supplier described above, the audit partner recognised that its owners and directors were none other than the company's own two transport managers. This was reported to the client company's managing director (MD), who then contacted the MD of the hauliers whose vehicles had been used by the suspect supplier. This MD reported that he had been fed the reciprocal explanation for the intermediate company: it had been created by the customer entity as a means of mitigating its tax liabilities!

Needless to say, the two culprits were apprehended and summarily dismissed. The client company commenced proceedings against the intermediate company and its owners to recoup the profits lost, represented by the difference in haulage rates negotiated with the independent carrier and those charged to the client company, amounting to more than £800,000 over a five-year period. An action was also commenced against the auditors for recovery of any sums not otherwise recouped.

Experts acting for the defendant firm reported that the audit files referred to suspicions regarding the conduct of the two managers, but that these had regrettably never been communicated to the company's senior management. One query concerned the two managers' lifestyle, one being seen by audit staff driving a Ferrari and the other a brand new Porsche. Another audit query, never resolved, concerned certain invoices from the suspect company for haulage jobs never undertaken, but which were nevertheless passed by the managers for payment.

A management letter had been drafted following each audit, but was never delivered to the Board of Directors 'in the interests of minimising costs'. The draft letters included reference to weaknesses in the transport department, notably the fact that the managers were autonomously responsible for

- placing business;
- negotiating terms; and
- approving invoices for payment.

The auditors had also noted the so-called 'tax avoidance' explanation given by the intermediate supplier, and should have appreciated its patently spurious nature.

In consideration for not pressing criminal charges against them, the two managers agreed to make substantial restitution from the past profits of their company, leaving approximately £200,000 in the claim against the auditors. A strong defence was pleaded, based on the management's own failure to control the responsibilities and actions of its managers, and on the accepted common law limitations of the scope of an audit and what might reasonably be expected from it. A settlement of £97,000, including costs, was negotiated.

Lessons to be noted

- Once auditors have recorded queries arising from their work, these should be followed up and pursued until satisfactorily resolved. Had they formally reported their suspicions to the Board, including the passing of invoices for jobs never undertaken, their position would have been less exposed when the fraud's nature and dimensions had been discovered.
- Although the client company's financial statements, on which the auditors reported in true and fair terms without qualification, correctly reflected its actual results, it is always difficult to plead this as a defence when more persistent audit work would have revealed the extent to which those results had been adversely affected by fraud on the part of the company's managers.
- Company management frequently relies on auditors to identify systems weaknesses that are susceptible to fraudulent abuse. Although in this case the client perennially complained about the audit costs, this would be an unacceptable defence for failing to issue formal management letters already in draft. Standards requiring formal communication between auditors and senior management have applied for many years, and this case highlights their importance as a means of reducing exposure to liability when there are genuine weaknesses to report.

2.9 USING THE COMPANY AS AN INSTRUMENT OF FRAUD BY SENIOR MANAGEMENT

This genre of fraud is characterised by the use of a corporate vehicle to enable its owners to steal money from third parties, whether financial institutions, investors or even government. In contrast to Section 2.8, which addresses instances of employees exploiting internal control lapses reflecting management failure to impose controls, the cases highlighted here set out the fraudulent exploits of top management (usually the owners). Since they hold dominant and powerful sway over other employees, the lack of internal control is often deliberate and is obviously to their advantage.

In such circumstances the obvious audit risk relates to the ability of senior management to exploit their control of the records to hide their illicit transactions. Consequently auditors should factor in the 'dominant director' syndrome when planning the audit. Attention should obviously be paid to such matters as directors' expenses to ensure that they are justifiably reimbursable, there being no independent authorisation involved.

F. Lack of independence

Guidance on professional conduct stipulates that members of the audit team should not risk compromising their audit independence by undertaking any executive or other non-audit roles for or on behalf of the client entity or its directors. It is the responsibility of the partner or manager to ensure that audit independence exists both in name and in substance and this review must be evidenced on the audit file every year. The guidance lists comprehensively the circumstances in which independence may be jeopardised – by making or receiving loans, gifts or even social invitations – and the process of affirming independence should always be vetted by a partner unconnected with the client to ensure that any compromising circumstances are taken fully into account.

Case F.1

This case concerns a sole practitioner, Henry Worrall, who in 2003 accepted an appointment as auditor of two small design companies offered to him by his oldest friend, Clarence Brighouse, who was the newly-appointed finance director of both companies. The two companies had a common shareholder who took full responsibility for the operations of the businesses but left financial matters entirely to Mr Brighouse.

Mr Worrall and Mr Brighouse had been at school together and 'best man' at each other's weddings, and were godfathers to each other's children and regularly attended social events together. Some years earlier Mr Brighouse had been articled to Mr Worrall's practice as a trainee and had spent several years with him post-qualification in an 'audit manager' role.

Naturally, having been appointed finance director to the two companies, Mr Brighouse lost little time in appointing his old friend Mr Worrall as auditor. Unfortunately, they were not particularly lucrative appointments from Mr Worrall's perspective because neither company was profitable and he was asked by Mr Brighouse to do what he could to keep his fees to a minimum.

The solution to the fees situation seemed obvious to Mr Worrall. Who better to undertake the necessary audit procedures than his old friend and former employee, who knew his audit system inside out? Without further ado he duly photocopied the entire audit programme and sent it to his old chum to complete.

Unsurprisingly, in his capacity as 'audit senior', Mr Brighouse succeeded in producing an immaculate audit file, complete with all the requisite planning documentation, diligently completed audit tests and fulsomely-worded conclusions. When Mr Brighouse's escapades finally led to the collapse of both companies, Mr Worrall found himself at the wrong end of negligence claims. Examination of the file by experts engaged by Mr Worrall's insurers, revealed that Mr Brighouse's answers to certain prescribed audit enquiries had been less than candid.

For example, in answer to the question on the professional independence questionnaire 'Is the partner or any senior employee on the audit joining in or involved in substantive negotiations with the client?', Mr Brighouse ticked 'no', presumably on the basis that he had not engaged in any substantive negotiations with himself!

He also assessed the risk of fraud on the part of himself as 'low', a somewhat inaccurate assessment given that over the course of his five-year tenure as finance director Mr Brighouse managed to misappropriate a sum in excess of £250,000 from the two companies using the age-old method of paying his personal expenses with company cheques.

Notwithstanding that he claimed on the face of the relevant audit schedules to have vouched 100% of the companies' purchase invoices, Mr Brighouse's 'rigorous' audit procedures somehow failed over the entire five-year period to detect any indication whatsoever of his own fraudulent activities, the fraud coming to light only when the principal shareholder, having become perplexed by his companies' perennial shortage of cash and failure to make a profit, decided in 2008 to glance through the cash books from which the fraud became immediately apparent.

The shareholder issued proceedings against Mr Worrall whose insurers responded by instructing an expert to report on the quality of the audit work. Needless to say the expert's advice was that the case against Mr Worrall was indefensible. Indeed the question arose as to whether professional indemnity (PI) insurance policies are obliged to cover instances of such reckless disregard for fundamental audit principles. Mr Worrall was indeed fortunate that his PI insurers decided in the end not to deny indemnity altogether.

Lessons to be noted

- At first glance there seems little to draw from such an extreme example of a practitioner's abject failure to understand the very essence of what constitutes an audit, namely its *independence*. Without this, the process is merely an accounting exercise, not an audit. This recent case demonstrates that even now, after the plethora of technical and ethical guidance issued by the accountancy authorities over the years, there are still some accountants who fail to grasp the principles at even the most basic level.
- In the current economic climate the greatest risk facing any accountancy practice is the threat of a claim for which their insurance policy proves invalid. There must be a limit to *how gross* a practitioner's recklessness can be before he or she loses the benefit of insurance cover!

Case F.2

This case centred on a UK company, which was part of an international group ultimately owned and controlled by an East African family based in Kenya. The company bought aero-engines and alternators and converted them into generator sets for sale to its customers. It won a Queen's Award for Exports in 1997 and 1998.

Over the seven-year period from 1994 to 2000, the directors of this company falsified the company's accounts by creating fictitious sales and debtors in order to obtain funding from its bank through an invoice discounting facility. They also defrauded the company itself by channelling money and assets into companies controlled by members of the same family in India and certain Middle Eastern countries. By the time the fraud was discovered the company had lost millions of pounds, and so had the bank that had been funding the scam.

The fraud was exposed when the bank became alarmed to note that the company was increasingly falling behind on its repayments and that many 90-day debtors had become nine-month debtors in the company's books. The bank, having been fobbed off with excuses for more than two years, was left with no option but to make direct contact with some of the longest outstanding debtors. The bank found out that those debtors did not exist and the invoices were false. In fact, the company's trading transactions amounted to little more than 30% of its size as shown in its records. It certainly could not afford to repay its obligations either on their due dates or at all. The company's actual turnover of £7 million was inflated to £28 million in the accounts of a single year.

The company was put into receivership and it soon became apparent that the bank would be able to recover no more than a fraction of the £7.5 million it was owed.

The Serious Fraud Office was brought in to investigate the fraud perpetrated by the directors, and this eventually led to them being charged with criminal offences to which they pleaded guilty.

Inevitably the role of the auditors was investigated by the receivers and a multi-million pound negligence action was commenced.

The auditors were a five-partner firm with a single office in North London, and the company in question was its largest client. Moreover, the exceptionally wealthy owners, all of whom were directors and members of the same family, were also personal clients of the practice. Consequently every conceivable incentive existed for the firm to ensure that nothing was done in the course of the audit that might cause the directors to become disaffected. These circumstances represent a recipe for audit failure given the degree to which independence is bound to be compromised and seen to be so.

A further obstacle to the auditors' defence was the departure of the manager responsible for the audit to join the board of the client company as finance director, without any 'cooling-off' period between jobs. When the time came for the following year's audit to commence he was contacted by his erstwhile firm and asked whether, since no one in the firm understood the client company's business as fully as he did, he would be kind enough to accept a secondment back to the firm for the sole purpose of supervising the audit!

It was alleged against the auditors that whenever faced with a query, they far too readily accepted explanations from the directors rather than pursuing their own enquiries through to a conclusion. The result was a settlement at close to the full amount claimed plus costs.

Lessons to be noted

- The close relationship between the audit firm and the management of the company clearly militated against a truly independent audit. The audit papers included lengthy schedules comprising the entire list of sales transactions, with audit marks entered whenever genuine supporting documentation (such as order numbers, delivery schedules) was available. The lists included all the fictitious sales transactions but there was no record of any query to the effect that they were unsupported. The 'audit' exercise was in fact a grand accounting reconciliation and involved no intelligent checking.

- It should have been obvious that there was a huge discrepancy between the VAT records and the sales records. Although this might have been partly explained by the volume of sales purporting to be exports, most of the difference arose because the sales had been fraudulently inflated to impress the bank in order to secure additional finance on fictitious invoices.
- Debtors were unsupported by any third party evidence, and it should have been clear to the auditors that direct confirmations were required.
- Stocks in the balance sheet included goods held on consignment belonging to suppliers and yet were shown in the records and draft accounts as company assets, despite documentation that clearly showed the true status of the goods in question.
- A great deal of creative work was performed with the use of the journal, always the most lethal accounting record. It was used to good effect in relation to substantial sums paid to the directors. Journal entries were made whereby these amounts were charged to other companies under their control and then written off as bad debts or recharged against the profit and loss account as an expense.

G. Lack of resources

Suspicions should always be aroused when a large company appoints a small firm of auditors. Why would a major entity with operations on three continents wish to appoint a three-partner provincial firm to act as its group auditors? The answer is that the directors, in all probability, have much to hide. It is the very fact that the audit firm's resources are so palpably inadequate to meet the requirements of a major audit that makes them such attractive appointees when the last thing the client wants is a pukka job done.

The temptation to the audit firm is obvious: very substantial fees on a recurring basis and a flow of work that will keep everyone fully occupied. For this reason the professional bodies set a limit on the percentage of total fees that the firm is allowed to receive from a single client source. Once the 10% threshold is reached alarm bells should be ringing, and in no circumstances should this level exceed 15%. This is no more than informal guidance, however, and it obviously does not guarantee independence – which can be compromised in many other ways as we have seen.

Firms should always ensure that they are adequately resourced before accepting an audit assignment, even if it means bringing in staff with appropriate experience and qualifications especially for the purpose.

Case G.1

The public company concerned was a national high street retailer of women's fashion clothing. Over a period of some four years its directors, who had retained significant shareholdings, boosted the company's assets by a process known as 'multi-financing'. The company had over 100 stores in most major cities and the directors used finance leasing (secured on company assets) to fund the construction of new shop fronts. The fraud consisted of the fact that a single shop front would typically have been used to raise finance from two separate finance companies.

The company's auditors were a two-partner firm in the North of England, and they quite simply lacked the resources to do justice to an audit of this size. This is a syndrome that is regularly encountered in the course of forensic work. Directors or owners of companies with complex systems and activities who seek to mask fraudulent activity will often appoint a small firm of auditors who

- lack the resources and experience to dig beyond the surface level of a web of transactions; and
- become financially dependent on the fees from the audit and hence reluctant to follow up suspicious circumstances in a manner that might incur the displeasure of the client company's management.

This degree of dependency will inevitably raise questions concerning complicity rather than mere incompetence and acquiescence. The 2008 Bernie Madoff scandal is clearly a case in point. Both the New York and London audit firms comprised little more than a front for producing audit certificates, apparently without any underlying attempt to verify the company's fraudulent or nonexistent investment transactions.

Even high profile frauds that implicate big-firm auditors in charges of negligent work will often rely on a single office of the audit firm to conduct most of the work, as happened with Enron. Although the auditors' name and reputation is used as a front for respectability, it is often the case that a small branch of the firm will depend for its internal viability on the retention of the audit in question. This was certainly true of the audit of the de Lorean car company in Northern Ireland.

Reverting to the case in question, to their credit the auditors noted in the course of their work a particular instance of finance being obtained twice on the same asset. Despite representations from the management that this was an administrative error, the auditors considered that they had been seriously misled and that they had little option but to resign, given that the all-important trust that should subsist between management and auditors had broken down. In their resignation letter, the auditors cited their reasons for resigning as 'falsification of company records, obtaining finance by fraud and failing to maintain proper accounting records'.

Two months later the company collapsed with over £60 million being owed to creditors. Investigations by the police and the serious fraud office were commenced, criminal actions were instituted and the directors were convicted and sentenced to varying terms of imprisonment.

Lessons to be noted

In this particular case the lessons are implicit in the narrative provided. The company's liquidators were, of course, duty-bound to investigate the conduct of the auditors given that a systematic fraud on several finance companies had continued undetected for so many years prior to the company's collapse. Scrutiny of the audit files and the relevant sections of the company's records showed a number of audit failings, and ensuing litigation was settled at an amount that approximated to the limit of the firm's indemnity. In particular:

- Although the files included pre-printed audit working papers, these enabled the auditors to go through the motions of audit testing without attempting to apply their critical faculties to the process in an intelligent manner. The impression was given of a firm who saw its task as simply to complete a series of prescribed audit tests without regard to the substance of what would have been obvious had they stepped back and looked at the evidence before them, rather than merely assuming that what was recorded was real. Indeed there was no evidential support recorded on files to substantiate the conclusion expressed in the audit opinion. The company's own records, understandably with the hindsight knowledge of a massive fraud, were incomplete to such a degree that they too provided no reliable basis for the production of financial statements.

- The audit files included copies of management letters issued by the auditors in successive years in which they highlighted their awareness of the inadequacy of the fixed asset register. Year after year they noted that it was impossible to relate leasehold costs or the cost of fixtures to any particular shop, and consequently that the company records may be carrying fixed assets that had already been disposed of. Despite recommendations concerning the information that a proper asset register would include, the company directors simply carried on as before.

Notwithstanding the above difficulties, the auditors included a schedule in their file that listed additions to the register of new shop fronts during each of the years in question. Reference to the equivalent schedule in the previous year's working papers clearly showed new shop fronts being added for the same branches, but with the name of a different finance company entered alongside.

H. Failure to obtain third party verification

Audit evidence used to support the audit opinion may be categorised in terms of quality. Simple word of mouth from members of the client staff, if relating to significant accounting issues, should never be relied upon without additional support in whatever form is appropriate. Written representations from an internal source, including the standard letter of representation from the directors, is normally acceptable as reliable evidence, provided that

- there are no circumstances that give rise to suspicion; and
- the auditor is satisfied that the directors do not stand to benefit personally from the matters that those representations address.

In the case of the City Equitable Fire Insurance Company (1924) the auditors were successfully charged with negligence because they accepted, from the insurance company's stockbrokers, a certificate confirming the custody of a substantial portfolio of securities representing the investment of premiums already received. The securities had in fact been fraudulently pledged by the stockbrokers (who were known to be heavily indebted to City Equitable) to outside parties in order to cover losses on unauthorised dealings in the investments of other clients. As a consequence City Equitable suffered severe losses.

Although it was acceptable practice for auditors to request certificates from third parties in appropriate circumstances, it was held that the auditors in this case had been negligent for two specific reasons:

- It is not normal for stockbrokers to act as the permanent custodians of clients' investments and securities. The company's own secured vaults or those of its bankers would have been an appropriate repository.
- The senior partner in the stockbroking firm, who subsequently faced criminal charges, was at the time of the audit the Chairman of City Equitable – a fact known to the auditors when they accepted his firm's external certificate.

Whenever a material asset is being verified, this should if at all possible be done directly. Had the auditors of City Equitable called for the securities for inspection, they would have discovered the fraud immediately. Certificates should be requested only from third parties whose ordinary course of business includes the activities or custodianship being certified.

Any certificate accepted must of course emanate from an independent source – which is the entire point of the exercise. Occasionally full independence is impossible, such as the receipt of certificates from staff confirming their indebtedness to the company. In such cases, however, the amounts involved are unlikely to be excessive or material.

Case H.1

The company in this case was set up by a highly inventive entrepreneur, Mr Simeon Ripley, for the sole purpose of fabricating a superstructure of false documentation that purported to reflect the manufacture and onward sale of a narrow range of easily erectable fairground equipment. Mr Ripley's real purpose, of course, was not to manufacture anything at all – other than documentation purporting to represent orders from local authorities and private fairground operators in the UK, Scandinavia, Italy and the Baltics.

The scam was to use the overseas orders for fairground equipment as a basis for gaining Bank of England ECGD approval, on the strength of which finance was raised under a revolving credit system from a major UK bank. Some £5 million was raised (and misappropriated) in this way over a four-year period. The auditors of Mr Ripley's company devoted excessive time to the production of accounting records sufficient to support a set of reasonably plausible financial statements. Their principal source for this exercise was, of course, the bogus documentation provided by Mr Ripley and a number of his servile acolytes working overseas, purporting to reflect high-value transactions whereby municipalities, communes and local authorities purchased merry-go-rounds, big wheels and dodgem cars.

No attempt was made by the auditors to test thc underlying veracity of the transactions themselves. They did not undertake debtor circularisations or enter into any direct communication with the overseas parties for the simple reason that Mr Ripley explicitly prohibited any such contact. He invariably protested that attempts of this nature on the part of the auditors would not be understood by the relevant parties and would serve only to upset them.

The successive use of equipment orders by Mr Ripley to settle liabilities to the bank arising from earlier orders would have achieved relatively little had there not been a gradual but irreversible escalation in the size of the facility balance over a period of some five years. The point was reached, however, when it became clear to Mr Ripley that the paltry sums received in respect of supposedly fulfilled orders were bound to generate a worrying credibility gap with the consequent risk of the entire structure crumbling. At this finely judged juncture he proceeded to put the company into insolvent liquidation and unceremoniously decamped to Sweden, where he was known to have a team of co-conspirators.

Lessons to be noted

- Regardless of obstacles put in the way of auditors by a powerful and persuasive managing director, the circumstances of this case made it imperative that material and long overdue debts (in some cases by 15 months after the balance sheet date) should be verified by direct communication. Furthermore there appeared from the audit files to have been no attempt to corroborate the substance of transactions for purchases of raw materials from which the equipment would have been produced.
- No tests were performed by the auditors on the outstanding liability to the finance company at various points in time or to reconcile the liability balance shown in the records with confirmations supplied by the finance company.

- An obvious audit failure was the absence of any 'plausibility test', which would have shown that the amounts actually received from 'customers' were woefully insufficient to support the level of exports purported to have occurred.
- In addition to the above, it was clear from the files that manager reviews undertaken prior to audit completion drew attention to matters requiring investigation, none of which were properly dealt with before the issue of an unqualified audit opinion. Such matters included the fact that there appeared to be no contracts with customers on file, and a note to the effect that stocks and work in progress 'appear to be totally unaudited and as such unacceptable'.

The sad fact is that the audit partner, whose sole responsibility it would have been to address the aforementioned queries, had established a close social relationship with Mr and Mrs Ripley, and had blinded himself to the potential consequences of signing off while such blatantly suspect discoveries remained unaddressed.

I. Improper reliance on management representations

The qualitative classification of audit evidence has already been mentioned in the previous section. The most reliable form of evidence for audit purposes is that which has been generated from a completely independent third party source. Obvious examples include suppliers' invoices and statements, which are clearly documents that originate outside the client entity.

This does not mean, of course, that they cannot be used in a fraudulent context, but this would usually involve collusion on the part of someone in the supplier's employment, and collusion always involves greater risk to fraudsters because one of the culprits may suddenly be beset by a fit of contrition and confess.

Sometimes it is not possible or practicable to obtain independent confirmation of important audit issues, such as an assessment of the amount that should safely be regarded as recoverable from debtors, or the valuation of shares in unlisted companies (although it may be possible to assess a range of reasonable valuations from a set of accounts, if recent and audited). In such cases, it is obviously acceptable for the auditor to rely on representations of senior management, always provided that he or she has no reservations concerning the honesty and integrity of those from whom the representations are received. Reliance on evidence of this nature should never be resorted to as the 'easy option'.

In this section we address three instances of inappropriate reliance on management representations.

Case I.1

In this case the liquidator brought an action (funded by HMRC) against the auditors of a company whose sole director had depleted the company's resources over a number of years in order to fund his own building developments. The company's principal activity was to lease trailers to haulage companies, and this was a successful and profitable enterprise – sadly brought down by the owner's frolic with residential building speculation.

The auditors had accepted the director's wholly unsupported assurances that the proceeds from the eventual sale of his own properties being developed would be sufficient to extinguish his debt to the company. In the event the properties were sold at a significant loss and the company was placed in the hands of a liquidator, who promptly sought compensation from the auditors on the basis that they had, all too readily, accepted the director's wishful thinking as valid audit evidence.

Lessons to be noted

- It is imperative that auditors give proper consideration to the validity and plausibility of any representations made by management and, where possible, that such representations are verified by reference to independent third party documentation.
- The significance of the representation in the context of the company's overall financial position must also be considered. In this case there was no recognition on the part of the auditors that the company's ability to continue to operate as a going concern was wholly dependent on the recoverability of the director's loan.

Case I.2

The claimant company was the sole UK agent and distributor of advanced technology colour printers manufactured in Germany. Its MD was the controlling shareholder and enjoyed almost complete autonomy in exercising his stewardship. The German supplier periodically provided its UK agent with substantial loan capital, but it appears that this was accounted for incorrectly as a credit to cost of sales, inflating profits accordingly. Loans in excess of £600,000 were treated in this way over a two-year period.

The MD then sold a substantial proportion of his shareholding to a third party investor, but continued to run the company. Over the ensuing 18 months the company became increasingly stretched for cash, with a rising overdraft secured by way of a floating charge over the company's assets. The bank became anxious over its margin of security, because title in the machine stocks was reserved by the German manufacturer. Sales declined as the recession hit the printing industry and the bank appointed a receiver.

Independent accountants called in by the receiver reported that the accounts of the company were materially defective in respect of each of the three most recent years of account, in each case overstating profits significantly due to:

- incorrect treatment of German loans as credits to costs of sales;
- disregard of exchange losses of £65,000;
- understating interest charges and administrative expenses to the extent of £42,000.

In addition, the independent accountants uncovered defalcations by the MD in excess of £150,000 – most of which comprised cash drawings charged against the intercompany account with the German suppliers. There appeared to be little prospect of significant recovery from the MD, who also faced police charges. The amount claimed in the Statement of Claim was £789,000, including the costs of the investigating accountants and the re-audit of the accounts in question, as well as consequential trading losses incurred after the audit of the first accounting period.

Inspection of the audit files showed little evidence of proper procedures having been performed, and that the auditors had relied excessively on the representations of the MD. Solicitors acting for the underwriters reported a serious risk of liability and recommended a negotiated settlement on the best terms possible, particularly since the partner in the firm responsible for the audit had retired due to a serious heart condition and was unable to provide more than token assistance.

Lessons to be noted

- This case highlights the determination with which receivers and liquidators will pursue auditors in the name of the company for recovery of the full amount of its losses even when the principal culprit is the company's own managing director. Unlike the UK's 'joint and several' system, most EU member states, by contrast, operate a fairer 'several' liability system as a result of which proportional liability is effectively applied by the Courts. One cannot, however, blame liquidators for their approach since they have a duty to recover as much as possible from all available sources, and may themselves become personally liable for any failure to act with vigour and alacrity in pursuit of this objective.
- The case also demonstrates the dangers of extensive reliance on the client company's management as a substitute for independent authentication of recorded transactions, possibly to save time costs. In this instance the auditors failed to obtain direct confirmation from the German supplier of the true nature of the substantial payments it made to its UK agents. In general, if the audit files do not pass muster by reference to contemporary standards the ability to marshall a proper defence will always be severely restricted.
- It seems clear that the audit in question had grown too large for the defendant firm's resources. This is a factor to which small firms should always remain alert. The firm in question appears to have been unable to cope with the size and complexity of the assignment, and over-reliance on the MD in the circumstances increased the risk factor disproportionately to any perceived advantage in retaining the audit.

Case I.3

In this case the client company was a motor vehicle time-share operator, pioneering a growing market in which customers purchase weekly time-share units in motor cars and other vehicles to be used during specific periods, such as holidays.

Time-share contracts were similar to leasing contracts, but were measured in the number of weekly units specifically purchased. Such contracts typically ran for three to five years, dependent on the quality and hence expected life of the vehicle selected.

Customers found the purchase of time-share units far more cost-effective than standard charges for vehicle hire, and the company's sale of units expanded dramatically in the first four years of business, branches being opened in all major holiday and business centres throughout Europe.

The expansion required a correspondingly larger vehicle fleet throughout the product range. Some vehicles were acquired on finance leases, but most were purchased outright by borrowing through a European bank consortium credit line. At its peak the company appears to have operated several thousand cars, vans and trucks, and sold over 700,000 time-share units of one week each.

With steep increases in finance costs applicable at the time, margins had to be reduced for the company to remain competitive by comparison with conventional vehicle hire. Insurance costs also increased as the cyclical market hardened and imposed steeper rates. The company's growth ceased, expiring time-shares were not renewed and many vehicles were underutilised.

The company began to default on finance leases and some vehicles were repossessed. To maintain cash flow, however, the directors continued, fraudulently, to present the fleet financiers with evidence of bogus time-share sales, thereby securing continuing credit lines and working capital. Far from acquiring more vehicles, however, the directors proceeded over an 18-month period to run down the fleet by selling all vehicles surplus to the much reduced requirements. In order to effect rapid sales many vehicles were disposed of for cash at rock-bottom prices, but the company's books recorded these receipts as sales of further time-share units in order to support the deception of continuing growth.

At the time of the audit in question the company's vehicle inventory at all its centres had dwindled to a few hundred vehicles, although its records continued to show the quantities needed to support the fictitious time-share unit sales. The auditors sought to verify vehicle stocks by attending selected depots in two separate locations for the purpose of identifying and counting a sample of vehicles included on lists of registration numbers taken from the records.

Selections made by the auditors from the lists included both genuine and bogus vehicles, and the auditors were advised that those missing from the depot were currently with time-share owners, and a return date was indicated in each instance. The auditors returned to one depot at a later date and duly inspected what appeared to be the bulk of the remaining cars. It later transpired, however, that all those checked at the second visit had already been inspected, only the number plates having been changed!

The company's financial statements, supported by an unqualified audit opinion, were issued to shareholders, banks and other lenders in the course of negotiating extended facilities.

Before the hopelessness of the company's position became apparent, a non-executive director and major shareholder in the client company complained to the auditors that the value of vehicles in the accounts had been inflated by a large number of fictitious items, and that the audit procedures had therefore been deficient. He sent a copy of the letter to the company's principal bankers.

The auditors, unwisely, replied (again supplying a copy to the bank) in terms that effectively acknowledged that the nature of their inspection of the physical inventory might have facilitated fraudulent duplication. Not yet appreciating the true position, no notification to underwriters took place.

Following the appointment of a receiver on behalf of the banking consortium, the company collapsed and a liquidator was appointed. The audit firm thereupon received claims from individual shareholders, the liquidator, various third-party creditors including finance companies and the lending banks, who claimed to have relied on negligently audited annual accounts when monitoring and extending their lending. Claims were also received from a handful of time-share owners with unexpired contracts.

Needless to say, a sustainable defence presented formidable difficulties given the variety of claims against the firm, the total quantum of claims being of the order of £7 million. Given the serious breach of policy conditions that the audit firm's acknowledgement of potentially defective procedures constituted, and the extent to which it may have prejudiced underwriters' interests, the firm's partners faced personal bankruptcy. Compromise of the insurer's position was evidenced by the inclusion of the auditor's stock observation admissions in the banks' and major shareholders' particulars of claim. The various claimants recognised that the partners' bankruptcy would yield them no compensation and a deal with the underwriters was struck at a much reduced level of indemnity.

Lessons to be noted

- The verification of the physical assets that are in continuous day-to-day use by a business to generate its income requires careful procedural planning by the auditors, particularly when those assets are of material value and are highly susceptible to manipulation.
- In this instance the directors' excuse that the missing vehicles were out on hire appeared superficially to be plausible to the auditors but, given the size of the amounts in question, they should not have simply agreed to return at a later date to complete their inspection, thereby allowing for the duplications and substitution of number plates.
- When directors offer an explanation for the fact that key assets are not available for direct verification, auditors need to think creatively and devise procedures that will either affirm or rebut the representations of management. In this case it would have been a simple matter for the auditors to request sight of the relevant hiring-out or time-sharing documents as evidence to support explanations of the whereabouts of the absent vehicles. They should, moreover, have insisted that those papers be produced there and then – not on a later, more convenient (for the directors) date!

J. Risks of international affiliations and inappropriate reliance on the work of others

There is ample guidance on the circumstances in which it is permissible to rely on the work of other auditors or appropriate professional parties. For example, auditors of the group accounts will not necessarily have any direct involvement with the audits of major subsidiaries, which may well be performed by firms in overseas jurisdictions.

Before simply taking the audited subsidiary accounts at face value the parent company auditors should at least adopt the prudent approach of making enquiries about the professional standing of the auditors in question, to whom comprehensive questionnaires should be sent for completion and return. These serve to satisfy the parent company auditors that the work was carried out to a standard consistent with that which they themselves would have adopted in terms of approach to sampling, attendance at stocktaking, circularisation of debtors, analytical procedures on the accounts as a whole and other key areas of work.

The same principles apply in any context in which reliance is placed on other experts. Auditors may, for example, seek an opinion on mining potential based on independently conducted geological surveys. As before, the auditors should ensure that those issuing the opinion are appropriately qualified, and they should examine the terms of reference given to the valuers to ensure that they were sufficiently comprehensive for the purposes that the auditors require.

Several UK firms have established continental and international links, including expansion into Eastern Europe, and cautious analysis is warranted. There are deep cultural attitudes that distinguish the role and status of professions in different countries. These differences are neither good nor bad, but it is wise to recognise their implications before entering into long-term relationships.

In France, for example, there are two accountancy bodies: one governing the whole field of general practice (answerable to the Ministry of Finance) in which even routine bookkeeping and tax advice must be carried out by a qualified accountant; and the other for regulating auditing (under the jurisdiction of the Ministry of Justice).

The audit requirement for French companies is based primarily on the size of share capital, and the status of French auditors is similar to that of UK solicitors in that they are regarded as officers of the Court. They are required to reveal any illegality encountered, and the effect of issuing an 'attestation' (the equivalent of a 'clean' report) is primarily to relieve the directors of liability. Auditors are not permitted to 'disclaim' an opinion and the worst situation from the directors' viewpoint is simply a refusal to attest.

This aspect of French law may be a major influence in the curtailment of corporate fraud and the issue of false financial statements in that country, compared with examples that have recently proved so rife both in the UK and the USA.

Distinctive features, analogous to the above, will no doubt apply in every other EU Member State, and knowledge of these is a sensible prerequisite to the establishment of formal links.

There are also practical risk-avoidance precautions that UK firms should apply, as follows:

- A firm should not be held out to be a multinational or international practice, especially if there is a US affiliation in the network. The possibility of being joined as a UK co-defendant should obviously be avoided, given the characteristics of US litigation: class actions, contingency legal fees, jury trials, punitive damages and no cost recovery even in successfully defended actions. For those reasons UK professional indemnity policies invariably exclude liability for US-based risks.

- It is essential to become familiar with the operation of the legal system in the other countries involved. Defence costs in Spain, for example, are usually assessed as a percentage of the claim. Furthermore, in both Italy and Spain the duration of civil trials is notoriously lengthy, and accumulating interest costs alone could well exceed indemnity limits!
- Accountants should ensure that their cross-border arrangements avoid the risk of 'forum shopping'. Liability laws in EU States vary greatly, and the UK could be a very attractive jurisdiction in which overseas claimants may seek to bring a claim, especially since most other countries with compulsory indemnity insurance for accountants has a corresponding liability 'cap'. In similar vein, both Belgium and the Netherlands operate a 'several' liability system (rather than 'joint and several' as in the UK), and this effectively allows damages to be apportioned judicially.
- Firms should give careful consideration to the operating style used to identify their overseas links. If it is intended by all participating offices, wherever located, to share each other's liability risks, an overt partnership structure is required. But each partner in each office must then accept that he or she could be jointly and severally liable to claimants worldwide for all acts or omissions of every partner and employee of the firm – also worldwide – and can be sued in any jurisdiction in which a member firm practices! The PI consequences hardly bear thinking about, especially as lower indemnity limits in one country will increase the potential liability of partners in other jurisdictions.
- Most firms therefore prefer to operate within an association of quite separate firms acting under an umbrella organisation, often carrying a common name, but overseas members must *never* be referred to as 'partners', especially in ambiguously phrased promotional brochures or on letterheads. In one instance a firm described its overseas affiliation in its promotional literature as 'an international practice with 65 offices worldwide'. This is potentially lethal.
- Firms should formalise relationships by means of binding written agreements. In an association structure the agreement should make it clear that no sharing of profits or losses will occur; there will be

no common partners in distinct firms; and there will be no element of control by one firm over the activities of another. This will help to avoid what happened in one case when an Italian claimant sued his Milan accountants, who in turn joined their UK associates as co-defendants. Although the UK firm had never been involved in the matter complained of, the lack of any formal agreement to this effect made it very difficult to resist the proceedings. Whatever arrangements the firm intends to make, appropriate advice should be taken and indemnity brokers must be kept fully informed.

Case J.1

The companies involved in this massive investment scam were all part of the same group and under common ultimate control, based in Switzerland. A network of 'loan salesmen' was engaged, situated in a variety of locations, including most European countries, Singapore, South Africa, Australasia and North America. The familiar refrain was that the group's investment expertise and inside understanding of global markets would guarantee returns that no high net worth individual could achieve on his or her own.

The Swiss auditors of the parent company never questioned the way in which investors' funds were channelled through no fewer than six group companies for no apparent commercial reason. Investment funds were received by the Swiss parent and passed via a series of 'secured' loans to other group companies, finishing up with two UK companies whose sole purpose was to apply these funds to profitable use. They purported to achieve this mainly through the purchase of a large number of financial services businesses and by direct investment in hedge funds and private equity. The two UK companies, which between them were responsible for the custody of average annual investment holdings of £48 million, were audited by a three-partner firm in Cardiff.

The Cardiff-based auditors' principal responsibility was to establish at each year-end the ability of the two UK companies to repay the loans made to them from Switzerland. Their instructions also required them to confirm that the amount of such loans was in turn sufficient to meet the ultimate capital repayments to investors together with accrued interest thereon. This responsibility should of course have rested with the Swiss companies and their auditors. Nevertheless, the form of certification provided by the Cardiff auditors each year included a statement of sufficiency that covered the whole of the sums owed to investors.

The masterminds presiding over the fraud relied on the improbability that investors would seek repayment of the capital funds in a way that would cause the illiquidity of the investment in other businesses to be a problem. In fact, many of the UK investment businesses acquired had been set up by the perpetrators themselves for the sole purpose of channelling funds into their own pockets.

Questions raised by the Swiss regulatory authorities and custodian banks concerning the apparent lack of inter-group inflows were met with no satisfactory replies, and new investments were put on hold, causing existing investors to seek repayment prematurely and the entire structure collapsed with the loss of well over £150 million.

The Swiss audit firm was an independent associate of an international network with a well known global brand. Since its local professional indemnity insurance cover was unable to make any impression on the scale of losses suffered, it was clearly in the interests of the claimants to allege that the mere use of that name was sufficient to suggest to investors that their funds were with companies audited by a firm of international standing and repute, and the lawsuits brought on behalf of investors therefore targeted the international firm.

There was uncertainty on the question of who was responsible for confirming the ability to repay investors. The Swiss audit office appointed to vet the accounts of the non-UK group companies believed that the UK auditor, who was in direct contact with the acquired entities, would carry out the necessary asset verification for this purpose; whereas the UK auditors, who had no direct access to the companies with whom the investors had established their contractual relationship, had good reason to believe that the Swiss auditors would certify adequacy. They nevertheless accepted representations by management that the necessary funds were available if required. Ultimate responsibility lay with the directors, but the relevant audit work was never undertaken.

Lessons to be noted

- It is crucial that instructions to auditors of a non-routine nature, such as certifying adequacy of funds for a particular purpose, should not only be properly understood but should also fall naturally within the scope of what it is reasonable to expect of them.

  In this instance the UK auditors were provided with documentation purporting to show the amount of funds held within the group on behalf of investors, to which accrued interest had been added. Even assuming the accuracy of the amounts at which the acquired

UK businesses were valued and the availability of liquid funds if and when required, the UK auditors were in no position to know that the said documentation accurately reflected the full liability for funds invested. It was therefore inappropriate for them to provide the certification in the terms of the formula requested. Not surprisingly, their indemnity insurers chose to negotiate a settlement within the limits of their cover.

- The parent company auditors in Switzerland lost track of the manner in which investors' funds were applied once they reached the UK companies and in turn relied upon the UK auditors to certify adequacy. This was a gross misjudgement on their part since, being auditors of the parent company, they had a duty to ensure that there would be no deficiency in the event of withdrawals, either large or small.

  Relying on a formulaic certification from a small UK audit practice, when it should have been obvious that those auditors had no means of checking what they were certifying, meant that responsibility for the growing deficiency on funds fell on the Swiss auditors' shoulders.
- This case amply highlights the hazards of 'holding out' that a firm is part of an international network, conveying the impression of mutuality of partnership responsibility and hence liability.

  The use of the international brand was the most dangerous element. Many large firms seek to exaggerate their international presence through the use of a common brand name, when the reality is that the network is a loose association of fully independent and autonomous firms that benefit from the association only through the process of cross-referrals and inward/outward investment. The system works well enough until there is trouble, as indeed was the case with Parmalat, when the UK auditors, being located in a favourable litigation jurisdiction with the perception of ample insurance cover, were targeted for the lapses committed by their North Italian associate.

K. Failure of analytical review

If routine audit procedures can be thought of as a 'bottom up' process, its complementary approach, known as *analytical review*, would be the 'top down' process. Broadly, analytical review requires an objective and intelligent review with the intention of assessing whether the financial statements subjected to audit make sense in their own terms.

No single blueprint can be used for analytical review, although it will invariably be necessary to begin the process by making comparisons of numbers and ratios with their counterpart figures in the accounts of earlier years. Any material variation will obviously require explanation.

If the entity trades in other jurisdictions, it may need to make payments and receive remittances in foreign currency. The auditor will need to familiarise him- or herself with dominant exchange rates in the period in question in order to make sense of the foreign exchange gains or losses per the accounts. If, for example, the company relies on supplies of raw materials that are traded on the commodity exchanges, the auditor will, again, be able to assess the reasonableness of the cost of sales shown in the accounts by reference to any significant movement in the price of the commodities in question.

Analytical procedures are the least mechanical feature of an audit and fraudulent operators often rely on the likelihood that auditors may skimp in this area, even though any intelligent appraisal would alert them to suspicious circumstances.

Case K.1

The client company in question was a family-controlled manufacturer of tinned meat, pies, pasties and sausages, based in Woolwich and within a comfortable distance from Smithfield meat market. In the four years from 2002 to 2005, it recorded increases in turnover from £14 million to £29 million to £63 million to £87 million. The company had an established relationship with the invoice-discounting subsidiary of a major bank. Every month the bank was sent summary sheets recording the total of sales transactions, and within seven days its account with the bank was credited with the discounted advance. Responsibility for managing the accounting and for the collection of debts remained with the company.

Under their own internal quality control procedures, the auditors were required to have the file independently reviewed by a partner wholly unconnected with the client company. This arose once the annual audit fees, which were clearly related to size, exceeded £50,000, one of the firm's thresholds for triggering a second-partner review.

The independent partner noted the dramatic, scarcely credible, increase in turnover, which prior to 2002 had generally been between

£7 million and £10 million for several years. His own Internet checks showed that the turnover of its basic meat products, if correct, exceeded sales of comparable items for the UK as a whole. He calculated that one of the company's own refrigerated meat transporters would have had to leave the Woolwich works every 12 minutes, 24 hours per day, seven days per week to achieve the purported level of business.

In view of the implausibility of the situation confronting him, he believed he had no alternative but to contact NCIS, the appropriate anti-fraud agency operating at that time. This led to an in-depth investigation, following which criminal charges were brought against the directors, resulting in custodial sentences. It was readily apparent to the liquidators of the company that its activities amounted to a massive invoice discounting fraud on the bank, on whose behalf the liquidator was effectively acting. Unsurprisingly, civil proceedings were taken out against the audit firm, alleging negligence in failing to detect the use of fictitious invoices in the three previous periods. Experts appointed by the firm's insurers reported that the audit work was deficient in several respects, but notably regarding standard analytical review tests. Negotiations resulted in a settlement at a substantial sum.

Lessons to be noted

- It is surprisingly common to find that smaller firms of auditors still spend prodigious amounts of time on a company's detailed records without standing back to assess the overall plausibility of what those records convey. It is of course encouraging to note that a client company's trade is improving and becoming more profitable, but an auditor should always ensure that the basic trading ratios continue to make sense within periods of expansion.
- Production in any industry requires raw material inputs yielding gross profit percentages taking account of opening and closing stock levels. The phenomenal growth in sales turnover shown in this case would have required a corresponding increase in the amount of meat and related products purchased, and invoices reflecting this increase should have been examined to ensure that they came from a bona fide external source.
- The expansion shown in the records would have necessitated an appropriate level of manufacturing capacity and the auditor should have visited the plant in Woolwich to ascertain whether the

purported throughput appeared to be realistic. If stock levels also increased, observation of a physical count would have helped to verify this. Direct contact with a sample of customers should have been undertaken to authenticate the validity of sales shown in the records.

The above is a summary of a few of the many audit procedures that should have been obvious to the firm when confronting yet another year of phenomenal growth on the part of its client.

L. Lack of awareness of risk

Risk assessment lies at the heart of systems-based auditing. One of the factors that obviously contributes to risk is the existence of major outside interests in the company's welfare, notably funding arrangements involving third party institutions. The audit risk is high because of the auditor's awareness of the reliance of those institutions on the borrower's audited financial statements as a significant element in the institutions' loan monitoring programmes.

Case L.1

A claim was brought against a firm of auditors by three major lending institutions that had provided finance to their client for the purchase of slot machines and other gaming equipment in Ireland. It was the client's practice to arrange hire purchase finance for the sale of equipment to casinos, nightclubs, gaming arcades and other operators and then to raise finance from lending institutions on the security of the HP contracts.

Unfortunately it was also the client's practice to deal with his cash flow shortages by generating forged HP contracts for onward sale to the institutions, remembering to keep up the monthly instalments on the fictitious contracts.

Over a period of some six years, the proportion of bogus contracts rose until they accounted for over 90% of the total contracts in force, at which point the client could no longer rely on his rudimentary computer system to distinguish real from false or calculate how much should be paid each month to whom, causing him great anxiety. He also realised that there were not enough casinos, pubs and clubs in the whole of Ireland to explain the amount of equipment passing through his records.

So one day he marched into his auditor's office and unburdened himself by confessing the whole scam.

Interestingly, his computer had proved to be the limiting factor in a fraud that could, in theory, have continued to expand indefinitely – presumably until someone noticed that the quantity of equipment 'sold' was more than enough for every casino on the planet!

The claimants, mainly finance houses, contended that they had relied extensively on the audited accounts for the purpose of monitoring their lending and they brought a claim against the audit firm for several million pounds. On disclosure it became clear that the lenders had sent in their own inspectors every six months to examine the borrower's records, including copies of contracts. The defendants therefore entered a strong defence based on the following:

- lack of proximity;
- lack of causation; and
- poor quality of inspections in fact carried out.

A year later the actions were struck out for want of prosecution.

Lessons to be noted

- Audit risk is invariably heightened when a company's financial stability is underpinned by a substantial rump of borrowings from independent financial institutions.
- Audit procedures and ensuing reports must therefore reflect auditors' responses to their awareness of the presence of those interests, and the extent of the institutions' alleged (real or supposed) reliance on audit opinions as the primary means of monitoring their loans.
- Despite auditors' relatively scarce on-site attendances in connection with their annual audits, it is always convenient for third party lenders to blame auditors when loans prove to be irrecoverable.
- Auditors' first steps in responding to an awareness of a particular source of risk is to ensure that they and their staff are thoroughly familiar with the client company's systems. In this instance the company's sole director was placing business on his computer that had never in fact been transacted. The convoluted processing of transactions was too difficult for the auditors to trace within the scope of standard audit procedures – always a warning sign. Had

the auditors probed the authenticity of those transactions as assiduously as was warranted, they would undoubtedly have detected the fictitious sales.

M. The practice ethical problem

When in partnership, mutual trust and understanding grows over the passage of time while working together. A partnership based purely on sharing of overheads is one in name only, and presents problems for the participants in many instances.

In the event of a partner leaving or dying, the remaining partners may find that the person has left them with horrendous unresolved issues relating to the affairs of clients that he or she was handling. It may even be impossible to determine whether the person was complicit in instances of fraud perpetrated by his or her clients, or whether incompetence was the problem.

Case M.1

Jolly & Partners was a two-partner firm that acted as accountants, auditors and tax consultants to a family company with jewellery shops in five West Country of England towns. In 2003, HMRC demanded additional tax, interest and penalties in respect of the accounts of the company from 1998 to 2002 inclusive. This demand was as a result of substantial loans to the managing director and largest shareholder not being disclosed in the accounts or otherwise notified to HMRC on the director's or company's tax returns, also submitted by Jolly & Partners.

The jewellery company and the shareholders, some of whom Jolly & Partners acted for, alleged that the relevant Jollys' partner had been negligent in the conduct of their accounts' preparation and audit work, in failing to draw the loans to the attention of the shareholders, and in properly advising them of the tax implications of the loans. Further investigation showed that the loans were unlawful: the managing director concerned had no current accounts in credit in any of the years in question.

The claimants' solicitors required that Jolly & Partners take responsibility for the following:

- the additional taxes; and
- the loans that had been made unlawfully and which were now irrecoverable from the director.

They also demanded that Jollys issue credit notes for all fees outstanding at the date of the solicitor's letter.

In their defence statement, Jolly & Partners maintained, based on the files in their possession, that they were totally unaware of the loans in question, but experts appointed by underwriters' solicitors reported that the audit files were singularly lacking in any evidence that they had performed the work necessary to discover that the loans had taken place, despite the fact that their amount exceeded £50,000 in each of the years in question.

The Jollys partner who had dealt with these matters proved to be uncooperative and retired in 2002. He is now living in Portugal, making it exceedingly difficult for the firm and its insurers to establish any plausible defence. Furthermore, the company's managing director died shortly after the commencement of litigation, leaving a very small estate with insufficient assets to make any worthwhile claim against it. How he had disposed of the loans, totalling £362,289 over the five-year period, was never ascertained.

In the circumstances the insurers were left with no alternative but to settle all the actions at a composite sum including claimants' costs.

Lessons to be noted

- This case demonstrates the plight of the remaining partner in a two-partner practice. Jolly & Partners was in fact the result of a merger of two sole practitioners primarily for the purpose of sharing overheads. After the merger, the partners continued as before to service the needs of their respective clients, without making any attempt to establish a unified practice ethic based on acceptable standards of professional work.
- The remaining partner acknowledged that basic audit procedures should have identified the cash drain on the business caused by the concealed loans. Although the retired partner maintained in his proof of evidence that he was unaware of the loan's existence, doubt remains as to whether he might have colluded with the managing director in their concealment. It seems, on the evidence, that such concealment was intended to deceive the other shareholders as much as to avoid the taxes arising on loans to participators.
- Loans to directors, legal or otherwise, must be disclosed in company accounts, and failure to do so triggers a requirement for

disclosure in the audit report. In the circumstances it would have been a very difficult case to defend at trial, and an expensive settlement was the only remaining option.

This case illustrates the dangers of viewing a multi-disciplinary engagement, variously involving tax advice and compliance, accounting, auditing and general financial supervision, as primarily tax-focused, with basic accounts preparation thrown in. Auditing is viewed by many clients as an expensive imposition that adds no value and practitioners may be tempted to spend as little time on it as they think they can get away with. Jolly & Partners misjudged the situation, with serious consequences. Had they undertaken the most basic audit checks on payments, they would have discovered the director's illicit loans.

N. Would any audit have picked this up?

There are some frauds that are either too simple or too complex to be detected by normal auditing procedures, particularly if they are masterminded by individuals who control and/or own the business.

Case N.1

The company in this case manufactures trumpets and other musical instruments for the brass section of bands and orchestras from its factory in Milton Keynes. Its most valuable raw material is brass, which is supplied in the form of long tubes obtained from specialist suppliers.

The proportion of each brass tube that is actually used in the manufacturing process is approximately 60%. The remainder emerges from the process covered in oil and water to form a black sludge-like substance, which is collected in large plastic bins as a by-product. The brass contained in this by-product, which is known as 'swarf', is almost as valuable in this state as in tubular form, because it is relatively simple to clean off the oil and melt it down to be moulded back into tubes.

In the summer of 2008 two of the company's directors, who were father and son and had been responsible for the main manufacturing process since the commencement of trading, left the company. Over the next few months the company's finance director noticed that the proceeds of the sale of swarf since the departure of the two directors were more than double what they had previously been over an equivalent period. Initially he assumed that there had been an error or misposting in the current year's accounting records and set about trying to find it. Eventually it dawned on him that the current year's accounting records were accurate and the accounting records, and the accounts, for all previous years were materially misstated.

The accounting records in respect of those earlier years revealed nothing untoward. It was only when he began questioning employees on the factory floor that he began to pick up rumours of dodgy practices. Apparently, throughout the tenure of the father and son's directorships, an arrangement was in place whereby the swarf would be collected by the company's brass supplier twice a week. On the first occasion it would be collected from the factory, an invoice would be raised and the proceeds of sale would be entered in the accounting records either as a receipt or by offset against the cost of brass supplies. On the second occasion, however, the two directors would load it on to the back of their van, which they would drive round to the local Tesco car park. The swarf would then be transferred on to the brass supplier's lorry and the cash proceeds handed over in the proverbial brown envelope: no invoice, no record of the transaction in the company's accounting records.

Legal proceedings have already been initiated against the two former directors and the company is currently contemplating its options with regard to a potential action against its auditors.

Lessons to be noted

- It would have been impossible for the company's auditors to detect a fraud of this type by reference to sales information, invoices, debtor accounts or any other record, because no trace of the fraudulent transactions existed therein. Nor would analytical review procedures based on year by year comparisons of swarf sale proceeds have assisted them, because revenue from the sale of swarf was understated by approximately 50% in each of the accounts that had been subject to audit.
- This case therefore highlights the need for auditors to gain a thorough understanding of all aspects of a company's operation from the outset of their engagement. The fact that the company's manufacturing process involved a very expensive raw material should have given rise to numerous enquiries during the initial familiarisation process – in particular with regard to the proportion of brass tubing that is actually used in that process and the amount of swarf that would normally be generated from each tube. The responses

to such enquiries may have enabled the auditors to form a view as to the amount of swarf that should be generated during a particular year by reference to the quantity of brass tubing utilised.

- The auditors, however, should have recognised that the individuals to whom any enquiries would most likely have been directed were the very individuals that were in a position to perpetrate a fraud with regard to the sale of such a valuable by-product. Such a risk may have been mitigated at the outset of an appointment by undertaking industry-related research. After all, the technicalities of manufacturing brass instruments are known to the relevant trade bodies, from whom sensible information could have been sought. If necessary, following such enquiries, the auditors may have needed to devise imaginative testing procedures to verify information provided to them by company personnel. The auditors might, for example, have tested the proposition that only 20% of brass tubing was converted into swarf (being half the actual figure of 40%) by weighing the amount of swarf generated from the processing of one batch of brass tubing.
- Notwithstanding the above comments, it is arguable that, unless the auditors caught wind of the rumours circulating the factory floor or encountered other suspicious circumstances during the course of their work, a fraud of the nature described above is likely to go undetected until other circumstances, such as the departure of the perpetrators, brings it to light.

2.10 SUMMARY OF KEY LESSONS

Fraud by employees

- Auditors should not allow budgetary constraints to restrict the scope of audit work that is necessary.
- When relying on an internal control system, auditors should check controls each year of the engagement to ensure that they are still applicable.
- Auditors should not forget that even the most basic checks can provide evidence of wrongdoing.
- Auditors often allocate a low-risk assessment on the basis of a false premise that management, by virtue of its proximate involvement with the accounting function, exerts effective supervisory controls:

in reality such apparent controls can be wholly inadequate or easily overridden.

- Audit fieldwork must be undertaken by personnel with sufficient experience to identify and recognise the significance of anomalies within the accounting records.
- Surprisingly little audit attention is often focused on the use of journal entries – always the most lethal accounting record.
- Suspicious circumstances, regardless of the materiality of the sums involved, should always be probed until resolved.

Using the company as an instrument of fraud by senior management

- Independence is a key constituent of an audit. Without it, the process is merely an accounting exercise.
- Small audit firms in particular must remain alert to the risk that an audit assignment may grow too large for the firm's resources.
- Auditors must have regard to the substance of what would have been obvious had they stepped back and looked at the evidence before them, rather than assuming that what was recorded is real.
- Auditors must not allow powerful and persuasive management to put obstacles in the way of a properly conducted and robust audit process.
- Auditors must give proper consideration to the validity and plausibility of representations made by management and must verify such representations to independent third party documentation.
- Audit procedures and audit reports must reflect the auditors' responses to their awareness of the interests of independent financial institutions and the extent of these institutions' reliance on audit opinions as the primary means of monitoring their loans.

3

Negligent Audit Work Not Involving Theft of Company Assets

3.1 INTRODUCTION

Both management and owners of businesses rely on audits as an independent authentication function. Financial statements carrying an unqualified audit opinion are endowed with a credibility that they would lack otherwise. Even the directors/owners of relatively small entities, which would otherwise be exempt from statutory audit requirements, may voluntarily opt for an audit in order to build confidence in the accounts; this is particularly the case where minority non-executive shareholders exist and/or the company depends on external bank finance to a large degree.

In such cases it is essential that the standard of auditing should fulfil the above purpose so that reliance may be placed by all interested parties on the accounts in question for any legitimate purpose. Several of the cases in this chapter arose in the disciplinary context, following complaints made to professional bodies regarding sub-standard work.

Some of these cases involved fraudulent manipulation of financial statements for the sole purpose of satisfying bank creditors and hence keeping the company afloat. Such cases are to be distinguished from instances of fraud that involve the embezzlement or other abstraction of company assets by employees or management, as illustrated in the previous chapter.

Claims under the auditing heading are, of course, legion. Bank managers, investors, suppliers and other creditors often assume, quite incorrectly, that because accounts carry an unqualified audit report they may be relied upon in any context. Liability in such cases will often depend on whether the auditors were aware at the time of signing their reports that the accounts were to be used for the purpose in question, and whether that purpose was reasonable. Wherever possible, carefully worded disclaimers against losses caused by inappropriate reliance should be used.

3.2 FUNDAMENTAL AUDITING PITFALLS

The majority of claims brought against accountants and auditors contest the adequacy of the work undertaken, often at a basic level. The most common allegations of auditors' negligence concern overvaluation of stocks or debtors, or understatement of liabilities, in circumstances where more careful and thorough work would have identified the misstatements.

In some cases work-in-progress is overvalued by including items already sold in the period; in others, sales are inflated by including items sold after the year-end. Manipulation of year-end 'cut-off' is one of the simplest methods of fabricating results and therefore represents an area with which auditors should always take great care.

Also in this category are claims against auditors of companies that are the subject of a disappointing acquisition, reliance having been placed by the purchaser on audited accounts in reaching the investment decision and the purchase consideration to be paid.

A. Failure to carry out basic procedures

In difficult economic times, when banks and outside investors need to be satisfied that a company's finances are on a solid footing, directors may be tempted to exploit the susceptibility of financial statements to manipulation within the variety of interpretations that may be placed on accounting standards. The result may be a set of accounts that show the company's financial position in a more favourable light than is warranted.

The role of auditors is, of course, to assess independently the judgements made by the directors in the context of the overriding need for accounts to show a true and fair view. The innate subjectivity involved in many accounting issues – from the valuation of aging stock to the recoverability of loans to other group companies and the identification of undisclosed tax liabilities – oblige auditors to take an objective stance and remedy, if necessary in their report, any undue bias in the accounts subject to audit. No matter how effectively and comprehensively basic audit procedures are performed, all this effort is to no avail if the auditors fail to evaluate the consequences of any innate misjudgements with the above objective in mind, prior to issuing their audit opinion.

Case A.1

The auditor's client was a profitable company that specialised in hiring out and selling exhibition scaffolding and show stands. Until 2001 the company's finance director, a qualified accountant, prepared draft accounts and supporting schedules to a good standard, which were then submitted to the firm for audit purposes.

In 2001 the finance director retired and no replacement was appointed, the audit firm itself taking over responsibility for preparing draft accounts from the company's records for audit purposes. Accounts for the years ended 31 March 2002, 2003 and 2004 were prepared and audited in this way, each year showing a small profit of no more than £2,000 or £3,000, despite turnover over the same period rising from £550,000 to £780,000.

In February 2005 the company's bankers expressed concern over its rising overdraft and were reluctant to renew its facility of £60,000. Another firm of auditors was then appointed at the bank's insistence, and the audit of the March 2005 accounts disclosed a loss of £67,000. The auditors reported to the directors and the bank that they could see no reasonable prospect of the company trading through its current difficulties. Shortly thereafter a receiver was appointed, and the company was taken over for nominal consideration by its largest creditor, a supplier of exhibition equipment.

In March 2006 the previous auditor received a Letter before Action from solicitors acting for the company's largest shareholder (who was also its managing director) alleging that the 2002, 2003 and 2004 audits had been negligently conducted and that a competent auditor would have detected that the company had incurred substantial trading losses in all three years, rather than breaking even. It was claimed that had the directors been made aware of the company's true position they would have taken the necessary remedial steps to reverse its decline, thus preserving the value of the shareholders' investment.

The defendant auditor dismissed the allegations as speculative at best and utterly spurious at worst, maintaining that the burden of proof that earlier losses had been concealed in the audited accounts could never be achieved by the claimant. Liability was denied and proceedings were commenced for recovery of alleged consequential losses of £212,000 from the defendants.

An expert accountant was appointed on the underwriters' behalf to report on the audits in question, and his preliminary opinion on the 2004 accounts was that they appeared to have been prepared and audited negligently. The company's stock figures were based on directors' 'valuations', no formal stock count having been performed. The audit file was completely disorganised and most working papers were scrappy, incomplete and illegible. There was no evidence of any independent audit work having been performed, and it seemed unlikely that the papers for earlier years would be any better.

Solicitors recommended to the underwriters that a commercial settlement should be negotiated rather than incur the heavy costs of proceeding to a full trial. A settlement at £176,000 plus costs was eventually agreed.

Lessons to be noted

- This case demonstrates that even a spurious action (the directors themselves having deliberately inflated the equipment stock figures) can succeed when defendant accountants are unable to support their rebuttals with adequate documentary evidence of competent work on their audit files.
- Litigation is conducted on the presumption that the issues will be determined at trial, and Court proceedings rely extensively on file evidence. It is rarely worth risking the very substantial costs of proceeding to trial when the defendants' files are woefully deficient in every material respect. Even when there is no causal connection between deficient work and the alleged losses, underwriters will be advised to settle on the best terms that can be negotiated. In such circumstances it is not difficult to imagine the impact of such a settlement on the auditor's renewal premium quotation.
- If the stock figure is material (as it was in this case) and it is not supported by any formal inventory inspection, the auditors would have no alternative but to qualify their opinion in appropriate terms.

Case A.2

The client company carried on business as painters and decorators, subcontracting much of the work. The company was a contractor within the relevant tax provisions, and was therefore bound to make basic rate tax deductions from payments to subcontractors who do not hold the relevant certificates under the Construction Industry Scheme. If such deductions are not made, the contractor remains liable to pay over the imputed tax.

The client company was required to complete and submit Returns sent to them by HMRC, detailing the subcontractors employed and the amounts paid to them. Holders of the certificates are themselves required to complete returns, and HMRC is thereby able to reconcile charges for subcontract labour in the accounts with the returns submitted.

HMRC wrote directly to the company's auditors, who had at all times acted for the company, drawing their attention to the fact that there were serious breaches of the regulations covering two financial years. In one fiscal period the company failed altogether to lodge its return, despite its audited accounts showing that over £250,000 was paid to subcontractors; and in respect of the ensuing period its return showed payments to subcontractors of some £80,000 whereas the equivalent charge in its audited accounts was over £350,000.

The matter was complicated by the likelihood, admitted by the firm, that the company was making gross payments to subcontractors irrespective of whether the required certificates were held.

Although no claim was received prior to the lapse of the limitation period, the firm notified underwriters of the possibility of a claim, following receipt of HMRC's letter. Solicitors advised them that they should write to the directors of their client company informing them that unless they made full disclosure to HMRC, the firm would no longer be able to act for them.

The directors refused to make such disclosure and the auditors resigned. However, as is prescribed in the formal guidance on changes in a professional appointment, the circumstances that led to the resignation were explained to a successor firm who the directors nominated. It is not known whether that firm was prepared to accept the appointment without an assurance from the directors that full disclosure to HMRC would be made.

Lessons to be noted

- The audit firm was clearly negligent in that it failed to spot the discrepancy between the amount of payments to subcontractors in the audited accounts and the returns to HMRC. However, it is difficult to see what the client company could have suffered through negligence on the part of the firm, since the directors were themselves responsible for the breaches referred to in HMRC's letter.

- There was, nevertheless, some vulnerability in that the firm clearly failed to perform audit procedures which would have identified the following:
  - the absence of a return in one year;
  - the discrepancy between the return and the accounts in the following year; and
  - the consequences of the above for the accounts that they were auditing.
- Furthermore, sound professional practice would have required the firm to
  - advise the client in writing, at the first moment it became aware of gross payments not covered by certificates, to discontinue this practice and to make full disclosure to HMRC; and
  - have qualified its audit opinion in respect of the omission of any tax liabilities of the company attributable to the gross payments in question.

B. Risks of undertaking work outside the scope of the auditor's expertise

Although auditing may be regarded as a discrete discipline, involving a methodology that practitioners and their professional bodies have developed over many years, situations arise when an auditor requires specialist knowledge before being able to issue a competent audit opinion.

This arises when undertaking audits of solicitor practices, estate agents and charities, to name but a few obvious examples, when the accounts of such entities are themselves governed by regulations and conventions with which the auditor must be familiar. If a firm has a number of clients that fall into this category, it will sensibly engage staff with the requisite skills who form themselves into a dedicated team charged with keeping up to date with developments in the relevant disciplines.

Such specialisms may, of course, relate to activities other than those of professional colleagues. For example, a client company engaged in mining and excavation would need to be audited by a firm capable of understanding the niceties of fault lines and geology in so far as it impinges on judgements affecting the accounts. More usually, auditors will become involved in specialist share valuation exercises when there is a dispute between shareholders requiring a minority interest to be purchased under the terms of the company's articles.

Historically, Information Technology (IT) auditing using specifically devised computer audit techniques was considered to be a separate area of specialisation. In view of the rapid rate of technical development, however, and the almost universal use of computerised accounting systems, almost all audits will require the application of such techniques to some degree.

Case B.1

Auditors of companies with the most usual form of Articles of Association may well find that they become involved in a dispute between shareholders. In such cases the articles include a clause which states that, in the event that one shareholder has agreed to be bought out by the other shareholders but agreement has not been reached on the value of his or her holding, the auditors will undertake the valuation and it will be binding on the parties.

In an early litigated case (Arenson v Casson Beckman Rutley & Co, House of Lords, 1975) auditors defended an allegation that their share valuation had been negligently performed on the grounds that they were acting in the capacity of arbitrators having to balance the arguments between two warring relatives. It was held, however, that auditors appointed to undertake a valuation under the articles were acting in the capacity of experts rather than arbitrators, and as such they could be held to account on the methodology applied by them.

For this reason most auditors appointed under the articles of association will take the precaution of issuing a 'non-speaking' valuation, which amounts to a statement of the monetary value of the shareholding without providing any documentary support or explanation of the valuation method adopted. This makes the valuation more difficult to attack, an important consideration given that in any such dispute at least one of the parties is likely to be aggrieved by the auditor's figure.

Although share valuations by accountants do not fall naturally into the scope of this chapter, such exercises arise in the ordinary course of acting for a limited company in an audit capacity. The auditor must therefore be prepared to apply an appropriate level of expertise to an assignment that is significantly different from routine auditing work.

It was in this context that the present case arose. The company's sole asset was a substantial collection of works of art, consisting of paintings and sculptures. As they were obviously not competent to undertake the specialist valuation of works of art, the auditors, with the agreement of the parties, instructed experts in the valuations department of a reputable firm of auctioneers to undertake this aspect of the assignment.

The claimant, who had been made redundant by the company following a dispute between the directors, alleged that the valuation undertaken by the auditors, in this instance issued on a 'speaking' basis, was negligent in a number of respects, the most pertinent being the valuation of the works of art.

The auditors had instructed the valuers to value the portfolio of artworks at their best price on the assumption that they would all be sold to a single purchaser in a single transaction. The specialist valuers stated in their report that they had allowed a discount of 15% of the gross value to reflect their valuation 'as a portfolio' and the auditors incorporated this discounted value in their valuation.

The issue in dispute was whether such an approach was reasonable. The claimant maintained that the 'job lot' approach was unnecessary and unrealistic. Making a large number of works available on the market at the same time would simulate the conditions of a 'fire sale' and would give rise to a sale at a depressed price compared with what each of the articles, placed in the appropriate market for a painting or sculpture of that type, might have fetched if the collection had been disposed of piecemeal.

The defendants argued that since a hypothetical purchaser of 100% of the company's shares would, in effect, be purchasing the entire portfolio in a single transaction, anyone buying the company would be obliged to purchase the works as a 'job lot', including those that the purchaser had no desire to own. They contended that such a purchaser may reasonably seek a discount from the best price to reflect the inconvenience factor of having to re-sell any unwanted works and the risk that their values may suffer a decline.

The articles also stipulated that no discount should be applied to the value of a minority holding to reflect the absence of control. However, for the purposes of their valuation the defendants had applied a discount of 10% to the value of the claimant's holding to reflect the absence of a readily available market place for the sale of shares in a private company. The claimant argued that such a discount was inappropriate being, in effect, a minority discount by another name.

The parties provided the judge with a template to enable him to calculate the range within which a reasonably competent accountant would have valued the claimant's shares. The judge held that the application of a discount to the gross values of the artworks was inappropriate. He also found that the auditors had displayed undue bias in the manner in which they raised questions and sought information from the parties in the course of their valuation exercise. Notwithstanding these criticisms the judge concluded that the defendant's valuation fell within the range that he considered reasonable. Accordingly, the claim was dismissed.

Lessons to be noted

- As this case demonstrates, the valuation of shares, particularly those of companies with diverse or unusual assets, can be a difficult exercise. It is not unusual for complex technical issues to arise part way through the assignment that could not have been predicted at the outset. The auditors had to contend with a number of issues for which they lacked the appropriate expertise and experience to handle. There are obvious dangers for a firm in being tempted or persuaded to take on tasks that are, in all honesty, outside the scope of its capability.
- Whenever accountants are appointed in the circumstances described above, it is imperative that they maintain a scrupulously impartial and unbiased attitude towards the parties. This did not happen in the case in point. Almost inevitably the accountants will have more cause to contact the company's directors, who are usually the majority shareholders, than the minority shareholder whose shares are the subject of the valuation, because the company is the source of the relevant financial information. However, it is essential that the minority shareholder is copied in to all correspondence and has the same opportunity as the majority shareholders to express his or her point of view on any appropriate issues.
- Above all, it is vital that each stage of the valuation process, including any preliminary research and discussions with partners or others within the firm, is documented in full. The file should contain sufficient information to enable a third party to understand precisely the accountant's approach to the valuation, the work undertaken and how the conclusions concerning each of the variables in the final calculation were arrived at.

Although the auditors and their insurers were not liable to make any payment to the claimant, their conduct was subject to trenchant criticism and, had their valuation not fallen fortuitously within the judge's range, the allegations against them would undoubtedly have resulted in a substantial payment of damages.

Case B.2

Accountants acting for a sole practitioner solicitor were sued by the solicitor as a result of a ruling by the Law Society that his practising certificate should be suspended indefinitely. The suspension was imposed following an investigation into the manner in which he conducted his practice and, in particular, his failure to observe the client money rules applicable to all solicitors.

The solicitor maintained that he had relied heavily on his accountants in all matters pertaining to compliance, and referred to the promotional 'puff' in the accountants' marketing literature regarding their specialist knowledge and experience of the audit of solicitors' practices.

Despite the accountants' claim regarding their expertise, it was clear that the partner concerned did not appreciate the most fundamental of the client money rules. In each of three years he confirmed to the Law Society that the total of client ledger balances equalled the credit balance held in the client bank account. However, the accountants appear to have completely overlooked the following:

- the fact that the clients' ledger included numerous debit balances, which is itself contrary to the rules;
- the fact that he should have been certifying that the bank balance equated to the *gross* credit balances, not the net;
- the fact that in the third of the three years the entire net balance on the clients' ledger was in debit – and equated to an overdrawn client bank account equal to that debit balance.

By merely certifying the equivalence of the monetary numbers the accountants undertook what amounted to no more than an arithmetical exercise, without any regard to the question of what the balances *should* have been. Consequently the Law Society issued an embargo on the firm, prohibiting it from undertaking any future work on solicitors' accounts.

In their defence, the accountants claimed that they accepted the verbal assurances of the solicitor that all negative balances on individual client accounts at the selected reporting dates had subsequently been repaid. The accountants reported to this effect in their certificate to the Law Society despite not having conducted any tests to confirm that the repayments had been made.

The case settled on terms recognising that the accountants' defence was unsustainable.

Lessons to be noted

- The majority of accounting firms undertake work under the solicitors' accounts rules, and yet the latter contain numerous pitfalls and only specialists within the firm should be engaged to perform such audits. Furthermore, the rules are subject to periodic revision and changes may easily be overlooked if specialists are not charged with keeping up to date. In the case in point the individual accountant did not understand even the most basic principles of client money compliance.
- Although the solicitor, in his own defence, claimed to have relied almost entirely on the supposed expertise of his accountant on matters of compliance, the accountant should have been at pains to point out explicitly that the matter of compliance with the rules is first and foremost the responsibility of the solicitor himself and cannot be left to other professionals.
- This case affords yet another illustration of the dangers of accepting representations from an unreliable client. An examination of the solicitor's correspondence files would have provided evidence to the accountant of acrimonious and lengthy disputes with building societies and banks concerning mortgage grants and redemptions, as well as numerous complaints from clients that their instructions regarding searches were being overlooked and that he had failed to credit them with interest under the rules.
- When the client is subject to the regulation of a government agency or a professional body, particular care must be exercised given the legitimate interest of the third party supervisor or regulator. It is incumbent on the accountant to have a sound grasp of the principles underlying the relevant rules and sufficient knowledge of their detailed working to avoid being caught out on inadvertent breaches.

Case B.3

On occasion, auditors will receive instructions that are not only outside their expertise, but also for which there can be no recognised expertise. In this instance the principal asset of the company whose shares were to be valued was an untested inventive process that existed only in the mind of its creator.

The audit firm was appointed in accordance with the articles of a company to value the shareholding of one of its former directors who had been dismissed from his position after it was discovered that he had falsified his expense claims. The company's principal asset was an experimental process for disposing of household waste. In brief, the idea, which was being promoted to a number of local authorities, was that organic household and garden waste should be tipped into specially dug ponds and then covered in plastic during the process of decomposition. This process would cause the temperature of the water to rise until it was ideal for farming crustaceans such as mussels, oysters and prawns.

The company also owned all the shares in a subsidiary enterprise whose principal asset was a local football club that played in the Conference League.

Some months after delivering their valuation, the auditors were notified that the minority shareholder was bringing a negligence action against them. The claimant alleged that the auditors had been negligent in their approach to the valuation of the waste disposal process, the freehold football ground and the players.

The auditors valued the waste disposal process on the basis of the costs incurred in developing it up to the valuation date. Some months later, but before the auditors had completed their valuation, the process was sold to another company for consideration that was more than three times the total development costs incurred. The claimant argued that the subsequent sale proceeds were the best indicator of the value of the asset, and the auditors' apparent disregard of the post-valuation transaction was therefore negligent.

On the issue of liability, the auditors argued that the sale of the process had not been negotiated at arm's length and that the consideration had been artificially inflated as a result.

Unbeknown to the auditors when they undertook their valuation, the purchasers of the process discovered shortly after buying it that it was fatally flawed on technical grounds and had been so from the outset. They had been obliged to consign it to scrap and write off the cost. Hence the process had not been undervalued since it was utterly worthless throughout the entirety of its life, and the claimant had therefore suffered no loss. If anything, the auditors had *overvalued* the process – the development costs incurred by the company could justifiably have been written off.

With regard to the shares in the company that owned the football club, it was contended by the claimant that the auditors should have valued the various individual players on the club's books rather than attempting a composite valuation.

Lessons to be noted

- Since the two main assets that formed the subject of the valuation were both bound to be problematic the auditors should not have agreed to undertake the assignment without securing the agreement of the parties to
  - permit reference to specialist expertise in the case of the football club and its players, an area known to have its own unique valuation methodology; and
  - sign a 'hold harmless' undertaking with regard to the untried and untested waste disposal process.
- Although the auditors would obviously attempt the exercise in good faith and to the best of their ability, the only evidence that the process constituted an asset at all was a file of correspondence with local authorities that had expressed interest in acquiring licences to use the process after its technical viability had been established. It was obvious that no specialist expertise pre-existed the valuation, which was therefore bound to be contentious.
- In the absence of evidence that the auditors had undertaken the valuation in bad faith by exercising undue favour towards the purchasers of the disaffected shareholder's interests, the effect of a hold harmless letter would serve to enable the auditors to proceed with their valuation without fear of consequential litigation. Such a strategy is unusual in the case of auditors' valuations under the Articles of Association but the circumstances of this case amply warranted it.

C. Improper reliance on management representations

The case in this category illustrates an instance of accounting manipulation that had no motivation on the part of the perpetrators to obtain company property for their personal benefit. The sole motivation was to improve the appearance of the company's accounts by making it seem more profitable than it really was. Inevitably, despite the best intentions of the falsifiers to reverse the deception 'when business improves', the manipulation strategy is always short term for the most obvious reason – accounting falsification cannot generate cash. The parties adversely affected are, of course, banks, shareholders and other external providers of working capital finance who rely on audited financial statements as a significant safeguard.

Case C.1

The company involved in this case was a grain merchant whose suppliers were local farmers and whose customers were wholesale and retail bakeries over a wide area. The company's handwritten accounting records were audited by a sole practitioner in East Anglia. The auditor faced allegations of negligence brought by the company's liquidators on the grounds that he had failed to discover material misstatements in the financial statements of successive years arising from the inclusion in turnover and debtors of sales approaching, in the final year, £1 million that had in fact been achieved *after* the year-end.

Unfortunately, this state of affairs could not have been discerned from an examination of the audit working papers. Indeed, the auditor had created a bespoke version of standard audit working paper formats, which appeared to have been completed satisfactorily. Every audit test undertaken had been meticulously planned, recorded and cross-referenced to underlying documentary evidence. The independent accountant instructed to investigate the allegations reported initially that they appeared wholly unfounded.

However, audit tests conducted without any intelligent appraisal of what is contained in the company's own records are bound to be inadequate. In this case, had the audit clerk to whom the work was entrusted stepped back from his programme and viewed the sales day book objectively, he would have noted no more than a handful of sales transactions in the early months of the following financial period, but that the final month of the year subject to audit had listed page after page of transactions, far more than could be explained by reference to normal trading patterns.

The sales invoices for an average month could normally be recorded on approximately a page and a half of the sales day book. In August, the final month of the accounting period, however, they occupied more than eight pages of the day book. By contrast, sales in the first three months of the succeeding year occupied only six lines in total! The merest glance at the day book should have alerted any auditor with a modicum of common sense that something was seriously amiss.

Such an auditor would also have noticed that when the date sequence had reached the 31 of the final month, it merely began again at 1, 2 and so on, recording the following month's sales as if they had taken place in the final month of the year.

The schedule of queries showed that the auditor had noticed that the record of sales entries was unusual, to say the least, but that he accepted as plausible the management response to the effect that August is the month of harvest and hence the busiest period for sales.

The case was settled before the trial at a sum that approximated to the company's losses after the conclusion of the first audit that should have detected the year-end manipulations.

Lessons to be noted

- The response given by management did not in fact make any sense at all. The company's main customers, being bakeries, required a supply of grain throughout the year, to reflect the even purchasing pattern of households. There was no reasonable explanation for such frenetic activity in the month of August. The implausibility of the explanation should have been apparent from the fact that the deliveries that followed the huge number of orders in August were met several months later, in some cases in late November. Why would a local bakery be making orders in August for a delivery three months later? The audit tests clinically related orders to deliveries and this puzzling timing feature should have alerted the audit clerk concerned.
- This was a case of a relatively inexperienced audit clerk being taken in by representations supplied by the client. He was far too keen to accept these representations as genuine, because not to do so would have created problems for the relationship. The sole practitioner himself, who had been on friendly terms with the client for many years, was similarly disinclined to investigate the anomalies thrown up in the course of the audit thereby risking the relationship. Independence was therefore more apparent than real.
- There were other indicators that might potentially have betrayed the client's dishonesty. In response to enquiries about stock levels, the auditor was told that the company's grain stores were located in silos rented from other entities near Felixstowe, and two stock certificates were produced as evidence. Although these purported to emanate from two different silo companies, they were printed

on almost identical notepaper and both quoted a registered address and phone number at the same office in The Strand in London. The auditor attempted to telephone this number for a verbal confirmation but obtained no reply, whereupon the client arranged to ensure that the silo proprietor would be present at the office in The Strand to receive a call at a designated time. When the auditor phoned, not surprisingly, his client was at the other end impersonating the third party silo owner. Naturally the quantities of grain and their ownership were duly confirmed.

Audits that do not adopt the requisite measure of objective rigour are a complete waste of time and resources.

D. Failure of analytical review

Prior to the sale of a business, there is a temptation on the part of the vendors – not necessarily fraudulently – to defer the settlement of liabilities, to conceal or understate the existence of creditors and to delay necessary expenditure on repairs and maintenance, all with the view to making the accounts look better than is justified. It is normal for completion accounts to be prepared in the context of settling the amount of purchase consideration payable, and to provide a benchmark against which any subsequent warranty claims may be tested.

In such circumstances auditors instructed to prepare, review or audit completion accounts, depending on the terms of the sale and purchase agreement, will need to ensure that these accounts are comfortably reconcilable with the company's internal management accounts and its final published accounts if recently filed. The chief characteristic of this work will involve a high-level review of any volatile and hence subjective elements in the accounting matrix, and this analytical review must be carefully planned and executed to afford an optimum opportunity to identify and explain any significant variations from what might have been expected.

Where completion accounts prior to the sale of a business are prepared at a date that does not coincide with the company's normal financial year-end, great care needs to be exercised to ensure that the adjustments normally applicable are given full consideration. Otherwise there is a risk that the completion accounts will not be directly comparable with the accounts for a full period, and could therefore be regarded as misleading by the purchaser of the business.

Case D.1

This situation is what occurred in the case of Paradise Palaces Limited, a national high street furniture retailer and manufacturer that entered insolvent administrative receivership in 2005, shortly after a planned sale by the family who had controlled the business from its inception in the early 20th century. The completion accounts had been prepared by the company's own accountant for a seven-month period ended 30 June 2004.

On advice given by lawyers acting for the vendors, the company's auditors were instructed to undertake a full audit for the period covered by the completion accounts. In so doing, however, the auditors failed to take into account the seasonality of retail furniture businesses. Had they done so in the course of their analytical assessment of the plausibility of the accounts, they would have recognised that the notoriously poor winter sales in 2003/2004 were not reflected in the surprisingly profitable completion accounts.

Had the auditors investigated the reasons for this apparent suspension of reality, they would undoubtedly have ascertained that a change of policy on recognising sales was behind it. The saga resulted in a claim by the vendor shareholders against the company's auditors for substantial damages based on the allegation that if they had performed their work to the standard of a reasonably competent auditor they would have identified the unauthorised change of sales policy. The sale of Paradise would have had to be postponed until an orderly expansion of the business was reflected in accounts that could once again have provided a potential purchaser with assurance that Paradise was a solid business.

The company's conservative policy, which had applied since it first began to manufacture and sell furniture, had been to recognise sales only on delivery of furniture in fulfilment of orders. This meant that all the costs of implementing orders, including administrative costs, showroom overheads and costs of direct manufacture were included in the balance sheet as work in progress at the lower of cost and net realisable value in accordance with applicable accounting standards. Only when signed delivery notes were copied to the sales department was the consignment treated as a sale and recognised as such in the accounts.

The change of policy, which had never been formally approved by the board, was instigated by senior managers motivated by bonus undertakings following the sale of the company. The managers, with the connivance of the senior financial officer, proceeded to recognise sales on receipt of a firm order, which in many cases preceded delivery by as much as three months. Consequently, in the three-month period ended 28 February 2004 the management accounts, which were subsequently audited, recorded sales at a record figure of £7.3 million, compared with budgeted sales of £5.6 million. Following investigation by the administrative receivers, it transpired that actual sales had been well below budget. Furthermore, by 'stealing' sales that would have been recorded in subsequent quarters, the budgeted cash flow failed to materialise and this was the effective cause of the company's demise.

When an undertaking is sold to a third party in its entirety it is normal that any untidy loose ends are 'cleaned up' to reduce the risk of subsequent allegations of breaches of warranty or inadequate disclosure. In this case, one of the main board directors, Mr Milton, owned two other companies to which Paradise Palaces Limited had made substantial loans, duly guaranteed by Mr Milton. The auditors of Paradise were also the auditors of the other two companies. The relationship between the companies had been disclosed in the accounts for successive periods under the usual 'related parties' note. It was agreed that prior to the sale the intercompany loans would be settled, and it appeared to the auditors that this had been achieved by a 'settlement in kind' comprising certain antiques owned by Mr Milton personally, which later proved to be worth no more than 25% of the amount of the outstanding loans.

Lessons to be noted

- No matter how anxious the directors and shareholders of a client company may be in seeking to achieve a profitable trade sale of the enterprise it is essential that the auditors distance themselves from the euphoric anticipations of the vendors and other members of senior management who stand to benefit from the transaction. In this instance the seven-month accounts were drawn from the company records and set out in the same format as the company's published year-end accounts. The conversion from computer-generated management accounts to full-format accounts was undertaken by the auditors, who were also charged with responsibility for authenticating the numbers and issuing an audit opinion on their truth and fairness.
- It is clear that the auditors failed to bring to bear the rigour of their year-end audit approach, mainly because the analytical review procedures that they adopted following their normal audits required careful adaptation for accounts ending on 30 June rather

than 30 November. This adaptation was without precedent for this company and would have required time and effort that may well have affected the deadlines that applied. The auditors took the line of least resistance and issued their opinion without undertaking the type of analysis that would have brought the sales cut-off aberration to light.

- The auditors accepted at face value that the intercompany loan had been settled by the transfer to Paradise of Mr Milton's antiques. Had they sought appropriate valuations based on the known provenance of the items in question, they would have discovered that even an optimistic valuation would have shown up a 75% shortfall on the amount of the loans. Although the valuation of antiques is not a matter within the expertise of an auditor, guidance published by the professional bodies caters for circumstances in which reliance on outside experts is warranted. This was an instance of blatant neglect of fundamental procedures for which the frenetic sale preparations afforded no valid excuse.

E. Inadequate assessment of going concern

Whenever a client entity is heavily dependent on external finance the renewal date for funding is critical in the context of going concern assessment. From the perspective of accounting and auditing standards, the relevant period for viewing going concern is 12 months following the date on which the financial statements are approved by the directors. Since the latter date may be several months after the year-end, it is possible that directors and auditors will need to view the adequacy of working capital facilities for a period that extends 18 months or more beyond the balance sheet date.

In troubled economic times the testing of the going concern assumption can no longer be regarded as an optional extra. If a company or group collapses within a matter of months after its accounts are published with an unqualified audit opinion, the auditors will undoubtedly find themselves in the firing line of shareholders and creditors who will claim to have relied on those accounts for the purpose of deciding whether to retain or even to increase their level of exposure.

A critical feature of such an audit exercise will always involve the testing of headroom calculations as at the future covenant assessment dates, usually quarterly. Covenant tests imposed by banks and other lenders will usually relate to multiples of core earnings, interest charges and net debt against the amount owed to the bank in question. Indications that the client company may fail the covenant test at any critical date over the ensuing 12–18 months will trigger a warning of a potentially terminal risk of failure.

Case E.1

In this case the company was involved predominantly in house-building and city centre construction activity and was listed on the secondary market. It had loan arrangements with three separate banks but the bulk of its funding requirement of £50 million fell due for renewal ten months following the year-end in question and its auditors, a mid-tier firm with offices in eight UK locations, were clearly required to assess the likelihood of the loan being either renewed or refinanced with another lender.

The audit procedures followed the familiar pattern of writing to each of the three banks, but received the equally familiar non-committal responses. Typically, the banks referred to the need to review the company's budgets; the need to undertake their own due diligence; and the company's ability to put together a proposal that would meet criteria for syndicated refinancing. It was clear that these responses provided the auditors with insufficient comfort.

It seems that the auditors did not examine the detailed correspondence files between the company and its bankers, which would have alerted them to a number of points throughout the year on which the banks had expressed anxiety, including the company's excessive dependence on its profitable house-building activity when many of its construction projects were patently in difficulty.

The company's finance director was the only member of the board who was sufficiently qualified to understand the ramifications of the refinancing necessity. He produced budgets for the board, a copy of which was found on the audit file. These showed that the group would have sufficient headroom on its existing facilities to satisfy its bankers that the facility should be renewed for a further term on the impending due date.

Unwisely, the auditors accepted the budgets at face value without undertaking their own independent tests on the validity of the many assumptions that those budgets incorporated. The group budget had been prepared on the most optimistic basis possible, anticipating returns from new projects still at the drawing board stage, and from recently acquired loss-making subsidiaries that were plagued with adverse post-acquisition problems.

These companies had previously been suppliers and the intention of management was to take control of the main elements in its own supply chain for products such as bricks, cement, timber and tiling, but these transactions left the company with untidy legal disputes, troubled labour relations and losses greater than anticipated. Yet the group budget incorporated earnings and income flows from these entities that were distinctly aspirational rather than conservative. The budgets also included full recovery on each of the company's own claims for variation under existing construction contracts.

Had the auditors insisted that the company revise its budgets on a realistically conservative basis they would have found that the cash flow tests in the covenants given to the banks showed that the company would find itself in breach on each of the quarter dates before and after the loan renewal. However, the budgets were accepted by the board without any serious questions being raised, and on the strength of management's own approval of the budget the auditors made no in-depth enquiries or stress tests that might have revealed prospective breaches of covenant.

The preparation of the draft financial statements was undertaken by the finance director and presented to the auditors for their consideration of the form and content of the accounts, notes and other matters included in the group report. Under the mandatory paragraph on going concern, and in the accounting policies note, the draft wording stated that the company's long-term facilities were coming up for renewal but that the directors were confident that the company 'has' sufficient funds to continue in operational existence for the foreseeable future.

This proved not to be the case because shortly after the renewal date for refinancing the group's bankers formally declined to continue to provide funding on comparable terms, or at all, and within six weeks administrative receivers were appointed. One of the allegations made by receivers against the auditors was that the wording in the notes to the accounts on going concern would have indicated to the ordinary reader that the question of renewal of facilities was a foregone conclusion because the necessary funding would be forthcoming, and was unaccompanied by any expression of caution or uncertainty.

The letter of representation from the directors to the auditors, which the latter drafted, purported to accept full responsibility for the budgets and forecasts. The management letter from the auditors to the Board adopted the same position, affirming that those forecasts were asserted by the directors and had not been audited.

Lessons to be noted

- Reliance on management representations, effectively given by the sole member of the board competent to give them, in circumstances where auditors should be forming their own independent assessment, is never acceptable. Management representations are a valid form of audit evidence only in circumstances where their subject matter is known to the directors alone and is not susceptible to independently executed verification.
- A competent audit would have analysed the budgets on which the going concern assumption was based in sufficient detail to identify instances of optimistic bias. For example, a number of projects undertaken by the company's construction arm were experiencing delays, in some cases beyond the company's control, which in all probability would have led to the exaction of penalties for late completion. A review of a sample of projects would have made this apparent, and yet the budgets took no account of this possibility. Certain of the recent acquisitions involved the phased payment of consideration subject to the absence of any breach of warranty. In two cases, however, it was clear that warranties regarding contingent liabilities had been breached. Although this allowed the company to withhold payment of further consideration, they were faced with having to deal with very substantial liabilities that were real rather than contingent in respect of intercompany guarantees.
- After substituting more realistic estimates the auditors should then have considered the impact of the budgets on the cash flow forecasts that were critical to the quarterly covenant tests. Had they done so they would have recognised that the going concern assumption was without foundation and this would in turn have required the directors to amend the wording in the accounting policies note so that the inherent uncertainty associated with the forthcoming refinancing date was properly highlighted. In turn, this would have required the auditors to refer specifically in their own report to the uncertainty expressed.

Case E.2

This case involved a parent company, Spiral Limited, which was incorporated for the sole purpose of acting as a vehicle for acquiring control of the share capital of an existing company, Ellipse Limited, a provider of general financial services. Both companies had common directors. The purchase consideration comprised an up-front cash payment of £500,000 and deferred consideration of a similar amount under an earn-out arrangement.

To make the initial payment Spiral borrowed £400,000 from a major bank and borrowed the remaining £100,000 from its own parent company, Conical Limited. The defendant auditors, George Muggeridge & Co, acted in that capacity for Spiral and Ellipse.

Since Spiral did not trade in its own right it was incapable of generating the income required to meet its own expenses, in particular:

- the debt servicing costs of its loans from the bank and its own parent;
- scheduled repayments of the capital sums;
- the deferred consideration due to the former shareholders of Ellipse.

Following consultation with the companies' auditors, it was envisaged that the resources required by Spiral to meet these expenses and capital outlays would in fact be provided by Ellipse in the form of dividends payable from its distributable profits. However, due to reduced profitability and changes in solvency criteria for financial services businesses, Ellipse was obliged to provide funds to its parent by way of loan rather than dividends. In fact a downturn in business caused Ellipse to incur annual losses. Eventually its cash ran out and both companies were forced into liquidation.

The above funding arrangements clearly constituted a breach of the Companies Act 1985 provisions on financial assistance, as a result of which the directors faced a successful disqualification action brought by the Secretary of State for Trade.

In a separate civil action the directors claimed that the auditors (who had acted for both companies) had a duty to warn them against the illegality of the loans made to Spiral, and it was also alleged that the statutory audited accounts of Ellipse failed to give a true and fair view of the companies' financial position because the illegal, and hence unenforceable, loans to Spiral were included in the balance sheet of Ellipse.

Furthermore it was alleged that the auditors, aside from the question of illegality, should have qualified their audit opinion on the accounts of Ellipse to the effect that if the loans to Spiral proved to be irrecoverable neither the company nor the group would be able to continue as a going concern without additional external funding. The directors alleged that a clear warning along these lines would have enabled them to make alternative funding arrangements before it was too late.

Eventually the matter went to mediation where it was settled at an undisclosed amount, borne by the audit firm's indemnity insurers and the self-insured deductible.

Lessons to be noted

- Going concern is usually assessed by auditors in the context of a company's liabilities to outside parties, and yet this case demonstrates the importance of considering the status of intercompany funding arrangements within a single group and the consequences of these for the viability of individual companies.
- The auditors, acting in a different capacity, were consulted on the arrangements for funding the initial £500,000 bank loan. It should have been obvious to them that this arrangement could continue only as long as the subsidiary generated sufficient profits and cash flow to make distributions of the required amount to the parent company. This was what may be termed a 'fair-weather' framework which, in adverse conditions, might easily prove to be untenable. Such a possibility should obviously have been within the auditors' contemplation.
- At the time of conducting their audit, George Muggeridge & Co would have been aware of the insufficiency of Ellipse's profits for the above purpose and they should not have simply turned a blind eye to the financial assistance consequences of treating the payment as loans rather than dividends. The arrangements had been put in place to enable Spiral to fund the purchase of Ellipse's shares and at that time the Companies Act expressly prohibited a company from providing assistance for the purchase of its own shares, subject only to certain specific 'gateway' exclusions set out in the Act. The Companies Act 2006 has since abolished these prohibitions for private companies.
- Even though private companies are no longer subject to the financial assistance prohibitions, the major going concern issue, which the auditors failed to address, was the irrecoverability of Ellipse's loans to Spiral. These continued at the level required by Spiral in the context of its own financial obligations, regardless of its complete

inability to repay them. The auditors should have recognised the inevitable consequences of such interdependence within a loss-making group, and should have forewarned the directors of where this path would lead.

F. Succumbing to client pressure

In this chapter, we address a variety of instances in which clients have a vested interest in making the accounts look better than is justifiable, and the potentiality for deviousness, even though it may be technically within the law, is virtually limitless. One of the most basic ploys is to attempt to delay audit completion until filing deadlines are imminent, and then applying pseudo-moral pressure on the auditors to sign off before the hour of expiry.

When the debacle eventually ends in tears it is difficult for auditors to provide chapter and verse on, say, the pre-arranged meetings at which outstanding audit queries were to be raised, but which the client, on some dubious pretext, failed to attend. Nevertheless, if major audit queries remain unresolved it is essential that auditors dig their heels in and refuse to sign off under pressure, regardless of the consequences for the client. It is simply never worth it.

In Chapter 2, we raised the question of what auditors should do when faced with the 'dominant director' syndrome (see page 62). Such characters invariably adopt a condescending attitude when auditors express serious reservations about accounting treatments involving, say, revenue recognition or the amount at which balance sheet items are stated. Auditors must take care not to be cowed into submission if their concerns are not fully alleviated. It is never wise to seek a confrontation, but if a clash of opinions concerning the truth and fairness of financial statements has not been resolved the only recourse for the auditor is to qualify his or her audit opinion.

Case F.1

This case involved the audit of a UK travel agency specialising in holiday flights to Caribbean destinations. It was a regulated business under which customers were given guarantees that, in the event of the failure of the agency's business, they would be transported back to the UK at the cost of the regulator. The case began as a complaint to the Institute of

Chartered Accountants brought by the Civil Aviation Authority (CAA), which had been obliged under the rules to transport a large number of holidaymakers back to the UK from a variety of Caribbean resorts, but mainly Barbados.

The travel agency was closed down by the CAA when it became aware of complaints from customers that reservations for hotels and return flights they were holding were not being honoured. On initial investigation it became clear that the agency's assets were deficient as compared with its latest filed accounts to the extent of £750,000. The audit firm, which had signed off on the accounts and audit opinion only two months before the company's failure, faced serious disciplinary allegations concerning its conduct of the audit.

The most critical asset in the balance sheet was a total of debtor balances representing monies supposedly advanced to various sub-agencies in the Caribbean to offset the cost of 'up-leg' return flights to the UK, and it was this asset that was discovered in the course of CAA investigations to be largely fictitious or in any event materially overstated.

The auditors encountered a difficulty that typifies many situations in which management set out deliberately to put the auditors under extreme time pressure thereby forcing them to take short cuts or otherwise curtail the audit process. Accounts of travel agencies must be filed with the CAA by specific deadlines failing which the agency runs the risk of losing its licence, and no laxity is permitted. In this case the agency promised their auditors that they would obtain certificates from the sub-agencies in Barbados confirming the existence and amount of the sums advanced, but with only 48 hours to go before the filing deadline no such confirmations had been received. The auditors warned the client that if the confirmations were not received by the next day they would have no option but to issue a heavily qualified opinion, with all the consequent risks for the survival of the client company business.

The following morning 26 faxed certificates arrived at the client's premises from each of the 26 sub-agencies in Barbados, confirming in every case the exact amount shown in the agency's books. The auditors' suspicions were aroused when they noted that the addressee's name was mis-spelt in exactly the same way on each fax, the lay-out of the supposed business notepaper of each of the sub-agencies was precisely the same on all the faxes and each confirmation was identically worded. It was subsequently held at the disciplinary hearing that a competent auditor would have refused to accept these faxes as evidence on the grounds that they had patently been fabricated.

In their defence the auditors pointed out that

- they were under extreme time pressure and the stakes for the survival of the agency could not have been higher;
- they had attempted to contact a sample of the sub-agencies by telephone prior to the midday expiry of the deadline, only to find that due to the time difference between London and Barbados (six hours) the calls were not answered. The audit manager stated in evidence that he took some comfort from the fact that the telephone actually rang at all and hence that it was indeed a bone fide number in Barbados!

The Tribunal concluded that the complaint against the firm should be upheld.

Lessons to be noted

- Although the audit manager, on whom the task of performing the audit fell, was an experienced auditor of travel agencies, he succumbed to the time pressure syndrome imposed by the client, which is often accompanied by threats of litigation or withholding payment of fees. He had used all means at his disposal to obtain the requisite evidence of the outstanding advances and he experienced profound relief when eventually, albeit up against the deadline, documentation suddenly appeared, which purported to provide the necessary evidence.
- Auditors must never allow their standards to lapse in the face of client pressure. If a client fails to meet its obligation to provide the auditor with evidence that would normally be available, thus causing delays that are the sole responsibility of the client, auditors must stand their ground and either refuse to sign off until the requirement for evidence is satisfied, or resign. Under no circumstances should evidence be accepted that, when subject to objective scrutiny, appears to have been manipulated or even fabricated.

Case F.2

This case did not involve litigation. The company's accounting methods attracted the attention of the Financial Reporting Review Panel (FRRP), a division of the UK's most senior accounting body, the Financial Reporting Council, because the company was a major player in the development of residential property estates and listed on the London Stock Exchange.

All such companies are obliged to incur very substantial up-front development costs. The prudent accounting treatment is obviously to treat such costs as part of the company's ongoing operational expenditure by writing the amounts off to the profit and loss account until the point is reached where a clearly identifiable project has received all the relevant planning consents and appears to be engaged in a viable, profitable project. At that stage all further development costs may be legitimately capitalised and held in the balance sheet as costs of the project, to be recouped from future sales revenues.

The company's accounting policies, which in themselves were never criticised by the FRRP, included its policy for the treatment of commercial property sales. This read: 'Commercial property sales are recognised at the date of exchange of contract, providing the Group is reasonably assured of the receipt of the sales proceeds.'

The FRRP appear to have been interested in the application of subjective judgement by the directors to the question of being 'reasonably assured' that the sale proceeds would be received. In particular, the FRRP argued that reasonable assurance, by implication, required the certainty or at least reasonable certainty of obtaining all the relevant planning consents.

The profitable operation of a residential property development company is dependent on a variety of factors completely outside its own control, notably the timing, agendas and frequency of Local Authority Council meetings at which grants of planning permission are discussed, as well as the application of government heritage guidelines on the facades of listed buildings, targets for sustainable housing in the context of environmental policy, changes in building legislation affecting site density and reaching agreement on infrastructure responsibility.

In such circumstances, given the number of variables involved, it is not surprising that many property companies opt for the most prudent policy of accounting for sales revenue on embryonic contracts with house-builders when (and only when) all the foregoing uncertainties have been resolved. In this case, however, the directors believed that their own experience of many years provided them with a reliable sense, based on firm assurances, albeit verbal, that they had received from key members of Council, planning authorities and other influential parties. Indeed, their track record supported this approach.

The question of revenue recognition is one of the most tortured in the entire accounting framework. Although national and international standards exist, none of these has been able to eliminate the element of subjective judgement on the question of when revenues may be treated as having been 'earned' rather than being merely prospective. It is generally agreed that an excessively conservative approach is just as capable of resulting in misleading accounts as its opposite approach, and it is the responsibility of the directors to strike a reasonable balance.

The permissive approach to revenue recognition runs the risk that a profitable outcome in any particular year's financial statements will be unmatched by the corresponding cash flows, which will materialise only when contracts are finalised, and that is what happened in this case. In two successive years final planning consents were delayed well beyond the directors' expectations, due allegedly to prevarication by the Office of the Deputy Prime Minister, and this led to serious disaffection on the part of the company's shareholders who, having seen spectacular profits being reported, were told that there was insufficient cash to pay a dividend.

Because of their acquiescent role in relation to the directors' application of the relevant policy the auditors (together with certain directors with accounting qualifications) were taken to task by the FRRP in a formal hearing before the Joint Disciplinary Scheme Tribunal. Charges brought by the FRRP covered the treatment of comparable issues in earlier years and the adequacy of explanatory notes in the accounts. The directors' response to the allegations was unhesitatingly to accede to the FRRP's requirement to amend and re-issue the financial statements for several years. This left the isolated auditors having to defend a position from which the directors had de facto capitulated.

On discovering that the FRRP were raising questions about the company's accounting policies the directors sought specialist advice from one of the large international accounting firms, and yet none of this advice was expressed in clear or unequivocal terms, indeed no formal written report was provided. The company's own auditors were effectively sidelined and were not invited to any meetings at which the areas of FRRP concern were discussed.

The auditors were a medium-sized national firm, but the office responsible for the audit comprised only four partners, a modest staff and was located in the English East Midlands. It acted somewhat autonomously, not seeking independent peer advice on the highly sensitive accounting issues involved with profit determination each year.

As is often the case communications within the confines of the small audit office were entirely informal and undocumented. This was understandable, but unacceptable from the standpoint of auditing standards when the firm's practices came under scrutiny.

The firm's procedures demanded that 'hot review' and second partner checklists should be completed, and indeed these steps were performed. However, their appearance betrayed a scanty 'lip service' approach indicating that they were regarded as a 'mere formality', and this did the firm little credit in the course of the hearing, particularly as the issues identified as part of the hot review included several that might have had a bearing on the acceptance or otherwise of the directors' interpretation of the company's policy on revenue. The Tribunal found against the auditors, both individually and as a firm, on a number of the key allegations.

Lessons to be noted

- Given the material effect on bottom line results of subjectivity in the interpretation of profit recognition standards and policies, it is essential for auditors to carry out the following:
  - Familiarise themselves with the range of factors impinging on the outcome. In this instance, the most important hurdle was the grant of irrevocable planning consent because until that was received none of the house-builders lining up to sign contracts would have been prepared to commit themselves.
  - Take account of a company's track record on achieving a resolution of the uncertainties within the time frame anticipated and, where that record is erratic, to insist on a more conservative application of the underlying policy.
  - Maintain a fully documented record of their findings that will make plain to any disinterested reader the facts and thought processes arising from them, as well as the overall conclusions reached.
- There are occasions when external auditors need to be more assertive when dealing with dominant characters on the client company's board who always appear to know better and who habitually adopt a condescending attitude to the auditors. Every corporate disaster includes within its wreckage a record of reluctance or inability on the part of the auditors to raise the appropriate questions and to hold firm until satisfactory replies are received. There is

no need to be deliberately confrontational, but auditors do well to remind the directors of the consequences for them if matters turn out adversely.

- National audit firms should adopt a clear supervisory policy when allowing their smaller offices in different parts of the country to undertake assignments for enterprises of such a size that could not possibly be justified but for the affiliation with a major national brand name firm. Although the firm's governing committees will provide facilities for research, enquiry and second opinions, they should be far more proactive in supervising the quality of audits undertaken by smaller offices in the firm's name.

Case F.3

Andrew Molehill was a partner in a medium-sized practice in the Midlands of England. A prospective client, Ivan de Paris, came to see him with a request to provide an auditor's report on financial statements of Mr de Paris' company, which was engaged on a secret process, virtually alchemical, whereby raw minerals forming part of the geology of certain Mid-Western states in the USA possessed properties that could be transmuted, by applying this process, into silver, platinum and other precious metals.

Mr de Paris claimed to have substantial financial backing from a consortium of finance houses for the further development of his process, technical information of which he could not provide for reasons of secrecy. The availability of such finance, and an appropriate level of credit insurance, was contingent upon the receipt of a set of audited accounts, including a balance sheet that reflected the principal intangible asset's value as representative of the mining rights to tracts of land in the Nevada desert.

No accounting records were provided to Mr Molehill for the purposes of his audit. The only information, on the strength of which he was asked to prepare and audit the de Paris company's accounts, consisted of the following:

- the representations of Mr de Paris himself;
- geological reports from assayers in Nevada attesting to the extractive potential of the relevant minerals and the production capability over a ten-year future period; and

- receipts supporting the purchase of mining machinery that was needed for the extraction of the said minerals.

On enquiry, Mr Molehill ascertained from Mr de Paris that no production had taken place to date, and the company had received no revenue. The potential, however, was virtually incalculable according to Mr de Paris.

It was clear to Mr Molehill, based on pressure applied by Mr de Paris, that the accounts and audit report were an essential element in oiling the wheels of the venture. After a good deal of cogitation and circumspection, Mr Molehill reasoned that, professionally, he was able to construct a set of financial statements and to provide an audit opinion, so long as he made it patently clear that the information on which those accounts and audit opinion were based had been derived from unverified and unsupported representations from the company's founder, chief executive and principal shareholder. On this premise Mr Molehill proceeded with the assignment, which resulted in a balance sheet that disclosed a capitalised present value of US$30 billion, reflecting Mr de Paris' estimate of future income streams.

Mr Molehill attached an audit report that disclaimed any ability to provide an opinion, given the virtual absence of any auditable data. In effect the report stated that the attached accounts were based on the unverified representations of Mr de Paris and hence were not susceptible to an opinion on their truth and fairness. Despite this, Mr de Paris appeared to be satisfied with the work of Mr Molehill and he proceeded to circulate the accounts and the attached audit report to his dedicated investors with an accompanying letter, effectively explaining that the disclaimer wording in the audit report was a mere technicality.

On the strength of the circularised data, funds in excess of £15 million were received from investors worldwide, all of which was banked in a UK account under the sole control of Mr de Paris personally. Over a two year period he proceeded to use this money to provide returns to investors in order to meet their promised expectations. However, his inability to raise sufficient new money forced his 'Ponzi' scheme into the open following complaints to the police from investors whose returns had dried up. Mr de Paris and four associates were indicted on criminal charges and given prison sentences.

In the course of police investigations Mr Molehill was subjected to extensive interrogation, following which he suffered a nervous breakdown despite the fact that at no stage were any charges levelled against him or his firm.

Lessons to be noted

- Mr Molehill had become an inadvertent accomplice to a major fraud without realising it. There is no doubt that Mr de Paris was an exceedingly powerful and domineering individual who, through sheer force of personality, coupled with Mr Molehill's regrettable gullibility, managed to get what he wanted – a set of accounts with an audit report set between the binders of a reputable accountancy practice, logo and all.
- At no stage did Mr Molehill share any misgivings that he must have felt with any of his partners, even though the firm's structure catered for consultations of this nature in appropriate circumstances. In short, Mr Molehill adopted the path of least resistance and mentally justified his actions on the basis that his and the firm's risk would be adequately mitigated by the fact that the audit report effectively disclaimed any responsibility whatsoever. In so doing he appears to have overlooked the very reason why Mr de Paris approached him in the first place. Specifically, he overlooked the fact that the mere association of the name of a reputable firm endows the accounts with a veneer of respectability that they otherwise would not be credited with.
- At some stage in their careers most accountants will encounter characters like Mr de Paris and, difficult though it may be, it is always advisable to put the onus on the client to demonstrate plausibility in circumstances when it is so obviously lacking. It is astonishing to any level-headed accountant that investors can be so easily gulled by a story such as that of Mr de Paris when the lure is to double their money within 12 months. Practising accountants should never participate in a ruse of this nature, in any capacity.

G. Risks associated with group structures and entities under common control

Major investors may seek and be granted board positions as a means of allowing them to have a voice when decisions are made affecting the company's operations. Unfortunately, such directors may be located some distance from the company's base and may find it difficult to attend board meetings.

This creates difficulties for the auditors who are obliged to consider whether communications, such as minutes of meetings not attended by all the directors, or management letters (in which significant risks are spelt out), need to be addressed to the company secretary for onward transmission to the directors or whether the information in question should be addressed to each of the directors personally.

If some companies in a complex structure are audited by other firms it may be necessary to deal with inter-firm questionnaires concerning the adequacy of audit procedures. The completion of these documents is itself an area of high risk.

Case G.1

The company, a wholesaler of motor spares and tyres, was based in Newcastle. It had two wholly owned subsidiaries. The parent company was owned 50/50 by its managing director and a Lincoln motor spares company. Its four directors were the managing director, his wife, the chairman of the Lincoln company and its managing director.

One of the two subsidiaries incurred losses in several successive years, to some extent because of commercially disadvantageous inter-group trading, and it required financial support from the parent. When the parent company itself experienced a downturn so that it could no longer support its loss-making subsidiary, the latter was placed in insolvent liquidation as a result of which the parent company lost the whole of its investment in that company.

Civil proceedings were taken out by the other 50% shareholder, the Lincoln based company, against the audit firm responsible for auditing the accounts of the group on the grounds that it had failed to report on the insolvent company's true position, directly or through a qualified audit opinion, or by means of an appropriately worded management letter.

In their defence the auditors vigorously denied that the Lincoln directors were unaware of the true state of the insolvent subsidiary. The documentary evidence showed that both Lincoln directors were present at critical meetings held in Newcastle at which the auditors set out at length the difficulties that were being faced by that company and its increasing dependency on the parent, clearly pointing out that there was insufficient cash generation in the group as a whole to continue to provide the required level of support. This evidence was, however, gleaned from a manuscript list of issues for discussion at that meeting, placed on the audit file, rather than distributed to the attendees. Regrettably, no minutes were taken.

The auditors attempted to rebut the allegation that the two Lincoln directors were not 'hands on' in the sense of being directly involved in management on a day-to-day basis, by pointing out that it is the responsibility of directors to ensure that they are informed of material developments at all times. In any case, auditors' duties do not require them to be present throughout the year and it is quite inappropriate for absentee directors subsequently to claim that the auditors were their sole information lifeline. Finally, the auditors' duty is owed to shareholders 'as a body' rather than to any individual shareholders.

Clearly, there were hurdles that both sides to the dispute had to overcome in order to feel confident of success at trial. In such circumstances the parties, advised by their respective legal teams and experts, would normally have had recourse to mediation as part of the process towards reaching a negotiated settlement. Given the prohibitive costs of a full trial a settlement is invariably sought as the most cost-effective solution. But not in this case: such was the intensity of mutual recrimination that neither side was prepared to listen to the voice of sweet reason.

The auditors were seething in their indignation at the very idea that they were being held accountable to the extent of several hundred thousand pounds for the consequences of the decision to close the subsidiary, reached at a meeting that lasted over two hours at which the claimants were present and fully involved. The weaknesses in their own defence, to which they had blinded themselves, were as follows:

- Their notes that effectively formed the agenda for the critical meeting were never typed up and distributed, and without these in documentary form it was impossible to establish after the event the extent to which the points listed were put to the meeting and discussed, nor was it possible to assess the 'tone' of what was said by the various parties and their responses to difficult questions.
- Although the auditors subsequently included their concerns in a formal management letter, they sent this to the managing director of the parent company, who neglected to pass it on to the other directors – he had his own reasons for not wishing to do so. Given the company's precarious financial circumstances, the auditors should have issued a copy of their management letter to each of the directors personally.

- The complexity of inter-company trading within the group and of the numerous management cross-charges left the inter-company accounts unreconciled when the time came to sign off. It is likely that a timely reconciliation exercise would have revealed the extent of the failing subsidiary's dependence at a much earlier date. The potential adjustments that might have been required and their implications for going concern should have formed the subject matter of a qualified audit opinion. Furthermore, the Companies Act requires auditors to state that proper accounting records have not been kept if that is indeed the case.
- The auditors had received a questionnaire from the audit firm responsible for the audit of the Lincoln company. Quite clearly the other auditors had a legitimate concern regarding the valuation in the Lincoln company's books of its 50% holding in the Newcastle parent company and the questionnaire was designed to provide relevant information in this context. It is reasonable to assume that any replies to its questions that gave cause for concern would have been conveyed to the directors of the Lincoln company by its own auditors. Inexplicably, the question that asked about going concern issues affecting any company in the group was dealt with by appending a 'not applicable' response. The sad reality was that the questionnaire had been passed to a member of the audit team who was far too junior to understand the key significance of the question, and no one more senior had reviewed it.

Lessons to be noted

- Auditors should always ensure that key findings are received by all the relevant officers of the client company, if necessary by contacting them directly. Reliance should not be placed on the Chairman or Managing Director to undertake the circularisation.
- Decisions taken at meetings must be supported by proper minutes, not only for the sake of good order and to comply with Companies Act requirements, but as a form of protection for the attending parties including, in this case, the auditors.
- Incomplete reconciliations, particularly when they relate to inter-company trading potentially affecting the viability of one of the companies concerned, should never be left unreported by the auditors. In some instances the auditors were being instructed in an accounting capacity to perform the reconciliations themselves, and if these efforts are successful they will certainly serve as audit

evidence. But simply to leave the work undone and 'hope for the best' will always render auditors vulnerable.

- Completing other firms' questionnaires is always a tedious exercise, but never one to be left to an unsupervised audit junior. Any document originated by an outside party who expects a competent and timely reply must be taken seriously, and should always be subjected to manager or partner review.

Although the parties were set for a full Court hearing, the audit firm's professional indemnity (PI) insurers assumed responsibility for negotiations at a very late stage, which resulted in a settlement two weeks before trial at an amount that was vastly excessive from the firm's point of view and woefully inadequate from the standpoint of the claimant. That's how it goes.

H. Risks inherent in subcontracting arrangements and joint audits

When the statutory regime in the UK relaxed the necessity for small companies to have their accounts audited, a number of firms entered into arrangements with larger practices under which the latter would undertake the 'official' audit of accounts that the smaller firm had prepared, hopefully to the requisite professional standard.

Effectively this means that the audit firm is subcontracting that part of the audit work that may be safely regarded as implicit in the accounts preparation process. Clearly, arrangements between the two firms and between them and the client must be properly understood by all the parties and set out in contractual terms and signed.

Far too many of these arrangements have led to serious problems – in one case the audit firm was sued for negligence in relying on work that the subcontractor firm had carried out. The audit firm's PI underwriters denied indemnity on the grounds that the declaration signed at the previous renewal date had failed to include the smaller firm's gross fees for the purposes of calculating the premium.

Similar problems arise when joint audits are undertaken without a clear delineation of responsibility agreed in writing in advance. In the event of subsequent claims, it must be remembered that the firms share joint and several liability in respect of each other's mistakes. Even though a right of indemnity may exist if liability can be clearly identified within the scope of work undertaken by one of the firms, this is not a remedy on which the other firm would wish to rely because it will be argued that its review of the papers, competently performed, may well have identified the mistakes made.

Case H.1

The Registered Auditor in this case had an informal working relationship with a smaller unregistered firm whereby it performed statutory audits for that firm's limited company clients. In these cases it relied extensively on the bookkeeping and accounts preparation work and schedules supplied by the smaller (sole practitioner) firm, which effectively acted as subcontractor but without any formal arrangements or proper planning and work allocation being established.

The audit client was a theatre and ballet company with a local base that also undertook national and international seasonal tours for which it received European and Arts Council awards and grants.

For grants purposes it was important to the client to have its statutory accounts prepared and audited to a tight timetable. After experiencing unwelcome delays in the production of both the 2005 and 2006 years' accounts, the theatre and ballet company changed to a different firm of auditors. Following advice from its new auditors, the company issued proceedings against its former auditors alleging negligent preparation of accounts and audits in respect of the 2005 and 2006 accounting periods.

It was claimed, specifically, that grants and awards were set off against expenditure to which they did not relate thereby inflating profits causing tax to be overpaid. In addition, grants and awards received in advance of specific productions or tours were allocated to the wrong accounting period, again resulting in tax overpayments. Unused or surplus grants that were non-repayable were treated as liabilities rather than as income, and PAYE and NIC on directors' bonuses were not properly dealt with in the records or accounts. The possibility of penalties and interest was raised by HMRC.

In response to the allegations the audit firm asserted that in respect of all the matters complained of they had relied on information supplied to them by the sole practitioner, who continued to act for the claimant company's directors personally. Unfortunately, the information in question had been supplied orally on an ad hoc basis and there was no file record of what had in fact been said on such occasions.

The case settled on terms favourable to the claimants.

Lessons to be noted

- The process of audit exemption resulted in a significant number of smaller practices de-registering as auditors, seeking suitable subcontracting arrangements with Registered Auditor firms. For the latter, this case exemplifies the warnings and precautions that apply to all such arrangements. If the accounts of client entities are shown to be materially defective, the Registered Auditor carries final responsibility. Unsupported reliance on a subcontractor is never a defence.
- It is essential that subcontracting arrangements between firms should be properly formalised, specifying the allocation of responsibilities between them, and all inter-firm communications should be in writing.
- Examination of the audit firm's files also revealed that no engagement letter was issued to the claimant company. The auditors' principal concern was with accounts preparation and no additional verification was recorded. There was no evidence of audit planning or risk assessment and only one meeting with the claimant company's directors took place in almost three years. No 'fit and proper' assessment of the sole practitioner's firm, on which extensive reliance was placed throughout, was ever undertaken by the auditors.
- Most significantly, the permanent file contained no notes relating to the grants and awards that represented a major source of funding, thus implying that the auditors failed to understand the accounting and tax implications of these receipts.

Case H.2

Boulder & Co is a six-partner firm with two offices in Essex. For 17 years the firm acted as accountants and auditors to Arrow Ltd, a company specialising in loft conversion work, building conservatories and house and factory extensions.

In November 2001 the five directors of Arrow Ltd, who were also its shareholders, sold their shares to Croft plc for a maximum consideration of £4.2 million in cash (achieved by arranging a vendor placing with a merchant bank), £750,000 in shares and the balance of £1.2 million deferred and dependent on achieving 'earn-out' targets in the three years ended 30 June 2002, 2003 and 2004.

The consideration was calculated by applying an agreed multiple of 6.75 to the weighted average of the company's profits per its audited accounts for the years ended 30 June 2000 and 2001. The draft accounts for these periods were prepared by Arrow Ltd's own staff, and were then submitted to Boulder & Co and Croft plc's auditors for correction as necessary, review and audit. (The auditors of Croft plc were appointed joint auditors of Arrow Ltd for the specific purpose of providing Croft plc with additional assurance regarding the 2000 and 2001 accounts.)

The recently computerised accounting system of Arrow Ltd proved unreliable throughout the accounts preparation period in question, and this created additional pressure on the company's staff and auditors to meet the target completion date for the sale and transfer of shares. Several of the key records had to be rewritten from original source documents.

It later transpired that Arrow's interim bills to customers in respect of work in progress were incorrectly entered in the June 2001 debtors' schedule. The value of work completed for these customers, amounting to £281,500, was covered by progress payments received before the year-end. The inclusion of this sum in debtors therefore gave rise to an overstatement of profits and net assets by that amount. After deducting Corporation Tax and applying the 6.75 agreed multiple, the inflation of purchase consideration for the shares amounted to some £996,000.

In its haste to finalise the 2001 accounts the double-counting errors were missed by Arrow Ltd's internal accountant, its managing director and both firms of joint auditors. The audit reports on the 2000 and 2001 accounts were signed without qualification.

The error was discovered by Croft plc in early 2002, following which Croft plc made a claim against the two audit firms, alleging negligence in the course of their work on the June 2000 and 2001 accounts. Both the solicitor's letter and the particulars of claim specified further alleged errors in the 2000 and 2001 accounts, giving rise to a claim for damages (based on the multiple) in excess of £2.8 million.

The directors also joined the auditors in respect of a more modest claim against them by Croft plc, although they unilaterally agreed to settle this by deduction from their future 'earn-out' payments.

Legal opinion suggested that Boulder may well have been negligent in its failure to detect the existence of material errors that came to light since the acquisition. Furthermore, the former auditors of Croft plc, since resigned, have filed a defence stating that

- their responsibility was limited to reviewing the work of Boulder;
- the alleged errors would in any case not have been apparent from the documents seen by them; and
- they were under no obligation to re-audit everything done by Boulder.

Lessons to be noted

- Auditors appointed to act jointly should establish, in writing, a clear definition of how procedures are to be allocated between them, and rotated in successive audits – although in this instance Croft plc's auditors were appointed as an ad hoc measure for a specific purpose. It is highly dangerous for either firm to make assumptions regarding the work of the other, in terms of specific procedures or the quality of their execution.
- It may sometimes be necessary for one of the joint audit firms to undertake work of an accounting nature. If so, the other should not automatically impute credibility to the resulting accounts purely because of that professional involvement. Each firm should review the work of the other with due circumspection. Remember – as far as the client and third parties are concerned the legal responsibilities (and hence potential liabilities) of the joint auditors are indivisible.

  In the case described it seems that Boulder & Co assumed that the other firm would double-check their accounts compilation work; and the auditors appointed to act jointly felt (incorrectly, as events showed) such checks to be superfluous because of Boulder's direct involvement. Ironically, a more effective independent scrutiny might have been achieved by one firm acting as sole auditors!
- Boulder's defence made several references to the twin pressures created by
  - externally imposed target completion deadlines; and
  - the untimely computer breakdowns, resulting in several crucial accounting records having to be recreated from original documentation.

  This untoward conjunction was, of course, regrettable – but afforded no legal defence whatsoever. It has long been established in codes of professional conduct that there must be sufficient time to enable auditors to complete assignments to the requisite standard; and if, circumstantially, such time is lacking they have no option but to issue a suitably qualified opinion, referring explicitly to the potential effect on their work and conclusions of the constraints in question.

- Auditors appear to be at their most vulnerable when auditing accounts that will form the basis, at least in part, of an important investment decision – in this case the determination of consideration for the sale of the whole of the shares in the client company.

  When auditors become aware of the potential dependence of others on accounts in such circumstances, they should appreciate that the context in which third party reliance takes place differs significantly from that of normal stewardship reporting – and they should make this position clear to all potential third party users.
- Although such awareness cannot of itself alter the statutory audit objectives, auditors should consider taking protective measures, including the issue of disclaimers, if the degree of third party reliance appears to be unwarranted given the limited usefulness of stewardship accounts as a basis for reaching investment decisions. This would apply particularly when a potential purchaser has no intention of engaging independent investigation accountants to assess the situation prior to purchase.
- It is unlikely that existing case law on proximity would provide automatic relief from legal action if the auditor of a private company has prior intimation that the accounts are to be used in this way. In any event the engagement partner in the audit firm should ensure that the auditing procedures, and the opinion that flows therefrom, are entirely beyond reproach by submitting working paper files to independent review by a partner unconnected with the work.
- An independent reviewing partner should, at the very least, undertake an objective analysis of the financial statements with a view to highlighting apparent anomalies and any material changes that require explanation – whether favourable or unfavourable.

I. Risks associated with disappointing acquisitions

Auditors acting for vendors or purchasers are equally vulnerable in the acquisition context. If the acquirers believe, after the event, that the completion accounts on which they relied were negligently prepared and audited, they will institute legal proceedings against their accountants to recover the difference between what they paid and what they believe they should have paid – in some cases they may sue on a 'non-transaction' basis, which means that they would not have entered into the deal in the first place if the accounts had shown what they believe to be the true position.

Conversely, accountants acting for the acquiring entity are at risk if any due diligence undertaken by them fails to uncover undisclosed liabilities, over-valued assets or inflated profits that provided the basis for multiples to determine the purchase consideration.

The former shareholders, usually the directors, may in practice be spared an involvement in allegations of misrepresentation if they remain as directors and are receiving their consideration by way of earn-out.

In such potentially fraught circumstances, it is obvious that the degree of care that auditors and advisers need to exercise is dramatically heightened.

Case I.1

In this case the claimants were partners in a recruitment agency business who acquired for a total consideration of £86,000 the whole of the share capital of a smaller company carrying on a similar trade in another town. The acquisition was based on trading accounts prepared by accountants who were also auditors of the acquired company for a seven-month period. These accounts showed a profit of £18,200. At the same time audited accounts for the full previous year, showed a profit of £27,900.

The claimants maintained that they relied on these two sets of accounts in deciding to acquire the company and in determining the purchase consideration. Subsequent to the acquisition, early the following year, the acquired company experienced cash flow problems and the new directors were obliged to issue personal guarantees to secure an overdraft facility in order to carry on trading. Three months later it was clear that the company could not continue to trade legally and the claimants repaid the overdraft, standing at £57,000. Liquidation followed shortly thereafter and proceedings were commenced against the auditors.

It was alleged in the Particulars of Claim that had the purchasers known the true position of the company they would not have acquired the shares and would certainly not have guaranteed its overdraft. The claim alleged that the accounts prepared and audited by the accountants had materially overstated debtors by including assignments in progress as if already billed to clients. It was also alleged that certain current expenditures had been invalidly deferred to future periods.

The defendant auditors contended that the claimants were already familiar with the company's affairs prior to purchase and that the causes of insolvency occurred following acquisition.

Although their files showed a lack of requisite professional care in preparing and auditing the accounts, the auditors argued that: negligence, if any, on their part was not causative of loss; the claimants were minded to purchase the company in any event; and hence the claimants had themselves been largely to blame for any loss suffered.

The sums involved hardly justified the wholly disproportionate weight of legal costs incurred in reaching a settlement.

Lessons to be noted

- The sale of a client company is always a high-risk situation. At such times, third parties are known to rely upon audited accounts and completion accounts for a purpose that differs significantly from the more usual stewardship context and particular care should be exercised with this additional risk in mind.
- The audited accounts and supporting files should be subjected to rigorous review by a partner unconnected with the assignment to ensure that all necessary procedures have been performed and recorded, and that the accounts themselves are in every way plausible.
- Unaudited completion accounts should similarly be scrutinised independently and any accompanying report should avoid giving greater credibility to the accounts than is strictly warranted by the work actually performed. Judicious use of disclaimers is certainly advisable.

Case I.2

The client of accountants Jason & Smith (J&S) was an acquisitive investment group with an AIM listing and a small but ardent group of institutional backers. In January 2000, the group purchased the whole of the share capital of a company producing rolls of patterned cloth for curtains, furniture coverings and wall hangings, J&S having first produced an Accountants' Report on the target company, after which the firm was appointed auditors.

The three vendor shareholders of the acquired company remained as directors under three-year services contracts, but were released after one year due to continuous disputes over management policy, and were each paid compensation for loss of office of £125,000, giving a total payment of £375,000.

The operating results of the plc parent and of the acquired subsidiary then began to deteriorate markedly, and two major contracts with furnishing companies were lost.

A national accounting firm was appointed joint auditors with J&S, and it prepared two reports for the group bankers on the parent and on the subsidiary respectively.

The 2001 published accounts showed group losses of £2.75 million, including a loss of £1.4 million for the subsidiary. The bank applied pressure for early reductions in borrowings, and in July 2002 receivers were appointed for both companies. The subsidiary's trade was successfully disposed of by sale to a major competitor, but this still left £420,000 owing to the bank and insolvency proceedings followed.

In February 2003 solicitors acting for the subsidiary's liquidator issued a writ against J&S, alleging negligent work in both the pre-acquisition Accountants' Report and the 2000 audit. It was stated that J&S's failure to detect material overvaluations in stock delayed the necessary remedial steps which, if undertaken in time, might have turned the company round and avoided losses to the bank and to other creditors in the sum of £690,000.

It was claimed that the company's stock recording system was defective in that the printing of cloth was often subcontracted to outside printers without recording the movement of materials from store. As a result stocks in the hands of subcontractors at the 2001 and 2002 year-ends were double-counted, giving substantially inflated inventory values in the balance sheet. It was further alleged that 40% of the 2002 year-end stocks were more than two years old, and no allowance was made for obsolete patterns or the substandard condition of rolls of cloth that had become unsaleable.

Although J&S believed that it had a strong defence with regard to its 2000 Accountants' Report, experts appointed by the underwriters reported that standard audit procedures should have detected the year-end overvaluations. The claimants indicated that due to the complexity of the legal issues on establishing quantum, and to avoid the costs of drawn out proceedings, they would be prepared to reduce the claim from £690,000 to £400,000 if early settlement could be achieved.

Based on their own legal and expert advice, the underwriters authorised negotiation and a final settlement at £345,000 was reached.

Lessons to be noted

- When undertaking pre-acquisition reporting assignments it is essential that the terms of reference are clearly set out to establish the extent of responsibility accepted for the accuracy of sums included in the report. In this instance no engagement letter was issued, leaving J&S vulnerable to claims that inaccurate stock values were accepted when these were in fact based on amounts in the 1999 audited accounts, on which J&S had performed no verification work since they were not the company's auditors at the time.
- The AIM-listed client had exerted considerable pressure to complete the report by the end of January 2000 and this caused J&S to work to unrealistic deadlines at a time when its staff were fully stretched on routine December year-end work for other clients.

Case I.3

Singlet Ltd, the wholly owned subsidiary of a major venture capital company, purchased ordinary shares in Slasto Ltd, a frozen foods wholesaler, on the strength of the first accounts audited following the appointment of Selig & Co as auditors. Singlet purchased the shares for £1.6 million.

Prior to making the investment, required by Slasto for expanding its warehousing capacity, Singlet appointed Violet & Co, another firm of accountants, to conduct an independent investigation and to report to them on the reliability of the accounts and the viability of the company in which the investment was contemplated.

In the course of the following year's audit, Selig & Co discovered that the stock calculation in the audited accounts submitted to Singlet had been vastly overstated. This overstatement, by over £2 million, had the effect of converting an actual net liabilities position of £900,000 into apparent net assets of over £1.2 million.

Shortly after this discovery a receiver was appointed, liquidation followed and the whole of Singlet's investment was lost. The ensuing action cited both Selig and Violet (the auditors and the investigating accountants respectively) as co-defendants, claiming recovery of the sums lost and interest thereon.

The case hinged on three issues:

- the alleged negligence of Selig & Co (the auditors) in failing to discover the stock overvaluation in the course of its first audit;
- the justification of Singlet's reliance upon the auditors' work when it had appointed another firm for the sole purpose of advising on the proposed investment; and
- the basis to be used for apportioning blame, if any, between the two firms.

The stock was the company's most significant asset, its properties all being leasehold. The overstatement of stock in the accounts was in fact a result of deliberate manipulation by one of the directors, and he had been doing this for several years. Computer generated stock lists had been produced by the director at each year-end against which the auditors checked stock sheets created in the course of a physical stocktaking.

Although aware that the stock sheets had no individual numbering or other distinguishing identification, the auditors did not impose their own identification for the purpose of establishing completeness or retain copies of the sheets they had examined while the physical count was being conducted.

Therefore, they failed to detect the fact that additional stock sheets were added to those used at the stocktaking in order to make up the discrepancy between stocktaking totals and computer lists.

Had the case gone to trial, however, it would have been argued for the auditors that, despite their awareness of the venture capital company's interest (and a 'letter of comfort' that they had gratuitously provided), any claim by Singlet Ltd that it had relied on the audited accounts should be discounted by its reliance on the report of Violet & Co, the other firm specially appointed by it. This independent firm's remit included the following:

- obtaining assurance from the auditors that the audited accounts for the year in question would not differ significantly from the drafts already in Singlet's hands;
- investigating the accuracy of the management accounts prepared to date; and
- reporting on the valuation of stock.

Therefore, Violet & Co's report was required to cover precisely the area that proved to be the problem, and an independent assignment couched in such specific terms could clearly not be fulfilled by tacitly relying on work already performed by the auditors.

Violet & Co, as independent accountants, reported within ten days of being instructed, and yet it included no caveat regarding time constraints. The firm reported positive conclusions on the company's viability and on the reliability of the accounts. The expert for Selig & Co, however, based upon his examination of the files of Violet & Co, was satisfied that the latter had not performed the work necessary to support those conclusions.

The claim was eventually settled before trial on the basis of a 50:50 split between the two firms of the sum claimed (less a 25% discount for contributory negligence on the claimant's part) and the costs of legal advisers and experts for the parties.

Lessons to be noted

- In the first audit of any company, particular caution should be exercised over the company's accounting practices, with special reference to stock identification, the counting of quantities, valuations and pre-numbering of stocksheets. Lacking a familiarity with these matters, Selig & Co's failure to perform the 'totality' tests on stocksheets stands out as a significant omission. It was these very tests in the second year's audit that led to the discovery of the fraudulent overstatements. Selig & Co should in any event have qualified its first report with regard to the potential impact of any misstatement of the value of opening stocks which, of course, it had had no opportunity to verify.
- The issue of 'letters of comfort' by auditors to third parties is a practice to be resisted, even when the subject matter of the letter appears to fall within the scope of audit work. The accounts subject to audit are produced to meet Companies Act requirements in a stewardship context and as such are filed at Companies House. It is neither feasible nor reasonable for auditors to assess the purpose for which third parties may require the accounts (or comfort relating to any particular feature included therein) and it is therefore unwise to risk unnecessary exposure to claims by agreeing to provide such letters. A polite 'letter of decline' is invariably preferable – at least to those supplying it!
- Although in this case the venture capital company agreed to a 25% discount for contributory negligence in proceeding with what

was obviously a risky investment, there is no established legal principle covering this issue on which firms can always rely. Case law suggests that contributory negligence can be claimed in cases of tort rather than contract, but there remains considerable doubt about the application of the principle in particular cases.

Case I.4

Spiral & Co had for many years acted as auditors of Natley Construction Ltd. In June 2004 the entire share capital of Natley was acquired by another construction company for a consideration of £12 million. Only eight months later, however, Natley's bankers appointed a receiver and manager and the shares were sold for £2.5 million, thereby crystallising a loss of £9.5 million.

The claimant company instituted proceedings against the directors of Natley, alleging fraudulent misrepresentation, and against Spiral & Co. The Claimant alleged that the audited accounts on which it had relied were materially misstated. Had these disclosed Natley's true losses and net liabilities, the purchase would never have taken place.

Independent expert accountants instructed by lawyers for Spiral's insurers reported that the audit work was negligent in connection with the valuation of the company's long-term contracts. Substantial amounts of attributable profit had been included on several contracts despite the anticipation, of which the auditors were aware, that work on those contracts would be subject to severe delays caused by structural faults not foreseen when the contracts were entered into.

Although Spiral & Co was unaware of the proposed acquisition at the time it issued its audit opinion, counsel for the defendant firm advised that the Court would in all probability find that an actionable duty of care existed, because Spiral & Co had previously advised the directors of Natley that they should seek a buyer for the company's shares, and had actively assisted in preparing a marketing description.

The directors carried no Directors' and Officers' (D&O) insurance cover, and in any case maintained that they too had relied upon the audit work of Spiral prior to signing the accounts.

In view of the opinions expressed by the counsel and expert accountants, a settlement of the action was negotiated at an agreed figure of £6.5 million.

Lessons to be noted

- In cases where joint and several liability applies, it is clearly in the interests of the auditors that they agree an upper limit on liability with the directors (subject to approval by the shareholders). In this case, however, the claimant was a third party and consequently no liability cap between the company and its auditors would have been binding on it.
- In similar vein, auditors should insist that the directors carry adequate D&O cover to ensure that, in the event of a negligence action, monetary liability is apportioned as equitably as possible.
- The valuation of long-term contracts in progress has always been a minefield for auditors in view of the number of variables that directly impact on the amount included in the balance sheet under this heading. Of these the most significant is 'attributable profit', which is permitted under the accounting rules provided that the contract in question has progressed successfully to a point where it would not be imprudent to recognise profit on work done to date. Indeed, in such circumstances, the accounting standard positively requires that profit be recognised.
- Once it is clear, however, from correspondence with the client or independent valuers that problematic issues have arisen, such as the discovery of weaknesses in the subsoil so that supporting piles cannot be driven, it is necessary to make a full provision or accrual for foreseeable losses on the contract, and these should be charged as part of cost of sales.
- A final value for 'amount recoverable on contracts' must be capable of being realised because it represents the excess of the valuation of work carried out to date (included in turnover) over payments received on account. The applicable Standard requires that this amount be included in debtors rather than stocks or work in progress.
- In light of the number of factors that impinge directly on the financial statements of a construction company, it is imperative that auditors fully appreciate the highly judgemental nature of contract appraisals, that they have a sound grasp of the accounting principles and that they seek and obtain appropriate written assurances from the directors on a contract-by-contract basis.

Case I.5

In this case, which is typical of the risks associated with acquisitions, the claimant company entered into a binding agreement to acquire the entire share capital of a company for whom Merry & Co acted as auditors. The agreed purchase consideration was £1,200,000, one half of which was paid at the date of the agreement.

The claimant, however, withheld payment of the remaining £600,000 and sought the return of the sum originally paid, on the grounds that the pre-acquisition accounts, on which it claimed to have relied, were prepared and audited negligently. As a consequence, according to the claimant the disclosed profit of approximately £249,000 should have been a £145,000 loss and the net assets shown in the balance sheet to be approximately £591,000 should have been net liabilities of £601,000.

The previous directors/shareholders (the vendors), having warranted the accuracy of debtors, creditors and other items in the balance sheet, were co-defendants in the action against the auditors who, it was alleged, owed the claimant a duty of care because they were aware that the accounts would be relied upon for the purpose of reaching a purchase decision, having attended several meetings at which negotiations took place.

Expert witness for the claimant severely criticised the quality of audit work and supported the contention that both profits and net assets had been materially overstated in the accounts. The expert for the defendant firm, retained by underwriters' solicitors, conceded that some of the criticisms of the audit were valid. In particular, the company, which acted as an agency providing part-time nursing care to retirement homes, had failed to provide for national insurance contributions for its agency staff at the appropriate rates, overstating profits to that extent.

Nevertheless, had the case gone to trial, counsel for the claimant would have had to establish not only negligence in performing the audit, but also that

- when entering into agreement to acquire the shares, the claimant had in fact relied upon the accounts; and
- the claimant had acted reasonably in exercising that reliance.

In the opinion of counsel for the claimant, such reliance would have been difficult to establish to the Court's satisfaction because

- the principal shareholder of the claimant company was a qualified accountant and had spent many months before the takeover at the assured firm's premises, had unrestricted access to the target company's books and generally became fully acquainted with all aspects of the business; and

- even if the accounts had been accurate, the results of the three years' trading prior to the takeover could not by any reasonable formula justify the purchase price agreed upon.

These considerations strongly suggested that other factors, notably the target company's near-monopoly position in its area of operations, had been instrumental in persuading the claimant to agree to purchase at the price of £1,200,000, and that the claimant was therefore using the alleged negligence as a device for avoiding settlement of the outstanding purchase price of £600,000.

Settlement, agreeable also to the co-defendants, was reached only days before trial whereby the claimant was persuaded to withdraw its action and to bear its own legal costs, but was not required to pay the balance of the outstanding purchase monies. The assured firm was required to pay £445,000 to its co-defendants, the vendors, an amount duly borne by the underwriters.

Lessons to be noted

- This case demonstrates how pre-trial uncertainty militates towards a settlement. The fact that the claimant appeared to be motivated to acquire the target company for reasons unrelated to the accounts, far from helping the auditors' case, illogically backfired on them by requiring them in effect to provide the vendors, their erstwhile clients, with a proportion of the monies due (but in the event unpaid) from the claimant. It could be argued that if the accounts had been audited to the requisite standard, the claimant would have had no case at all and hence no grounds for withholding payment.
- Assertions that the claimant did not rely upon the negligently audited accounts is clearly an uncertain form of defence in such cases.
- Rather than checking for themselves that national insurance deductions were being made at the appropriate rate for a nursing agency, the auditors simply assumed that the directors' interpretation of the legislation was correct. The omission of this liability had a significant impact on the company's earnings and on its net assets.

3.3 SUMMARY OF KEY LESSONS

- Auditors must not undertake assignments that are outside the scope of their expertise.
- Auditors should be wary of accepting representations from management merely because not to do so would risk the client relationship. Reliance on management representations in circumstances where auditors should be forming their own independent assessment is never acceptable.
- Auditors must never allow their standards to lapse in the face of client pressure. Auditors must stand their ground and either refuse to sign off until the requirement for evidence is satisfied, or resign.
- In high-risk situations, the audited accounts and supporting files should be subjected to rigorous review by a partner unconnected with the assignment.
- Auditors should remember that they lend credibility to financial statements by the mere association of their name with those statements.
- Auditors should insist that directors carry adequate Directors' and Officers' insurance cover to ensure that, in the event of a negligence action, monetary liability is apportioned as equitably as possible.

4

Professional Pitfalls for Accountants

4.1 IMPORTANCE OF ENGAGEMENT LETTERS

When accountants undertake assignments that (unlike auditing) are not governed by statute, whether on a single or recurring basis, it is imperative that the terms of engagement are clearly set out in writing to ensure that, as far as possible, the parties are of one mind as to where responsibility lies.

The importance of the engagement letter, the most obvious (and usually the only) written evidence of the contractual terms existing between accountant and client, cannot be overemphasised. In practice an accurate and well-drafted engagement letter may serve as the most straightforward and effective defence of all.

It is strongly recommended that an engagement letter, drafted in accordance with the professional guidelines on this subject, be sent to the following: all new clients; all existing clients to whom one has not already been sent; and those clients who have received engagement letters in the past that do not incorporate terms governing assignments currently being undertaken.

The accountant is the professional party in the relationship and it is therefore incumbent upon him or her to ensure that the parties are *ad idem* as to the contractual responsibilities involved. This is the principal purpose of the engagement letter.

4.2 COMPARISON WITH THE USA

Conventional wisdom proclaims that the notoriously litigious commercial environment in the USA is largely attributable to the twin institutions of class actions and contingency fees, and that since these are not precisely paralleled in the UK no comparable risk exists. This proposition is no more than partly valid.

The UK Civil Procedure Rules encourage lawyers to charge fees on a conditional basis which reflects the success or failure of the outcome.

This arrangement serves partly to deal with the consequences of the abolition of legal aid in its most frequently abused form. A distinction should be drawn between, respectively, a 'contingency' and 'conditional' fee arrangement. The former, common in the USA, connotes 'no win, no fee', with the lawyer taking 40% or more of the damages if the case is won; whereas conditional fee arrangements in the UK (which have to be declared to litigation opponents and the judge) may relate to differentials in charge-out rates and the contractual award of a 'success fee' in the event of a favourable outcome.

Lawyers themselves may, for obvious reasons, not be totally averse to a conditional fee system and there are strong social arguments in its favour, especially the assurance that everyone with a genuine grievance, actionable at law, has access to the courts, irrespective of his or her means. This would partially redress the inequity that favours those with the prodigious means required to fight actions in the courts. Furthermore, if fees are charged on a conditional basis solicitors would be disinclined to take meritless cases to court.

Irrespective of the existence or otherwise of class actions and conditional fees in the UK judicial system, it should be recognised that the main thrust of US litigation involving the professions in recent years does not necessarily arise under these headings anyway. Actions currently waged in the USA are more generally brought by financial institutions, mainly as investors, who have suffered loss through relying on audited financial statements or reports prepared by investigating accountants.

A feature of the prevailing consumerist notion is that buyers, depositors, lenders and investors should be protected at all costs, coupled with the understandable, if illogical, practice of suing the party deemed to have the deepest pocket (albeit via insurance) rather than the party on whom the blame most justifiably falls.

This 'no fault' style of litigation has reached extreme proportions in certain US states, in many cases auditors finding themselves liable to third parties for their failure to predict financial disasters rather than for negligent auditing, as UK readers might understand this phrase.

Providing a satisfactory professional service in an irrationally litigious environment is understandably difficult, and the cost of normal indemnity insurance has become almost prohibitive; some firms are obliged to insure for 'catastrophe' risks only, in effect carrying a level of excess (the self-insured deductible) that would be regarded as unacceptable in the UK.

There is also much practical disruption, not to mention emotional disturbance, associated with the massive lawsuits in the USA. In the New York case of Saxon Industries all 300 partners of the accounting firm in question were named as defendants and all their personal assets placed at the disposal of the court for execution if required. Partners in firms implicated in the many scandals that have taken place between 2002 and 2009 may well find themselves in the same position.

It is also common for USA auditors to be charged with fraud, because this automatically allows triple damages to be claimed under racketeering legislation originally enacted to aid the prosecution of Mafia bosses! Defendants, even if successful, have to bear their own legal costs in the USA – another factor that serves to encourage frivolous claims. Finally, civil actions in the USA courts of first instance are heard by juries, who tend, often irrationally, to favour the claimant and make prodigious awards accordingly.

4.3 LIABILITY EXPOSURE TO THIRD PARTIES

Over the years a considerable body of case law has served to interpret the meaning of 'proximity' in establishing the duty of care owed by auditors to third parties. Yet there is correspondingly less guidance available on liability in tort arising from *non-audit* assignments, such as reports included in acquisition circulars and other invitations to subscribe for shares.

Obviously the Courts will apply the relevant principles in the circumstances, but accountants are in any event strongly advised to

- accompany any report with a clear and concise statement of its purpose;
- include a rubric specifically restricting circulation to those whom the accountant had in mind when preparing the report;
- stamp all pages of a document 'unrevised draft', or 'for discussion purposes only', as appropriate, when the document is issued before it is in its final form;
- consider reasonable use of a disclaimer formula, especially when wide circulation is anticipated;
- make use of general indemnities wherever possible, according to the nature of the work (e.g., trusteeship and receivership);
- consider the use of a reasonable contractual 'cap' on any liability attributable to negligent conduct;

- refuse to release working papers to clients or to third parties in the context of a prospective acquisition, liquidation or receivership, unless the request is accompanied by a 'hold harmless' letter, drafted by legal experts and signed by all parties who will see or make use of the papers in question, directly or indirectly;
- avoid making any verbal or written comment on past accounts in circumstances where the party to whom the comment is made may subsequently purport to have relied upon it in reaching a business or financial decision;
- avoid making any admissions of error – indemnity insurance cover could be lost by so doing.

Some disclaimers can be highly effective in appropriate circumstances. Their nature may be precautionary, such as 'non-engagement' letters. These make it clear to any third party to whom information is provided at a client's request that such provision is made in good faith and does not create any contractual relationship, nor does it establish a duty of care. In some cases it may require written acknowledgement by the third party to guarantee legal effect.

'Disengagement' letters are equally important when a professional relationship is being terminated. In our experience, the 'change of adviser' context generates a surprising number of disputes, particularly when it relates to tax. Computations have been submitted but assessments have not been agreed; the submission of elections, claims and other notices is necessary, but which adviser is responsible? Time limits are approaching but, again, who is responsible for any necessary action? A well-drafted disengagement letter will serve both to inform and forewarn a former client and the successor adviser of exactly where you perceive the line to be drawn, putting the onus on them to say otherwise or accept its contents.

The cases in this section reflect assignments that accountants accept on a regular basis, but which involve work and methodology not laid down in professional standards or company law.

A. Preparation of unaudited accounts

Even though a set of accounts has not been subject to audit and carries no audit opinion, the mere fact that it has been prepared by a professional accountant endows it with a level of credibility that may be ill-understood by those who seek to place reliance upon the accounts, including banks and other lenders. Members of professional bodies have an obligation to review the financial statements they or others have prepared to satisfy themselves that there is nothing obviously amiss. This process is no substitute for an audit but is designed to provide some comfort that there is nothing glaringly misleading.

If, for example, the level of work in progress in the accounts is double the amount included in any previous year, without further explanation sensible accountants would be reluctant to allow their name to be associated with those accounts in any capacity whatsoever.

In view of the subjective nature of interpretations that may be placed on unaudited accounts and the range of uses to which they may be put by third parties, it is clearly an area in which accountants must exercise great caution by protecting themselves through the medium of carefully worded reports that make plain the limitations of the authentication process.

Case A.1

Pickles & Co had acted for the client company for the 18 years since its inception. The company's business was the manufacture of electronic components for incorporation in the products of its customers. The collapse of two major customers in 2005 caused a significant loss of turnover and the scale of the company's business was necessarily curtailed.

At this point extended overdraft facilities were sought, for which purpose the bank requested up-to-date accounts and other evidence from the directors regarding efforts to obtain new outlets and customers.

Pickles & Co prepared the accounts to meet the bank's deadline and additional overdraft facilities of £100,000 were granted, making a total of £180,000 available. Two months later, in January 2006, it became apparent to the bank that the company's position had seriously worsened, at which point the overdraft stood at £150,000. The bank appointed a receiver and liquidation followed.

The bank issued proceedings against Pickles & Co when it became clear that there would be a shortfall of at least £120,000. The bank alleged that the accounts on which it had relied in reaching a lending decision had materially overstated the value of work in progress, which was the second largest figure in the balance sheet.

In their defence, Pickles & Co pointed out the following:

- the work had been done at short notice at the bank's request;
- Pickles & Co's report stated that it had relied on information supplied by the directors regarding work in progress – an asset that the directors were far more competent to value within the bank's allowed timescale;
- the report noted that no audit verification had taken place prior to the issue of the accounts, for which the directors were solely responsible.

However, experts engaged by underwriters' solicitors raised doubts concerning the correctness of the work-in-progress values in earlier audited accounts. They also believed that, despite restrictions in scope and time, Pickles & Co should have undertaken a review of the plausibility of the accounts prior to releasing them, rather than rely on the disclaimer of responsibility. Such a review would, in the experts' opinion, immediately have raised doubts regarding the work-in-progress valuation.

In the light of this opinion, the legal advice to underwriters was to settle on the most favourable terms possible, taking into account the extent to which the bank may have carelessly contributed to its own loss. An agreed settlement was reached at £90,000 including interest, plus half of the bank's legal costs.

Lessons to be noted

- Chartered accountants lend credibility to financial statements by the mere association of their name with those statements. The circumstances of this case and, regrettably, its outcome, are by no means unusual – banks always show a marked propensity to sue accountants in order to recover their losses, particularly in the recent recessionary period, even when it is known that the accounts were unaudited.
- Given foreknowledge of the bank's reliance, it is essential that any disclaimer issued by the accountants, such as in this case, should not be able to be set aside as unreasonable or unprofessional. A review designed to test the plausibility of the accounts is therefore essential before they are released.
- In the event that
  - the review raises serious questions regarding the reasonableness of information in the accounts, or

- insufficient time is allowed for such a review to take place, the accountants should inform both the client and the bank that they are not prepared to allow their name to be associated with the accounts in any capacity whatsoever unless adequate further time is allowed for the purpose of removing any suspicions they may hold that the accounts could be misleading.
- Although this review need not amount to a full audit, a separate letter of engagement should be issued that incorporates the form of words to be used in the report to the bank, and ensures that the accountants' fees for this work are satisfactorily covered.
- As long as banks continue, unwisely, to regard the preparation of accounts as equivalent to audit, and are ready to sue on that basis, accountants must take all practical steps to protect themselves.

Case A.2

The claimant in this case was employed by a company client of accountants Tyler & Co as office manager and accountant. The company's principal business was the supply of twines, cords and ropes to shipyards and harbour authorities in Teeside. The claimant received a legacy from her late mother's estate in the sum of £152,000, which she intimated to her employer that she would like to invest in the company, subject to being shown up-to-date financial statements.

The company's 2003 audit had commenced and Tyler & Co, in their capacity as accountants, had prepared the draft accounts from the underlying records. At the managing director's request these draft accounts were shown to the claimant who then agreed to make the investment, £15,000 for shares in the company and £137,000 as an unsecured loan.

Five months after making her investment the company lost a major contract and this, coupled with the decline in UK shipbuilding generally, caused the company to go into insolvent liquidation, the 2003 accounts having never been finalised.

Solicitors acting for the claimant maintained that she relied on Tyler & Co's draft accounts in deciding whether or not to proceed with her investment, and this was followed by a formal claim in which it was further alleged that the accounts were grossly misleading. In their defence Tyler & Co confirmed that it had shown the claimant the draft accounts but maintained that she had not relied on them, having already made up her mind to invest regardless of the accounts. Indeed, Tyler &

Co had advised her to consult a solicitor with a view to protecting her position as shareholder and lender.

Furthermore, Tyler & Co stated that the accounts were not misleading for the purposes for which they had been drafted. As the company's own internal accountant the claimant would have been well aware of the extent of the adjustments needed before finalisation. Tyler & Co also stated that the cause of the company's demise had in any event occurred in the following period, after the draft accounts had been prepared.

Unfortunately the accountants retained no file notes of the advice to the claimant that she should consult a solicitor, and the release to her of the draft accounts was not accompanied by any written caveat as to use, or disclaimer of responsibility. In the event it would have been difficult for Tyler & Co to establish that no reliance had been placed on the accounts, because the partner concerned was aware at the time of issuing the accounts that an investment of some sort was in contemplation. Indeed, his advice to her to see a solicitor confirms this awareness. It was therefore decided to negotiate a settlement on the most favourable terms possible.

To assist underwriters in the negotiation process an expert accountant was appointed to provide an opinion on the merits of the claimant's case. The expert reported that the draft accounts were in fact grossly misleading in that large quantities of water-damaged stocks of ropes were included at original cost, despite being rotten and worth no more than scrap value. Although substantial write-downs may well have occurred if final accounts had been produced, this possibility did not help Tyler & Co's case, and the expert concluded that, on the evidence, the claimant had placed material reliance on the draft accounts.

Given the obvious commercial considerations and the weaknesses in Tyler & Co's case, solicitors agreed to a settlement at the full amount lost, plus costs.

Lessons to be noted

- This regrettably typical set of circumstances highlights the hazards of releasing unaudited accounts to third parties without taking protective measures. Would it have made any difference, for example, if the draft accounts in question had been supplied to the claimant by the directors rather than by Tyler & Co?

The answer, emphatically, would be yes, provided such release of the accounts had occurred without Tyler & Co's prior knowledge. If Tyler had subsequently become aware of the claimant's potential investment it would have been necessary immediately to issue her with a written disclaimer of responsibility on the basis that

- custodianship of the draft accounts lay with the company's directors;
- in their draft form, the draft accounts were unreliable for all purposes other than as a basis for preparing statutory accounts;
- even in their final statutory form for stewardship and filing purposes, the draft accounts would be wholly unsuitable for investment assessment, for which purpose many significant adjustments may be necessary;
- Tyler & Co's involvement in the preparation of the drafts arose in its capacity as agent of the directors, with whom lay the full statutory responsibility for producing true and fair accounts;
- the draft accounts, not having been subjected to any conclusive audit scrutiny, should not in any event be regarded as having in any degree been authenticated by the audit process.

- Essentially, the proximity required for a duty of care to a third party might be evidenced by
  - actual reliance on the document in question;
  - the accountants' prior knowledge of such reliance or that such reliance was within the accountants' reasonable contemplation;
  - the reliance was reasonable and consistent with the context in which the document in question had been prepared.

B. Preparation of independent reports

In contrast to the preceding section on unaudited accounts, accountants are sometimes commissioned to provide a report at the behest of a third party lender, possible purchaser of a business or other interested entity or individual.

In such circumstances the accountant must establish the identity of 'the client'. Is it the party for whom the report is being prepared? Or is it the company whose accounts are to be the subject of the report? There is scope for confusion and, indeed, the question of responsibility for the accountant's fees is also an important aspect of such assignments. The scope of the assignment, the party/parties entitled to rely on the accountant's report, the timescale and agreement on fees should all form the subject matter of a letter of engagement, which the accountant should draft and the relevant parties should sign.

If, for example, a company that is clearly in financial difficulties is to be the subject of a report that its bankers require before agreeing to advance any further sums, the bank would normally make the appointment, but the borrowing company would be expected to pay for it. In such circumstances the accountants should insist that, in the event that their report concludes that the company is unlikely to be able to continue as a going concern, the bank should guarantee their fees.

Case B.1

Pluto Ltd urgently required increased overdraft facilities but its bankers insisted on seeing a report on the company's financial position as a pre-condition of any further lending.

The bank therefore commissioned Lane & Co to prepare such a report as independent accountants, the costs to be borne by Pluto Ltd. Lane & Co discussed its concerns about the company's finances at two successive meetings with the directors, who suggested certain amendments to the draft report prior to its submission to the bank. In view of the urgency the final version of the report was sent to the bank without first showing it to the company's directors.

The bank declined the request for increased facilities, and the directors reacted by seeking a second opinion from their own auditors. The auditors contacted Lane & Co and provided them with further information concerning Pluto Ltd which, had it been known at the time, might have influenced the report. Lane & Co nevertheless refused to withdraw its report to the bank, but passed on the information in question, merely commenting on how it would have affected the report, whereupon the bank agreed to provide the finance sought.

Lane & Co's bill for fees was met with a counterclaim comprising the costs of the additional work carried out by the company's auditors, and the value of orders allegedly lost due to the delay between the submission of the first report and the eventual overdraft approval.

Lessons to be noted

- A counterclaim is often purely a device to avoid payment of professional fees for a report that leads to a decline of further bank facilities. The report was largely factual, and made no recommendation. The bank's initial decision, though no doubt influenced by the report, was reached independently without disclosure of reasons. The issue of a counterclaim that is made as a device to avoid settlement of outstanding professional fees should be rebutted and firms should pursue the demand for fees regardless, subject of course to legal advice and underwriters' views.
- In the case outlined, however, the original arrangements for dealing with fees clouded the contractual relationships: the bank commissioned and received the report, and nominated the accountants; the fees, however, were to be paid and borne by the company. There is no clear legal precedent that serves to establish the extent of any duty of care owed by the accountants to the company or to its individual shareholders in these circumstances.
- With hindsight, it can be said that the danger of non-recovery of fees (and of counterclaim) in the event of the report failing to achieve the objective sought by the company, should have been evident to the accountants at the outset. It is therefore advisable for firms acting in such a capacity to establish a clear contractual relationship with the bank *ab initio*, whereby bills are submitted to the bank for settlement, and the bank recovers same by direct debit to the company's account with the bank. On the evidence of the case described (and of many other cases like it) an arrangement on any other basis is unnecessarily risky.
- The possibility of a claim still exists, of course, but
  - might be less tempting to mount after the accountants' professional fees have already been settled; and
  - with the contractual responsibility clearly being owed to the bank the accountants would be under no obligation to show the report to the company, still less its own auditors.
- A defence in the case described would have been hampered by the absence of detailed attendance notes of the meetings between the accountants and the directors, and of any record of the substance of subsequent telephone conversations. It is essential that this

rudimentary discipline be established and observed by partners and managers as a matter of routine. Oral evidence is always less authentic and hence less convincing as the basis for establishing the facts in complex circumstances.

C. Counterclaims following pursuit of outstanding fees

Accountants' billing practices play a crucial role in the generation of litigation. Work performed to the appropriate professional standard and completed on time in accordance with statutory requirements or the client's instructions may well lead to the issue of a counterclaim when the fees for the assignment fall overdue and are, rightly, pursued – if necessary through a debt collection agency or even the Court.

Counterclaims brought in such circumstances will obviously lack merit and include spurious allegations to the effect that the work was incompetently conducted or that appropriate warnings were not given in time. There is no limit to the resourcefulness of wayward clients and certain lawyers who are prepared to go along with a trumped-up claim.

For these reasons accountants should always keep a close watch on the time costs while an assignment is progressing. If these are mounting to a degree that the client may believe, rightly or wrongly, to be excessive compared with his or her expectations, it is important to discuss the reasons for the level of charges being incurred and either to agree that the work may continue or that it should be terminated. The art is to send clients bills that do not shock them!

If the overrun gets out of control it will usually be preferable for the accountant to suffer a modest write-off rather than offend the client, enter into dispute and face the probability of a counterclaim – which may well exceed the value of outstanding fees.

Case C.1

In this case the accountant's client was a group of companies comprising several subsidiaries, each of which specialised in the production and supply of outdoor units, ranging from garden sheds and conservatories to swimming pools. The group's turnover in the year to 31 December 2006 was £38.3 million. Following a period of rapid expansion through the acquisition of small companies, the group's accounting and financial control became seriously disorganised, compounded by high staff turnover and the departure of key members of senior management.

Assistance was sought from Corey & Co, specifically to reorganise the computerised group accounting system on a uniform basis; to bring the accounting and stores records up to date; to establish the intercompany indebtedness and the overall financial position of the group; and to make recommendations for achieving sound future financial management, at both the company and group levels. A letter of engagement setting out these objectives was sent by Corey & Co to the parent company board, and its acceptance was indicated by signature on a copy, which was then duly returned to the accountant.

Work on the assignment commenced in February 2006, much of it being undertaken by the engagement partner directly with the ad hoc assistance of his in-house computer specialists. By the end of September 2007 interim monthly bills, issued without specifying details, amounted to £258,000, of which £218,000 had been paid. Although no formal report was issued, the engagement partner had at this stage become aware that the group's financial viability was questionable and he, without reference to the client, requested one of his partners, a licensed insolvency practitioner, to report on the position and to take over the conduct of the assignment. During October and November 2007, additional fee notes for £43,617 were issued, and a further £21,000 was received from the client.

In early December the replacement partner issued a report on the financial position of the individual subsidiaries and on the group as a whole, supported by analysed accounts in columnar form, with additional comments on future viability offered on the basis of stated assumptions. The report concluded that the group's solvency, as at the end of October, was seriously in doubt, particularly at the onset of the traditionally quiet winter season. No recommendations were made regarding accounting systems improvements, or enhanced stores control, as per the engagement terms.

In February 2008 the accountant issued a claim for the outstanding fees and this was met with a defence and counterclaim. This alleged, *inter alia*, that

- the accountant's work had involved considerable duplication of effort as between the partners and staff;
- such advice as had been received had in the main been worthless;
- severe delays in giving the advice sought resulted in heavy additional costs being incurred unnecessarily;

- wholly unnecessary attendances by the initial partner and his computer staff had generated fees for the accountant that could not be justified.

Based on advice of solicitors acting for underwriters, settlement negotiations were commenced on a without prejudice basis, and were eventually concluded by agreement that the accountant's claim for outstanding fees would be dropped and an additional payment of £150,000 would be made to the claimants, each side bearing its own costs.

Lessons to be noted

- The client's expectations were adequately set out in the engagement letter, but were not met by the accountant's performance. It appears that the work leading to systems improvements for the future was overtaken by the realisation that the group may not actually have a future – but it should not have required huge time costs to be incurred before coming to that view!
- The story strongly suggests that the accountant's approach to the work was devoid of intelligent planning from the outset. The work should have been prioritised, initial emphasis being given to ascertainment of the group's current financial position, followed by detailed accounts preparation work for the subsidiaries. Recommendations for systems improvements and the computerisation of stores records should have come later. Yet it was with the latter that the accountant began – 'the specialist computer staff being available at that time', as it was put in his witness statement.
- The reasons for the transfer of responsibility to another partner should first have been discussed with the client, whose forecasts of future trading patterns would have been highly pertinent to the going concern issues. Indeed, it is relevant to note that the group succeeded in avoiding receivership and, although now somewhat slimmed down, continues to trade profitably on a reduced turnover.
- The accountant's monthly bills simply read 'for professional services during the month of . . .', which is always a recipe for disagreement and dispute. The accountant should, at the very least, have explained exactly what work had been done in the month, by whom and how it related to the engagement letter's statement of objectives. Detailed progress reports and provisional conclusions should have been issued bi-monthly. Brief fortnightly meetings with the client should also have been arranged at which progress

to date could have been discussed and any client queries – particularly about the escalating costs – dealt with and satisfactorily resolved at an early stage.

D. Dangers of administrative foul-ups

Throughout this book, we identify the many circumstances in which accountants land in trouble because of sub-standard work – be it under the headings of auditing, tax advice or simply a failure to apply an appropriate level of specialist knowledge. In the cases that follow it will be seen that claims against accountants may arise under a different heading altogether: namely a failure at the purely administrative level of running a practice, using staff who are simply incompetent. Even a partner or manager may be guilty of the oversight that leads to an expensive claim.

Case D.1

The client company was a property developer who required funding for a new leisure complex, including an estuary marina, for which EU grants were available. Additional finance was forthcoming from the client's own family resources and from a venture capital company. The venture finance was, however, contingent upon the EU grant being secured as a condition precedent to contract completion.

The accountant was instructed by the developer to complete the EU grant application form and supply detailed financial information to support the application. The EU's UK agents at the Department of Trade & Industry in London advised the accountant that in principle the proposed venture was eligible for a grant of the amount applied for.

Unfortunately, however, unknown to the accountant, the grant application forms and supporting documentation had not in fact been despatched, due to being mislaid in his firm's post department.

The accountant informed his client that the grant had been sanctioned in principle and the developer authorised work to commence on the building foundations and on dredging the estuary. The venture capital company, however, refused to release its share of the investment prior to having sight of the formal EU grant concession certificate. It was then that the accountant discovered the omission to forward the papers to the Department.

A late application by the accountant to the EU on the client's behalf was then made, but was turned down on the grounds that work on the project had already commenced!

Lessons to be noted

- It is noteworthy that a high percentage of claims notifications received under all claims headings arise from internal administrative failures rather than negligent professional work or advice. This case provides dramatic evidence of how a post-room oversight can lead to a very substantial claim against the firm.
- As practices grow in size and take on work outside the conventional range of mainstream accountancy, the resulting complexity creates a need for partners to pay special attention to the organisational aspects of the firm.
- In this particular instance neither the partner nor his secretary had a record of the name of the official to whom the grant information and forms should be sent for processing, and the unaddressed packet was swept up with the day's post and passed for franking. On receipt in the post-room, it was placed by a member of staff in a drawer, the firm having imposed a 'clear desk' policy as a feature of its quality procedures. Unfortunately it was then a case of 'out of sight, out of mind' and no further attention was given to the matter – until it was too late!

Case D.2

In this case, a personal tax client of one of the partners in a firm of accountants started a new management training company with two colleagues in February 2004. The partner accepted oral instructions to deal with the preparation, audit and filing of the company's initial and subsequent accounts.

Accounts for the year ended 31 January 2005 were prepared and sent to the directors for approval, but no response was received and no follow-up action was taken. In June 2006 the Registrar of Companies wrote to the company's registered office at the accountant's address, warning that the company would be struck off after a further three months unless signed accounts were received for filing before that date.

The partner responsible was on holiday when the warning letter was received, and the firm's post-room staff were unable to trace the company, for which no previous accounts had been prepared. The letter was therefore not dealt with until circulated around the firm nearly two months later. The partner then wrote to the Registrar to the effect that the company was actively trading and should not be struck off; he also undertook to secure the accounts for filing within the ensuing four weeks. He then wrote to the directors and enclosed a further copy of the initial draft accounts and his correspondence with the Registrar, stressing the urgency of approving them.

The directors, all heavily involved in running management seminars for clients, failed to respond, and there was again no follow-up by the accountant. In February 2007 the company's bank manager informed the directors that formal notice of striking off had appeared in the London Gazette in November 2006. The accountant took immediate steps to have the company restored to the Register by bringing the filing of its accounts up to date for the years ended 31 January 2005, 2006 and 2007, all of which were audited by the accountant's firm before being approved by the directors.

The accountant then billed the client company for the time charges it had incurred since the formation of the company but this was met by a counterclaim for damages, including costs of restoring the company to the Register in July 2007, interest and loss of goodwill. The Letter before Action received from the company's solicitors implied, however, that the action would be dropped if a credit note were issued for all outstanding fees.

Although directors' contributory negligence could have been pleaded, the defence was not strong enough to justify heavy legal and experts' costs and the case was subsequently settled.

Lessons to be noted

- This case again illustrates the consequences of poor administration for a professional firm. As the professional party in the relationship, the onus is on the firm to accept written instructions only, as incorporated in an engagement letter that sets out the respective responsibilities of the directors and advisers/auditors, billing arrangements and fee settlement terms.

- On acceptance of a new client the firm's records must reflect all relevant details (assignments accepted, time ledger codes, contact partners, client contract names, etc.). Arrangements must be in force to deal promptly with any matters arising in a partner's absence. Lack of response from clients must be systematically followed up by the firm, if necessary culminating in a refusal to continue to act.
- On the face of it, it seems outrageous that matters falling wholly within directors' statutory responsibilities, and persistently ignored by them, should lead to a claim by them against their accountants. Yet it is common practice for directors' duties to be subcontracted out to their professional advisers, and once these are accepted it is essential that procedures are in place to ensure that the necessary work is done to the requisite standard on a timely basis so that deadlines are met, and that the directors' own lapses do not jeopardise compliance.

Case D.3

Ballard & Co and its predecessor firms had acted for the client company for over 25 years and during this period had served in the capacity of accountants, auditors and tax advisers. The firm always prepared the company's statutory financial statements from detailed books and filed documents produced by the client company's internal accounting staff. Latterly this included comprehensive computer output comprising the period's transactions listing and detailed inventories. Due to shortage of space at the client's premises the accounts preparation work was habitually done in Ballard's own offices.

On 1 January 2005, Ballard & Co entered into a new contract with a cleaning company for the nightly cleaning of their offices. On one morning during March 2005, when work on the client's 2004 accounts was nearing completion, it was discovered that all of the client's books and records, as well as the current audit files, were missing. Immediate contact was made with cleaning contractors to ascertain whether the missing items had been improperly removed by the cleaning staff, and Ballard's office manager interviewed each cleaner who had been on the premises the previous evening.

Although it was initially denied that any papers had been wrongly taken, further detailed questioning of the cleaning supervisor led to a full admission of the error. It transpired that all the client's books, files and other papers had been placed in a large solid plastic document bin, which an inexperienced cleaner had assumed contained items to be thrown out. It was, however, too late to recover the records since the waste from the whole building had already been transported to a central refuse site.

Work was immediately commenced on reconstruction of the client's records to the extent possible from previous years' accounts and files and computer back-up data retained by the client for security purposes.

The total time costs for this exercise at the firm's standard charge-out rates amounted to £52,500 excluding disbursements and VAT. Underwriters then appointed loss adjusters to assess the value of any claim that might reasonably be made by Ballard under its policy. This was then reduced by the profit element and certain charges not attributable to the reconstruction, leaving an agreed claim of £39,200.

Ballard's own records showed that at the time of entering into the new cleaning contract the office manager had spoken to the contractor's operations supervisor in detail about its requirements for the disposal of items on the premises, and had pointed out that the grey plastic document containers were often in use.

The contractors conceded full responsibility but recovery was limited under their standard contract terms to three times their basic annual cleaning charge leaving the balance to be settled by underwriters.

Lessons to be noted

- This case shows the importance of checking that the firm's professional indemnity policy gives cover for loss of documents and similar risks. It also highlights the need to ascertain the adequacy of recovery possible under contracts with independent providers of services in the event of their negligence.
- Most important, however, was the firm's own policy on office tidiness when staff go home after work. If at all feasible, desks should be left clear and books and papers deposited in cupboards and cabinets so as to minimise the risk of erroneous disposal.
- Staff should, of course, be deputed to check that post and other documents received for colleagues who are temporarily away from the office is dealt with appropriately, otherwise such a 'clean-desk' policy can itself result in claims.

E. Coping with clients whose record-keeping is chaotic

Every sensible accountant will attempt to persuade clients to take responsibility for punctual and accurate record-keeping. Although it is within the competence of any accountant to perform basic bookkeeping services, it is always recommended that clients should be made aware of the advantages of maintaining records that they themselves can refer to as a means of assessing and monitoring their financial position. Furthermore, leaving the most basic procedures to a professional person is not cost-effective and runs the risk of leading to a fee dispute.

Case E.1

Regarding payment of outstanding fees, there are certain categories of client who should carry a health warning. This applied to the case in question, with a vengeance. A small boutique firm specialised in providing accountancy and tax advice to clients in media and entertainment. Such clients are notoriously difficult to manage because they are characteristically poor at keeping reliable accounting records or even to attending to routine correspondence. They place no priority on 'mundane' financial matters until things go wrong, and they are rarely in one place for any length of time.

One particular client, Bingey Brennan, generated significant earnings from a variety of sources, having achieved modest success in the music industry and roles in TV 'soaps'. From his accountants' perspective, however, his financial affairs were a nightmare. His records consisted of little more than jottings on scraps of paper. Repeated requests from his accountants for basic information such as bank statements were ignored for months and any information eventually provided was incomplete and invariably gave rise to further queries. The scope of the work undertaken by the accountants by way of compilation of basic accounting information far exceeded the terms of the engagement letter, which the client had in any event failed to sign!

The accountants did their best to keep Mr Brennan's affairs in some semblance of order in near impossible circumstances. Inevitably, however, they fell into disarray and Mr Brennan eventually became the focus of HMRC investigations that resulted in the imposition of substantial interest charges and penalties in respect of late settlement of income tax, NI and VAT liabilities. During the course of the investigations, which lasted some four years, the time cost of work undertaken by his accountants reached awesome heights, on which Mr Brennan's erratic and relatively small round sum payments on account had scant impact. The accountants' numerous pleas by telephone for further funds resulted in little more than empty promises.

Although reluctant to lose their increasingly high-profile client, the accountants eventually carried out their repeated threat to cease work and issued a formal claim demanding payment of their outstanding fees. Brennan's response in his formal defence, drafted by his media lawyer, was to allege that

- he was not informed of the build-up of work in progress;
- the work undertaken exceeded the scope of the accountants' remit;
- his accounts and returns were prepared negligently.

Unsurprisingly, Brennan issued a counterclaim that substantially exceeded the outstanding accountancy fees, alleging that

- the penalties imposed by HMRC arose from his accountants' negligence in not completing accounts and returns on time; and
- fines, penalties and extra work undertaken in relation to HMRC investigations were a consequence of the accountants' failure to deal with his affairs properly.

The matter was eventually disposed of by means of a 'drop hands' settlement whereby neither party received any damages and each settled their own costs. The accountant's fees were never paid.

Lessons to be noted

This case encapsulates many of the features that are most likely to lead to a claim against an accountant:

- There are several basic procedures that should serve to rebut allegations made by a client who is not minded to pay outstanding fees and these procedures may even pre-empt such a situation arising in the first place. Contriving a pretext for litigation is commonly resorted to as a device for simply refusing to settle professional fees properly incurred and billed.
- Without having a signed letter of engagement the rule is that no work should be performed, no matter how keen the accountant

is to acquire a celebrity client. Insistence on this basic procedure demonstrates to the client that the accountant is subject to a discipline that may be alien to the client but which he or she is obliged to respect.

- Every engagement letter should spell out the responsibilities of the client as well as the accountant, and if the client fails to meet those responsibilities the accountant, instead of simply doing the work for him or her, should advise the client in writing that the further work is outside the scope of the engagement and therefore subject to a supplementary engagement for which an additional fee will be charged.
- The accountant should submit a detailed checklist of the documents needed before any work is commenced. It may be practical to arrange a meeting at the client's premises at which the necessary documents can be assembled and any missing information identified.
- If delays in providing the necessary information are creating problems with HMRC, the client should be informed in writing of the nature of the problem, what he or she has to do to resolve it and the potential consequences of failing to respond fully and promptly. Accountants should not chase for information by telephone without making notes of the conversation.
- Accountants should never allow unbilled time costs to build up by default. While work is ongoing, bills should be sent out on a regular monthly basis and these should include an accurate description of the work to which that time relates, including the names of staff members involved and the hourly rate applied. The use of unparticularised general terms such as 'professional services rendered' should be avoided.
- Arrangements for settling fees should be clearly set out as part of the terms of engagement, together with an explanation that if these are not complied with the accountant will be obliged to stop work, regardless of the consequences.

All accountants can think of at least one client they wish was someone else's! The truth is that there are some clients that are simply not worth having.

F. Conflicts of interest

When a prospective purchaser of a client's business raises questions that the vendor is unable to deal with satisfactorily, it is all too easy for the vendor to pass the queries to his or her own accountants, who may then find themselves giving information to the purchaser that includes estimates, even forecasts or projections. This is a dangerous situation, particularly when the information in question concerns the financial position of the business being sold.

Accountants are obviously not averse to assisting their clients with transactions involving the purchase or sale of a business, but they become vulnerable when the prospective purchaser/vendor places a high degree of reliance on the information supplied. It is always preferable to recommend to such parties that they should instruct their own independent advisers.

Case F.1

The accountant in this case had acted for the proprietor of four high street mobile phone retailing outlets for many years. When the client decided to sell the business, the accountant assisted him by providing financial information to a prospective purchaser who was not independently advised.

Over a period of some four months the accountant dealt with the purchaser's enquiries about the business operations, its costs, supplies and margins. As the negotiations between the client and purchaser progressed, the accountant was gradually drawn into a more proactive involvement, and eventually went so far as to provide the purchaser with cash flow and profit projections for each of the outlets, based on the purchaser's own assumptions regarding financing, the involvement in the business of members of his family and the level of drawings. The accountant also indicated that he would be happy to act for the purchaser after the sale.

In order to fund the purchase it was necessary for the purchaser to take out a second mortgage on his home, in connection with which the accountant assisted with tax advice and by speaking to the bank on his behalf. By this stage, even though no formal engagement had been entered into and no fees were charged, the purchaser's reliance on the accountant should have been plainly evident.

The sale went through on the basis that the vendor was prepared to accept delayed payment for part of the consideration, the outstanding balance being secured on the purchaser's home and on the business itself.

Despite the purchaser's family working long hours for minimal drawings the return proved insufficient to meet the payments to the vendor. The business was repossessed and the purchaser lost his home. The vendor had, in effect been paid out for his business and yet ended up owning it all over again! A claim for very substantial damages was made against the accountant, the claimant being legally aided.

Lessons to be noted

- In his defence the accountant cited the fact that there had been no formal engagement and no fees were charged. He maintained that he had been acting throughout, in good faith, on his own client's instructions to provide the purchaser with such information on the business as was necessary to deal with his enquiries. He was adamant that simply by being helpful and courteous in every way, and charging no fees, no duty of care to the purchaser had been created. He stated that the purchaser had reached his own decision to proceed independently, on the basis of information that had properly and honestly been provided to him.
- However the accountant knew, as a fact, that the purchaser was not separately advised and consequently should have realised that the degree of reliance placed on information provided by him was bound to be a major determining factor in the purchaser's decision to proceed with the acquisition. Indeed, the purchaser regularly approached the accountant directly for information and assistance. The accountant went so far as to issue spreadsheet projections and to provide tax and mortgage advice. This amounted to an acceptance of a responsibility that went beyond the passing on of purely historic data.
- The appropriate action, which should have applied at the outset, would have been to advise the purchaser to appoint his own accountant to undertake basic due diligence enquiries. In the event that such advice was ignored, the accountant should have issued a formal disclaimer of responsibility for the consequences of relying on information selected by the purchaser as relevant, and insisted that the purchaser add his signature.

- Having disregarded the need to take steps to avoid the assumption of a duty of care, the degree of competence displayed by the accountant was called into question during legal proceedings. It became apparent that the projections were grossly optimistic in disregarding any charges for debt-servicing or allowing for a reasonable level of drawings. The accountant failed to issue appropriate warnings on the slender margin of error built in to the projections and the dire consequences of not meeting the income figures.
- Any independent accountant advising the purchaser would have drawn attention to the hazards of proceeding when the commerciality of the purchase was so patently suspect. He would also have pointed to the potential loss of a home when using it as security for a loan that could not possibly have been repaid or serviced if turnover failed to match expectations by even a few percentage points.

Case F.2

In a similar case, an elderly retired couple decided to acquire a general trading store in a small town on the south coast of England. They responded positively to an advertisement in a local newspaper for the sale of a small general store whose owner wished to sell the business and retire. The couple contacted the advertiser, who turned out to be an accountant engaged by the storekeeper to deal with the sale.

Based on minimal financial information provided by the accountant, the couple produced their own handwritten spreadsheets and asked the accountant to have them typed and passed to a local bank manager with a loan application to fund the purchase. The accountant obliged but the bank manager emphatically rejected the proposition, which included an offer of the couple's matrimonial home as security for the bank loan. The bank manager's refusal was based on the improbability of the venture succeeding in the light of the skimpy business plan, and he commented that he was not a 'pawnbroker'.

The accountant helpfully introduced the couple to a mortgage broker who proceeded to arrange a loan of £200,000 secured on the matrimonial home. Following the introductory meeting the accountant reviewed the spreadsheets and made a few inconsequential changes. The couple then committed themselves to purchasing the leasehold store and its shop fittings and stock. Being without any relevant business experience, and despite the best of intentions and efforts, the actual turnover fell far below the level required to ensure viability. Together with crippling interest costs, this caused the business to fail and foreclosure of their home loan followed.

A short time later the husband died and his widow, legally aided, commenced proceedings against the accountant. Despite the latter's protests that he had acted as little more than an introducer, his insurers settled the case after an expert's report concluded that the projections adjusted and passed on by the accountant were grossly optimistic and hence misleading.

Lessons to be noted

- This case exemplifies the risks taken by accountants who overplay their part in seeking to achieve their clients' objectives – in this case going so far as to act as the advertiser and negotiator for the sale of the client's business. It would have been clear to a more sophisticated purchaser that the accountant was far from impartial, but the claimant in this action was naive in the extreme. Indeed, she did not recognise the extent to which she needed protection from her own innocence in matters of business.
- The prospective purchaser presented certain business plans and projections to the accountant for comment. He should immediately have advised that it was inappropriate for him to respond to this request and instead recommended that the purchaser seek independent advice elsewhere.
- By accepting and amending the claimant's projections the accountant was effectively precluded from subsequently claiming that he had acted as little more than an introducer. The fact that the spreadsheets shown to him were overoptimistic and patently misleading rendered a sustainable defence impossible, particularly after the accountant became aware that the bank manager to whom he had sent the documents had already concluded that the business was not viable.

Case F.3

Mr Adams inherited £360,000 and sought the advice of Gritty & Co, accountants who had acted for him for some years, on how to invest it. At the relevant time Gritty & Co had another client, Abacus Ltd, which was experiencing liquidity problems, believed to be short term. Mr Adams, acting on the advice of Gritty & Co, agreed to invest a total of £280,000 by way of loan capital, payable in monthly instalments over a six-month period. The arrangement was that the payments would be made to Gritty & Co who would, in turn, invest these sums on Mr Adams' behalf in Abacus Ltd. However Gritty & Co paid the relevant sums to Abacus Ltd in instalments over an extended period of 18 months, rather than on the dates that the cash was received from Mr Adams.

Mr Adams was told that the investment would yield interest at 24% per annum. However, over the 18-month period during which the investment was being made, interest of only £43,050 was received by Gritty & Co on behalf of Mr Adams.

Although it was Gritty & Co's intention that Mr Adams should assign the investment to a company (Yucca Ltd) formed for tax purposes, no formal assignment was executed, although Abacus Ltd did issue a debenture in favour of Yucca Ltd when the final instalment was received.

Six months later Abacus Ltd went into liquidation with a declared deficiency of £550,000. This was followed by a statement of claim alleging negligence on the part of Gritty & Co, claiming damages of the capital sum loaned and interest at 24% per annum, after giving credit for the £43,050 received.

Legal advice was that there was no reliable defence against the claim, Gritty & Co having admitted the following:

- If Mr Adams had sought advice on the investment, and had the firm not acted for Abacus Ltd, they would have advised against it because the financial position of Abacus Ltd was too precarious to have justified the recommendation to invest.
- They did not advise Mr Adams to seek independent advice, despite there being a lack of independence, given that Abacus Ltd was an existing client of the firm.
- There was an inexcusable delay between the date of receiving monies from Mr Adams and the date of passing it over to Abacus Ltd. There was also a delay in issuing the debenture, which in the event proved to be worthless anyway.

The matter was settled at the full amount claimed.

Lessons to be noted

- Despite the temptation to match the respective needs of two separate clients by bringing them together for their mutual benefit, the hazards implicit in the possibility of either party (or in some cases both) being dissatisfied should be fully recognised. When things go wrong the accountant adviser is faced with the additional difficulty of having to disprove the obvious implication of his or her own personal interest (albeit indirect) in the arrangement – in this case the advantage of avoiding Abacus Ltd's failure and hence the loss of outstanding and future fees.
- The intermediary role of Gritty & Co appeared to give it an indirect financial interest in Abacus Ltd. The possible breaches of professional ethics rules would have required full examination.
- If the arrangement between two clients was a possibility to be pursued (itself of dubious wisdom), at the very least the partner advising Mr Adams should have enlisted the assistance of a partner uninvolved in the affairs of either client, with a view to arriving at an independent assessment of the merits of the proposed investment. Assuming such assessment resulted in a recommendation to proceed, the uninvolved partner should thereafter have acted for Mr Adams in all matters pertaining to the investment.
- By retaining investment monies before passing them to Abacus Ltd, Gritty & Co may well have compromised the ability of Abacus Ltd to survive its funding difficulties. There was never any overt intention that monies received over six months should be delayed until the lapse of 18 months. This behaviour was both unethical and arguably dishonest.

G. Unwittingly becoming a shadow director

A *shadow director* is defined in company law as any person in accordance with whose instructions or directions the directors of a company are accustomed to act. As noted elsewhere in this book, it is unwise for an accountant to subsume responsibilities within the business of a client simply by default. There is no demarcation line on the duties that only the company's officers or employees should undertake. However, if an accountant undertakes responsibility for payroll preparation based on information held on the client's wages records and personnel files, that of itself would pose no risk. It is a responsibility that many companies pass to their accountants because it is cost-effective to do so compared with the cost of employing a full-time payroll clerk.

If, by contrast, the accountant is given cheque signatory status and retains the company cheque book, prioritising payments to suppliers and other creditors as a financial control, he or she runs the grave risk of executing functions that fall exclusively within the scope of the company's directors.

Case G.1

There are many accountants whose practice consists primarily of acting as 'company doctor' for clients whose businesses are in difficult financial circumstances of varying degrees. This was the case with Mr Eric Plowman's practice in which he acted as a sole practitioner, personally seeing to the needs of his various clients. One such client was a large machine tool manufacturing group in Scotland, with an annual turnover in excess of £75 million.

Mr Plowman was instructed by the managing director (MD), who was the major shareholder, to provide services as a consultant and to attend the company's premises in that capacity for five hours per week for an indefinite future period. The reason for engaging a consultant was that the MD had become increasingly concerned over the fact that despite the management accounts showing increasing profitability the high level of bank borrowings showed no sign of being reduced. It was also suspected that the company's own in-house accountant might be embezzling funds on a large scale. Mr Plowman's retainer was stated verbally to be limited to reviewing the monthly management accounts so that the company's true profitability could be established and any necessary remedial action taken to reduce borrowings. The scope of his engagement was never expressed in writing.

Over the period of Mr Plowman's retainer, which lasted less than one year, he made brief handwritten schedules of action points arising from his review of the monthly profit and loss accounts and balance sheets of each company in the group and conveyed his findings and suggestions to the MD verbally. Owing to the limited amount of time available, Mr Plowman relied extensively on the work of the in-house accountant, despite the MD's misgivings regarding his honesty and competence.

The company's finances became more precarious over this period and the MD decided to appoint an independent firm of accountants to undertake an in-depth investigation to ascertain the cause of this worsening position. One month later they reported that, far from being profitable, the company was losing money at an average rate of £25,000 per month. The MD took immediate remedial action to cut overheads drastically. He also sacked the in-house accountant and terminated Mr Plowman's consultancy. Furthermore, proceedings were commenced against Mr Plowman alleging that his work had been conducted negligently in failing to highlight the company's losses, and thereby preventing it from taking remedial action at least eight months earlier.

Mr Plowman's defence stated that, given the limited scope of his retainer and the time he was able to devote to it, he could not reasonably have been expected to discover the fact that the management accounts prepared by the in-house accountant so grossly misrepresented the company's true state of affairs. He claimed that the MD was well aware of his reliance on the company's own records and the accounts prepared from them.

After a prolonged and exceedingly acrimonious litigation process the matter was referred to mediation and the resulting settlement was reached at an amount well below the MD's expectations. Nevertheless, particularly in view of the hazardous nature of Mr Plowman's professional work, his insurers refused to grant him cover at the next policy renewal date. As invariably happens in such cases the rest of the insurance market followed the renewing insurer's lead and Mr Plowman was left with no alternative but to apply to his professional body for entry into its Assigned Risks Pool (ARP). The ARP accommodates accountants in a default situation as insurer of last resort, an arrangement set up to ensure that every practising accountant is able to provide clients with the comfort of having professional indemnity insurance.

Lessons to be noted

- Mr Plowman was, to a large degree, the author of his own misfortune. Given his experience as a 'company doctor' of many years' standing he should have appreciated the hazards of such a degree of informality in accepting an ill-understood consultancy. He should have ensured that the scope of his assignment was clearly defined and set out in writing in an engagement letter signed by the MD on behalf of the company. What could comfortably and reasonably be achieved in a few hours per week should have been clearly stated in that letter. This would have overcome the risk that the MD's expectations might exceed what could safely be warranted. It was Mr Plowman's belief throughout the progress of the litigation that the MD had fully recognised the unreasonableness of his claim, but exploited the lack of clarity in the assignment solely to obtain an award of damages funded by Mr Plowman's insurers.

- Although it was understandable that Mr Plowman's notes, queries and comments were expressed in highly abbreviated, handwritten form, he should not have allowed time constraints to prevent him from at least submitting weekly or monthly highlights typed-up in a form that the MD could readily digest and act upon.
- When it became apparent to him that the unqualified in-house accountant was patently incapable of producing timely and accurate management accounts, and that many of the records from which they were drawn had not been properly written up, he should have made it clear that unless the situation was rectified it would be pointless to continue his consultancy.

H. Negligent certification of creditworthiness

Clients used to instruct accountants regularly to provide certificates of creditworthiness to support loan or mortgage applications to lending institutions on their behalf. The mere association of the certificate with the name of a qualified accountant endowed it with a level of credibility that afforded a significant measure of comfort to the lender, and for this reason accountants providing such certificates in the ordinary course of their professional work were wise to exercise the requisite degree of caution.

Evidence emerging from the saga of sub-prime lending shows that in the years leading to the 2007/2008 credit crisis, banks were so desperately keen to 'sell' loans to individual borrowers that they adopted the practice of 'no status' lending, whereby borrowers were simply asked to 'self-certify' details of income and other relevant disclosures without the involvement of an independent accountant. Now that the dire consequences of such gross neglect have been recognised, it is inevitable that banks will revert to the practice of seeking a scapegoat for the results of bad lending practices in the shape of accountants who are over-eager to assist their clients.

Case H.1

In the case reviewed here, the accountants wrote a letter to a major mortgage institution in the following terms:

> *We confirm that we act as accountants for Mr Figleaf. In respect of Mr Figleaf's recent mortgage application we confirm that in our opinion he has sufficient income to service a loan of £282,000.*
>
> *Whilst this information is given in good faith, we do not accept any responsibility for any default which may occur or any problems arising therefrom, appertaining to the above credit reference.*

In the event Mr Figleaf defaulted on his mortgage and the proceeds of sale of the repossessed property fell well short of the amount of the outstanding loan and accrued interest. The mortgage company instituted proceedings against the accountants claiming that they had acted negligently, and that their gross negligence served to deprive the purported disclaimer of responsibility of any legal effect.

The litigation was protracted and costly but settlement was eventually reached between the mortgage company and the accountants' insurers.

Lessons to be noted

- The accountants appear to have been unaware of formal guidance issued by the major accountancy bodies to their members on the subject of confirming details of clients' income or assets to third party lenders. This guidance emphasises the need for accountants to consider the limits of what may safely be certified.
- It is dangerous for accountants to imply to a lender that their client is capable of meeting future mortgage instalments when they obviously cannot predict the effect of either changes in interest rates or changes in the client's circumstances. The term of the loan in this instance was 20 years, a period during which the client's ability to service the loan could alter significantly. Consequently, accountants should limit the scope of any certificates of this nature to information consistent with that shown in the client's most recent tax returns, provided these have been prepared on the client's behalf by the certifying accountants.

- Similar considerations apply when clients pledge assets as security for loans and their accountants are requested to provide valuations directly to third party lenders. Where the asset concerned is a property, accountants should respond by declining to provide a certificate because valuing property does not fall within their expertise. Where, however, the security takes the form of shares in a private company, the accountants may undertake the valuation exercise but should seek an indemnity from the client in respect of any liability arising from a claim brought by the lender. The lender should be required to confirm in advance that a 'non-speaking' valuation, which will declare the valuation without any accompanying calculations or statement of methodology, will be acceptable.

I. Vicarious liability following actions of consultants and staff

It should be impressed on staff (whether subcontracted, ex-agency or full time) that they stand for the firm in all their dealings with clients. There have been many claims caused by failure of even senior staff to make adequate file notes of seemingly casual conversations with client company directors or shareholders.

Over a period of years members of staff who regularly visit particular clients are bound to establish a cordial relationship with the client entity and its own staff and a relationship of mutual trust will arise quite naturally. There are dangers, however, that in the course of their work at the client's offices, staff members will feel no inhibitions about discussing their findings in a casual, informal manner without recognising that the listener may place a surprising degree of reliance on the substance of what is being said. If caution is not exercised and notes are not taken, the partners may find themselves vicariously liable for the consequences of what the client alleges was said at the time.

Case I.1

In one such instance the firm's manager was visiting the client's offices on a brief bookkeeping assignment. While he was working there he was introduced by the managing director to a non-executive shareholder who asked him 'how the company was doing'. The firm's manager maintains that he replied in a non-committal manner, in keeping with the apparently informal question, along the lines of 'it all seems to be okay'. The shareholder, from recollection, responded with 'good, then it's a safe investment', to which no further reply was given.

The manager was, however, later accused of having explicitly given the company a clean bill of health, something he was obviously in no position to do, not only because of his lack of authority but – far more to the point – because the position of the company could be determined only after his bookkeeping had been completed and full financial statements prepared.

Unknown to the manager, that question was put to him by the shareholder immediately prior to the latter's purchase of 50% of the MD's own holding. The accounts subsequently prepared by the firm showed that the company's finances were precarious and the partner responsible advised immediate cessation of trading. This was followed five months later by insolvent liquidation and the shareholders lost the whole of their investment.

The firm was sued by the shareholder for vicarious liability based on the negligent 'advice' tendered by its manager. A secure defence was difficult to establish because

- there was no documentary evidence of what was actually said;
- the manager had since left the firm; and
- the claimant was an exceptionally determined litigant.

As a result, settlement was reached at a substantial amount – a particularly expensive lesson on the subject of vicarious responsibility!

Lesson to be noted

- Most other claims in this area are less dramatic, but they all point to the need for a clear policy on client communications and where consultants (often ex-partners) are concerned, the need for proper agreements on the use of office and secretarial facilities, and limits on the consultant's ability to bind the firm.

Case I.2

This case concerns a partner in a six-partner firm of accountants who was retained to advise and otherwise assist a client to raise initial capital for the construction of a new marina planned to open in 2005 on a river in Dorset. During late 2002 and early 2003, the partner contacted several venture capital companies and government grant agencies, produced the necessary brochures and prospectuses, and dealt with the local authority's planning enquiries in anticipation of the issue of the necessary consents. The partner issued fee notes for only 50% of his time costs on the understanding, set out in an exchange of letters, that he would personally retain a £10,000 investment in the venture. The accountant did not act as auditor to the client, which was a consortium of joint venture interests held as shares in a limited company, the size of shareholdings being proportionate to the amount of seed capital committed.

In performing these services the partner was assisted by a qualified senior, who was fully aware of the project's details. Twice in the course of the work the partner recommended an investment in the project to his assistant, who then acted on this advice to the extent of £98,000, representing a recently received bequest from his late father's estate.

The project then encountered serious difficulties: two prospective contributors were made personally bankrupt having overextended themselves on another commercial property venture, and local residents successfully petitioned the planning authority to reduce the scale of the enterprise materially, causing other backers to withdraw.

By May 2003 it was clear that there was no reasonable prospect of success and, to avoid allegations of wrongful trading, the directors decided to discontinue operations and appointed a liquidator to wind up the company. The Statement of Affairs showed that the assistant's investment, the largest contributed in cash, was irretrievable, and certain creditors for architects' and legal fees remained unpaid.

The assistant resigned from the firm and immediately instituted proceedings for recovery of the £98,000 plus interest lost on the capital sum. The partner concerned denied liability on the grounds that

- he owed the assistant no duty of care, there being no professional relationship between them;
- his advice, being based on the best of his knowledge, honestly held at the time, was not in any event negligent;
- the claimant's awareness of the potential risks and rewards implicit in such a venture was by no means inferior to or otherwise materially different from his own awareness of same.

Despite the apparent strength of the accountant's case, he was clearly in a conflict of interest situation in that while recommending the investment he was actively seeking finance for the client. His advice to the assistant could not therefore be described as impartial. His insurers negotiated a settlement at £60,000, plus costs.

Lessons to be noted

- Advice given by a professional, even casually, to any listening party can prove to be extremely costly, as this case shows. Similar considerations apply to comments, often incorrectly construed as advice, made by a firm's staff, for which the firm itself might be held vicariously liable.
- The partner was undoubtedly out of order in encouraging his assistant to invest in this way. Indeed, firms should have a rule that personal investments by partners or staff in client ventures are explicitly prohibited. It is an abiding principle that all professional activities should be characterised by actual and perceived impartiality and objectivity.

Case I.3

The claimant company had been formed as a single venture company, committed to produce a modern ballet scheduled for a run in provincial theatres and finally in London. Fountain & Co was engaged by the company to prepare weekly management accounts for use by the directors when approaching potential backers ('angels'). Fountain & Co had a reputation for specialising in work for actors' agencies, dance production ventures and theatres.

The directors of the company also required the weekly accounts to assess the ongoing viability of the ballet following its London opening, in order to determine the length of its run and hence the contracts with dancers, orchestra and the theatre.

Contractual arrangements with the orchestra required provision to be made for NI deductions from its members' wages, and this Fountain & Co failed to do, the member of staff working on the assignment lacking the relevant experience. As a consequence of this omission, the profit of the production was inflated in each set of weekly accounts, and by the time the run ended the total amount owing to HMRC for NI exceeded £102,000.

In accordance with agreements already entered into with the investing angels, many of whom were shareholders in the company, the major part of the disclosed profit, including the erroneous overstatement, had already been distributed by instalments. The client's share of the distributed profits had in turn been invested in two plays, both apparently loss-makers.

When the error was discovered by the partner in Fountain & Co he advised the client that the overstatement of profit was due to an 'innocent mistake' and recommended that repayment of the relevant amounts should be requested. The client, however, refused to accept this advice on the following grounds:

- a request for repayment of sums already distributed would bring the company and its director into serious discredit and embarrassment;
- many of the angels were US nationals and legal complications could ensue;
- the recipients of the distributions could legitimately resist repayment on the basis that they had 'changed their position'; that is, that the relevant sums had already been spent or otherwise committed.

The client then instituted proceedings against Fountain & Co on the basis that its negligence had left a liability to HMRC for which no resources were now available. The claim added further damages by including losses incurred by the production itself. It was alleged that had the weekly accounts shown the true position, the ballet's run would have been terminated at an early stage and its losses therefore avoided.

On the basis of legal advice, insurers agreed to meet the claim to the extent of the liability to HMRC plus legal costs.

Lessons to be noted

- The periodic distributions to shareholders based on the weekly accounts were made on account of the company's supposed profits for the venture as a whole or, if it extended its period of operation, for its first accounting reference period. As such, distributions are permitted under the Companies Act 1985 only if they are made out of 'profits available for purpose'; that is, its accumulated realised profits less any accumulated realised losses, as defined under the Act. Strictly, therefore, the directors were obliged to prepare full format quasi-statutory accounts before paying any dividends to shareholders (as opposed to lenders). Apart from the shareholding directors themselves it is not known precisely how many of the other financial supporters were also members of the company.

- In the practical context of this unusual case, however, any claim against the company for wrongful distribution would have had to be brought by the directors themselves in their capacity as shareholders and by other shareholder recipients of the unlawful payments – a highly unlikely development. Whether the defendants in such an action were to be the directors or the company itself, it would no doubt be argued that complete reliance had been placed on the work of Fountain & Co prior to reaching successive decisions to make interim distributions. Directors of companies should nevertheless be aware of the risk of personal responsibility for making distributions that are found subsequently to be unlawful.
- Fountain & Co should similarly have been sufficiently familiar with the Act's provisions on distributable profits to have appreciated the risk of blithely paying out sums on account of profits, when the existence of those profits could not reliably be established at the time of payment.

Case I.4

This claim was one of several arising from the dishonest acts of a partner, since dismissed. The remaining partners have had to accept vicarious liability for losses suffered by clients and third parties stemming from such acts.

The former partner persuaded a personal 'client', an elderly widow, to advance him £220,000 for investment on her behalf, which he undertook to arrange. Approximately £150,000 was to be used to purchase high-yield bonds and the balance would be loaned, at 3% over base rate, to other clients of the firm. These details were established from correspondence in the claimant's possession, the firm being unable to find any record of the client's existence, let alone details of advice or business transacted.

Since, however, the letters from the former partner were typed on his firm's notepaper and the investments undertaken involved other clients of the firm, remaining partners were advised by solicitors that it would be difficult to avoid vicarious liability.

A total of £68,000 was in fact loaned on a short-term basis to three clients, interest was remitted and paid over, and the loans were duly repaid – although never accounted for to the lender. The balance, exceeding £150,000, was never invested in bonds or units for the client's benefit as agreed, and its ultimate destination was never ascertained.

The matter came to light when the client complained to a manager of the firm on the telephone that she had not received any interest on the bulk of her investment. This was then reported to the senior partner, the partner in question being on holiday.

The claim was settled at the full amount lost, including interest, and the claimant's legal costs.

Lessons to be noted

- Regrettably, claims under the heading of partner and employee dishonesty and fraud are not as rare as might be expected. Audit regulation requires partners and all professional staff, including subcontract and agency personnel, to complete comprehensive 'fit and proper' questionnaires, and this may assist the firm to identify risk factors associated with 'suspect' characters with dubious backgrounds – although anyone with a propensity for dishonest dealings is unlikely to reveal any compromising information when filling in a questionnaire.
- The best form of risk mitigation in this area is to build in a system of internal monitoring, which involves recorded details of incoming calls and independent opening of mail, periodically supervised by partners on a rotation system.
- Spot checks should be conducted on delays in dealing with clients' tax affairs and – above all – regular partners' and managers' meetings should be held at which problems can be discussed. Signs of personal financial difficulties and the effect of pressure of work should be periodically dealt with at private meetings with the senior partner. Dishonest actions by professionals will often stem from financial pressures which, if known in time, may be dealt with before any serious damage is done.
- None of these precautions can guarantee the discovery of deliberately planned and executed fraud, but the best chance is always based on how well you know your people!

Case I.5

Severe problems will sometimes be caused by mental anxiety and stress when practitioners cannot cope with their workload. In one extremely unfortunate instance a member of a two-partner practice neglected to prepare any accounts for a newly qualified dentist client who therefore fell into severe arrears with HMRC, leading to heavy penalties.

The partner had failed to keep abreast of his client's needs following a breakdown in his marriage and harrowing divorce proceedings. He made promises to catch up but was never able to honour deadlines; nor did he delegate work to others or discuss his problems with his partner – indeed it seems to have been a partnership in name only, for they rarely communicated on any practice issues.

After three years of escalating neglect on the accountant's part, and despite all the necessary records and vouchers having been supplied to him, the client applied for a mortgage and the building society sought proof of income. Hastily prepared figures were submitted in order to satisfy the society, despite the fact that no accounts had ever been prepared as a basis. The client sent his mortgage details to the local HMRC office to obtain relief on the interest and this triggered enquiries into the client's sources of income.

Only then did the extent of the accountant's neglect come to light, the excuse proffered being the fact that he had been verging on the edge of a nervous breakdown for some time. Accounts were hastily prepared but were not accepted by HMRC, who insisted on seeing all the supporting records.

At this stage other accountants were appointed and substantial fees incurred in reaching an acceptable settlement with HMRC, which necessarily included heavy penalties. Not surprisingly, the former client issued proceedings against the accountant for recovery of tax penalties, interest rate differentials, further professional and legal costs, as well as a claim for general damages for practice disruption. A settlement at close to the sum claimed was reached.

Lesson to be noted

- If accountants fail to recognise the hazards of allowing a backlog to develop in dealing with their client's affairs, no lessons will ever be learnt until it is too late. However, any responsible professional will find the personal resources to deal with domestic upheavals in a manner that minimises their impact on the affairs of clients. One of the advantages of being in partnership is to be able to call on others to assist before a crisis develops. The lesson is therefore to recognise the probability that clients will become disaffected and leave the firm, or that legal claims may arise, if the reasons for the backlog are not dealt with firmly as soon as they manifest. In the case of sole practitioners it is essential to have a relationship of mutual trust with another practitioner who would be prepared to assist if called upon.

Case I.6

Mr Arthur Willis, a founder equity partner in Willis & Co, became a salaried partner and then a consultant as he approached retirement age. His arrangements with the firm included restrictions governing the practice of accountancy, but allowed him to pursue other business interests and to retain fees or profits arising therefrom. Mr Willis nevertheless continued to use the firm's offices for meetings with business associates. When still a salaried partner he formed and built up a double-glazing company in Hull in association with other parties.

His company's minutes referred to the appointment of Willis & Co as auditors, but

- this was never communicated to the other partners in the firm;
- no engagement letter had ever been issued;
- such an appointment would in any case have been void in law because Mr Willis was both a partner in the accountancy firm and a director of the double-glazing company at the relevant time.

A short time later the company was sold to a third party at a price based, in part at least, on accounts prepared by Mr Willis. Unfortunately Mr Willis bound the accounts in Willis & Co standard folders and conducted all correspondence, which he signed in the firm's name, on the firm's headed notepaper (on which he appeared either as partner or as consultant), despite the fact that all income from the company was received by Mr Willis personally.

The company's new owners subsequently claimed that the amounts shown in the pre-acquisition accounts for debtors and work in progress were substantially overstated and that the company's true trading position was near hopeless. They claimed that if they had been aware of the true position they would not have acquired the company.

They then started proceedings against Willis & Co (with strong encouragement from their own bank to whom their personal assets were pledged against loans to the company). Following receipt of the claim, Mr Willis fled the country, leaving no assets of any substance. His final whereabouts were never satisfactorily established.

Counsel's assessment, based on such scant documentary evidence as was available (bearing in mind that the partners in Willis & Co had no knowledge of the existence of either the double-glazing company or the claimant prior to receipt of the claim) was that

- the accounts shown to the claimants prior to their investment appear to have been negligently prepared, and gave rise to a material overstatement of the company's net assets, as alleged; and
- it would be difficult for Willis & Co to argue that Mr Willis lacked ostensible authority to act on its behalf.

The underwriters accepted counsel's advice and negotiated a settlement of the claim at 70% of the amount claimed, plus costs.

Lessons to be noted

- Fortunately it is rare (but by no means unknown) to find partners behaving in such cavalier fashion against the interests of their own firm. Nevertheless it serves to remind partners in professional practice of the dangers of failing to lay down limits of authority (and to supervise their observance), particularly in relation to partners adopting altered status when leaving full-time practice.
- In this instance, Mr Willis continued to visit the firm's premises and use its offices for his meetings, apparently in full harness as a personality of some significance in the practice. A defence based on lack of ostensible authority was obviously difficult to establish, and the firm therefore had to accept vicarious liability for the claimant's loss, despite having had nothing whatever to do with its cause.

Case I.7

Mr Ackroyd and Mr Dalton, the two partners of an accountancy practice known as Collard & Co, each supervised one of the firm's two offices in adjacent towns. The partners split up after Mr Ackroyd became aware of a number of complaints from clients about Mr Dalton's work. Mr Ackroyd continued to practice as Collard & Co, but on his own.

Clients of the firm were advised accordingly and some of those for whom Mr Dalton had been acting (including the claimant company) chose to remain with him following the practice split. Collard & Co then gave permission for Mr Dalton to remove all the related client working papers, files and statutory records from its offices.

A short time later complaints against Mr Dalton were investigated by his professional body and, following disciplinary proceedings, he ceased to be a member. He then relocated and his subsequent whereabouts and practising style were never reliably ascertained.

A claim against Collard & Co by the liquidator of the claimant company was then received, alleging that accounts prepared by Mr Dalton (while still a partner in Collard & Co) had shown a profit for the period to 30 June 2002 of some £220,000, whereas the true result was a loss of over £140,000.

This was discovered by the claimant company's new auditor (appointed to replace Mr Dalton due to the latter's poor service following his severance from Collard & Co) when attempting to reconcile the 2002 accounts with the company's records as a basis for his work on the 2003 accounts. He sought the assistance of Collard & Co, but due to the removal of all the relevant files and papers, the firm was unable to help. The revised 2002 result therefore was arrived at by the new auditor having to rework the 2002 accounts from the company's original records and documents. The 2003 accounts showed a similar loss, and management accounts to February 2004 showed further trading losses. The company, by then clearly insolvent, ceased trading and went into liquidation. The disclosed creditors' deficiency exceeded £1.2 million.

The liquidator (bringing the action against Collard & Co on behalf of the claimant company) maintained that had the 2002 accounts been correctly prepared by Collard & Co the directors would have called a creditors' meeting at an earlier date when the deficiency would have been comparatively small.

The company's overdrafts had been personally guaranteed by the directors and recourse to such guarantees by the bank featured as a separate head of claim against Collard & Co, in addition to the other components of the overall deficiency.

Liability under the policy at the full sum claimed was very difficult to deny, given that

- the errors in the 2002 accounts prepared by Mr Dalton were of such an elementary nature that negligence was virtually indisputable;

- the absence of working papers made it impossible to mount a defence;
- neither Mr Ackroyd nor any present member of Collard & Co had ever been involved in any work for the claimant company.

The claim was therefore settled at the full amount claimed of £1.2 million plus costs.

The problems implicit in these circumstances were further compounded by two additional discoveries:

- Mr Dalton had acted for all the directors of the claimant company and their families personally in regard to their tax affairs which, at the time of the practice split, were substantially in arrears, no tax returns having been prepared or submitted for several years. Penalties and interest charges under this head of claim alone amounted to over £120,000.
- Underwriters were advised of two further and totally independent claims against Collard & Co also arising from Mr Dalton's alleged negligence when still a partner in that firm. The circumstances and sums involved in these additional claims are similar to those described above.

Lessons to be noted

There are numerous noteworthy aspects to the lessons of this claim.

- No partnership can function properly without mutual trust in the absolute integrity, technical competence, and administrative and organisational capacity of the partners.
- Yet this catalogue of disaster (the aftermath of which has well-nigh crippled the firm and Mr Ackroyd's professional career – despite his own complete personal innocence of all the matters complained of) clearly demonstrates the potential consequences of what can happen when that trust proves to have been misplaced.
- The case suggests the need for some form of internal monitoring system, which although not seeking directly to call partners' integrity into question, serves to ensure that the firm's operational standards are rigorously observed. Many larger firms have had such systems in place for years – this case shows its necessity in even a two-partner firm. A basic system of regular and independent file reviews and of monitoring taxation deadlines would, for example, have a good chance of bringing any untoward developments to light.

- At a more fundamental level the case highlights the need for carefully designed run-off insurance following a practice split. Since Mr Ackroyd had decided to continue to practice as Collard & Co he should have insisted, as a term of severance before releasing any papers, that Mr Dalton take out separate insurance for six years specifically covering Collard & Co in respect of any claims arising from Dalton's presplit work. In addition to providing extra cover, this would avoid any such claims affecting the terms of Collard's & Co's own ongoing indemnity arrangements and creating an adverse claims record due to no fault of its proprietor and professional staff.
- The directors of the now insolvent claimant company should have borne some responsibility for having continued to trade while insolvent. They were in day-to-day charge of the company's management, controlled its costs and determined its prices and margins. It is unreasonable that they should claim to be totally dependent on the formal annual historic accounts for knowing whether their company was solvent.

As usual with claims settled before trial, it is impossible to know how the Court might have ruled on the question of the directors' own negligence had they been joined as co-defendants. Under the UK system of joint and several liability, however, the liquidator had a choice of defendant and selected Collard & Co, the company's auditors at the relevant date.

Case I.8

Andrew Sanchez, one of the partners in a three-partner practice, Astoria & Co, showed signs of excessive strain and the quality of his work suffered. His behaviour deteriorated to the point that the other two partners felt obliged to serve him with a notice of expulsion.

For several years the expelled partner had acted for a close business and personal friend, and advice was usually given informally, few file notes being made. Following expulsion Mr Sanchez handed one of the files pertaining to the client's affairs to the client himself.

It then transpired that the client's building company, Biscuit Ltd, had acquired another of the firm's client companies, Pastry Ltd, for which Mr Sanchez also acted, the introduction having been effected by him. The acquisition was based on the latest audited accounts and other information supplied, but without full investigation or insistence on warranties. The terms of sale required payment for the shares by instalments, and included a golden handshake and pension for the vendor of the shares.

Biscuit Ltd then complained to the firm about the audited accounts of Pastry Ltd, alleging that they had overstated the company's net assets and that their former partner, Mr Sanchez, had made specific representations regarding the accuracy of sums included in current assets and liabilities. Although Mr Sanchez denied this, there was no file support for any work he may have done in relation to the acquisition.

Although no claim had been specifically threatened at that stage, Astoria agreed to waive unpaid fees of several thousand pounds in deference to the dissatisfaction expressed concerning Mr Sanchez's work.

A claim against Astoria was then received from Biscuit Ltd, seeking recovery of the sums already paid over to the vendors, alleging that the accounts of Pastry had been negligently audited and that as a result the investment was now worthless.

No doubt in part due to his mental state, Mr Sanchez proved to be of little use in defending the claim, and his attitude remained one of almost total non-cooperation, despite warnings of potential recourse against him personally.

Lessons to be noted

- The case described again highlights the extent to which one partner's unsound behaviour can rebound to the detriment of the entire firm. Although the nature of a partnership is one of complete trust and integrity, consideration could be given to setting up systems of independent monitoring of client files for completeness of information on advice given and work done. There is no reason why peer reviews and quality control checks should be confined to audit files.
- Ideally, files should be sufficiently clear and complete to enable another partner to take over an assignment at short notice in the event of the assignment partner's unscheduled and enforced absence for any reason. Such a clear record is of course de rigueur for investment business clients and it should set the standard for all the firm's files.
- Partners should be encouraged to discuss pressures and anxieties before they get out of hand, and regular health checks are to be welcomed.

- The waiver of fees prior to receipt of the claim could, at worst, be construed as an admission of liability in negligence whereas, at best, it could give a dissatisfied client further inducement to pursue a claim in law.
- In this instance Astoria & Co failed to appreciate the extent to which the potential claim against it could exceed the fees waived. It is for this reason that underwriter's policy terms prohibit admission of liability. The fees waived in this case totalled £24,800, whereas the subsequent claim was in excess of £180,000, including estimated costs of £32,000.
- Underwriters are also concerned that such an admission could have the effect of prejudicing a legal defence, including the possibility, no matter how apparently remote, of alleging contributory negligence. For example in this case, as we have seen, the claimant did not commission an independent investigation prior to purchase, nor did he seek any warranty from the vendors. He relied solely on accounts prepared and audited, as it happens, by the firm that audited his own company's accounts.

Case I.9

The client company, Sylvester Ltd, operated a public house and engaged Deronda & Co to write up the accounting records and prepare VAT returns. This work was performed by a junior member of the firm, Rufus Hubble, who had only recently been employed.

To enable the work to be done at Deronda's premises, the client sent the accountants the relevant returns, vouchers and cheque books, sometimes partially used. Mr Hubble forged the client director's signature and wrote out cheques for substantial sums in favour of his wife. From time to time he asked the client director for cheques with which to pay the VAT, indicating that he was as yet uncertain of the amount, which therefore was left blank when the cheques were signed. Similar cheques were requested for purposes of remitting PAYE.

Surprisingly, when signing cheques the client director also left the name of the payee blank despite it being obvious that this should be HMRC.

Legal advice stated that since the frauds were committed in the course of Mr Hubble's employment, Deronda was vicariously liable for the client company's losses attributable thereto. Settlement negotiations addressed the following issues:

- the bank's (at least partial) liability for paying on forged cheques;
- the client's contributory negligence in leaving the payee blank when the purpose of the cheques in question was known;
- Mrs Hubble's liability to refund sums paid to her (she would certainly have been liable if it could be shown that she spent sums to which she knew she was not entitled, but the situation was rendered far more difficult by the fact that the cheques made payable to her were lodged in a joint account with her husband).

Full settlement was reached taking account of sums recovered from the bank and from Mr and Mrs Hubble.

Lessons to be noted

- Those in professional practice must accept that in the eyes of their clients all partners and staff in a firm of chartered accountants are automatically assumed to behave in a manner that is scrupulously and at all times beyond reproach. Although such an assumption is a welcome compliment to the profession as a whole, and is fully justified in the vast majority of cases, there are notable exceptions that manifest from time to time, with severe repercussions for the firms affected.
- As this case shows, based on assumptions of absolute honesty and integrity, clients will often dispense with the most basic standards of caution. For this very reason, it is vital that firms' quality control criteria extend to the most thorough enquiry into the background and personal circumstances of applicants for staff positions, and an insistence on character references for all prospective recruits, which should of course be taken up and followed by further enquiry if doubt persists. In recent years the laws on defamation have rendered the receipt of character references highly problematic. Nevertheless, it is important to seek these on the understanding that if a previous employer was aware of dishonesty, it would probably decline to issue a reference altogether.
- It should be specifically noted that PI insurance gives no protection to fraudulent parties themselves, or those who condone it either openly or by implication through inaction. The policy is therefore

voidable in cases where the guilty party signs the firm's insurance proposal and in this event the 'Special Institute Conditions' would not apply to the guilty party. These conditions require underwriters to provide cover even in circumstances where the assured firm is technically in breach of policy terms but not to the extent of jeopardising the insurer's legal position vis-à-vis the claim.

J. Provision of advice outside the scope of an accountant's expertise

There are occasions when accountants are caught out by changes in legislation or market conditions, notably in the area of investment advice, leading to the issue of recommendations on which a client acts that have consequences contrary to intentions. If, for example, a client requires a sensible retirement plan based on the investment of the proceeds of the sale of his or her business, it may be preferable for the matter to be referred to a specialist firm of financial consultants.

Accountants may be able to give sensible 'generic' advice on investing a proportion of available funds in a pension scheme, but even advice such as 'place one third of the fund in UK gilts, one third in Asian growth funds and the remainder in solid UK blue chip equities', would in all probability exceed the scope of what an accountant is qualified to undertake under both ethical rules and financial services legislation. Anything more specific than that would be excessively risky.

Similar comments apply to specialist areas such as corporate recovery and insolvency, which not only require the accountant to be licensed but also are in any event so fraught with technical and legal difficulty that assignments under this heading should not be undertaken by the general practitioner.

Case J.1

The accountant in this case had acted for many years for Mr and Mrs Armstrong who were partners in an architects' practice. Mr Armstrong retired due to ill health and sold the practice and the freehold premises for £745,000. After purchasing a small home in Wales, Mr Armstrong sought his accountant's advice on how best to invest his remaining funds, totalling £402,000, and various options were discussed at a meeting held for the purpose, but of which no record was made.

Mr Armstrong then decided, based on the accountant's advice, to invest half his capital in building society accounts, and the other half in high growth off-shore funds. Instructions were accordingly given to the accountant to effect these investments on Mr Armstrong's behalf. The accountant failed to disclose his commissions on these transactions.

Mr Armstrong expressed dissatisfaction with the performance of the growth stocks and believed a better return could be obtained in alternative investments. He eventually issued instructions to surrender his off-shore holdings, despite incurring a substantial loss in so doing.

He then commenced proceedings for recovery of the loss on surrender and the difference in performance between his actual returns and what, he alleged, proper advice would have yielded, plus interest. To support his claim he contended that his instructions had been to select 'high growth units that did not fluctuate in value' and that after the meeting he had instructed the accountant to cancel the application, an instruction that had been disregarded.

The accountant denied both contentions categorically. However, his defence was seriously weakened by the fact that he had made no notes whatsoever of the meeting or any discussions pertaining to the claimant's investments. Furthermore, he had given Mr Armstrong no written information on the investments recommended to assist him in reaching a decision and had not advised the claimant of his statutory 'cooling off' period before committing himself to the investments.

He also failed to disclose to Mr Armstrong his entitlement to commissions on the transactions, and had been in breach of numerous other investment business regulations of his professional body.

Lesson to be noted

- It is hard to believe that some practitioners still continue to act as if financial services legislation had never been enacted, although such blatant breaches of the regulations are rare. In this instance the accountant also disregarded the Investment Business Rules of his own Institute, and disciplinary proceedings against him followed formal complaints by Mr Armstrong.

Case J.2

Eltham & Co acted for two companies, A Ltd and B Ltd, under common control. A Ltd was a manufacturer of children's furniture, and B Ltd acted as distributor and marketing agent for A's products. The companies traded with each other on a regular arm's length basis, as a result of which inter-company indebtedness in A's favour had accumulated to approximately £68,000 by February 2002. Profits that would have been earned by B Ltd were each year subvented to A Ltd by means of an inter-company management charge that effectively caused B's accounts to show a break-even position.

The owner of the controlling interests in A Ltd and B Ltd then instructed a partner in Eltham & Co to put in place a standard form of debenture in order to secure the debt owed by B Ltd to A Ltd by means of a floating charge over the assets of B Ltd.

The partner is adamant that he warned his client that this device could prove to be ineffective against any receiver or liquidator subsequently appointed, Section 245 of the Insolvency Act 1986 providing for the avoidance of a floating charge if no new consideration is given on or after the date when the charge is created. Sums already outstanding at the date of the debenture could not therefore be validly secured by the means proposed. Unfortunately, Eltham & Co's files contained no record of the client's instructions or of the warning claimed to have been given and which the client denied having received. The form of debenture actually drafted by Eltham & Co, however, purported to be a fixed charge over the company's leasehold property, plant and book debts.

In May 2003, B Ltd gave notice of a creditors' meeting, at which a liquidator was appointed. The liquidator rejected the validity of the debenture in favour of A Ltd on the grounds that it gave the debenture holder insufficient control over the assets purportedly subject to the fixed charge. The liquidator also questioned whether the debenture gave its holder any security at all because

- it contained no clause that expressly charged specific assets of B Ltd; and
- no debenture trust, as evidenced by deed, was in fact created.

Following communication from the liquidator to this effect, A Ltd issued proceedings against Eltham & Co for recovery of any shortfall in the debt owed to it by B Ltd. Eltham & Co's defence pointed out that it had never been instructed to consider the validity of the debenture, merely to prepare it and lodge it with the registrar. Eltham's solicitors believed, however, that there was definitely some exposure due to the fact that Eltham & Co apparently failed to achieve the fixed charge security when the degree of A Ltd's management control over B Ltd should have made this a relatively simple matter.

Following prolonged negotiations, and in order to avoid the expense of proceeding to a trial of uncertain outcome, settlement between the parties was eventually reached on the basis of a 50:50 split of the claimant's losses and costs.

Lessons to be noted

- Insolvency is a highly specialised activity in which non-practitioners become involved at their peril. Insurers' claims statistics show that defence costs per £1 of settled claims are higher in dealing with insolvency cases than in any other claims category.
- In this case the Eltham & Co partner should have
  - taken proper specialist advice at his client's expense prior to attempting to act on the defective instructions given;
  - provided written advice, including any alternative approach with a greater prospect of success, once he was aware of the problems in the way of achieving the client's objectives;
  - retained all the relevant evidence of advice sought and provided, including file notes of relevant conversations.

K. Accountants acting as trustees

Prior to the heavily regulated period that now exists it was common for testators to appoint a family friend, preferably one with a professional qualification in law or accountancy, as executor and trustee. As long as the appointee followed the directions of the will and acted in an honest and timely fashion, the beneficiaries were generally well satisfied and there was rarely any trouble.

The areas of executorship and trusteeship now come under much greater scrutiny and should be considered by accountants and lawyers to be specialist disciplines in their own right because case law has taken a much stricter line on the manner in which trusts are administered, with special reference to investment safety and returns. Both cases in this section highlight the dangers of failing to remain vigilant in meeting the terms of the trust and in supervising and monitoring the administrative process. Beneficiaries are particularly watchful concerning their own financial interests and will not hesitate to litigate against trustees (individually or collectively) who they believe have caused trust funds to be depleted negligently or trust income to be less than optimal.

Case K.1

A partner in a firm of accountants was appointed trustee under the will of a deceased client. There were three other trustees, one of whom died shortly after appointment and was not replaced. After making bequests in accordance with the will, the trust assets were realised and the funds held in approved short-term rolling one-month deposits pending determination of tax liabilities.

The trustees enjoyed wide powers under the will, which gave them complete discretion on distributions to beneficiaries, advances of capital, selection of investments and the retention of funds to cover tax liabilities, expenses and trustees' professional fees.

Due to difficulties in resolving the trust's tax liabilities, particularly Capital Gains Tax and Inheritance Tax, the trust funds were left in the original one-month deposit accounts for more than five years, after which the beneficiaries (all children of the testator) brought proceedings against the trustees, claiming the following:

- they had been dilatory in administering the trust and, in particular, in finalising its tax liabilities; and
- all funds not required for tax payments and expenses should have been invested in growth stocks to offset the erosion of the estate capital by inflation.

Solicitors advised underwriters that trustees appointed due to their professional qualifications and entitled to charge fees are expected to exercise a higher standard of diligence than that which might be exercised by a prudent person of business in the conduct of his or her own affairs; and that this higher standard would apply to the partner in an accountancy firm and one of the other trustees, a practising solicitor.

Subsequent investigation demonstrated that the trustees had never held any formal meetings at which trust affairs were discussed. Sporadic contact took place by telephone, and each trustee believed that the others were more heavily involved than they were. Matters were allowed to slide through inaction.

Underwriters were advised that there was no defence against the allegations, and that only sums required in the short-term should have been retained on one-month fixed deposits. The balance could have been invested far more beneficially.

Negotiations between defendant trustees resulted in the accountant and the solicitor co-trustee sharing the claim and costs on a 50:50 basis.

Lessons to be noted

- Partners in accountancy practices are often appointed as trustees under clients' wills. It is the individual rather than the firm that holds the appointment, although any fees charged would normally accrue to the firm.
- This case demonstrates the importance of establishing, between the trustees, their respective and collective duties and responsibilities. In this instance the partner believed that his sole function was to prepare the periodic trust accounts and investment decisions fell within the province of the solicitor; the latter, in turn, believed that he was no more than a cheque co-signatory, other responsibilities belonging to the accountant who had for so many years acted for the testator and his family business.
- Clarity of individual responsibilities, although having no bearing on the collective role of trustees, will at least provide a viable modus operandi that avoids such costly misunderstandings as those presented here.
- The case also highlights that, regardless of the trustees' virtually unfettered powers under the will, they must conduct the trust's affairs with all diligence and expedition in the best interests of the beneficiaries alone.

Case K.2

The partners in Phillipsons, accountants, regularly acted as trustees for several substantial family trusts, which in some instances allowed them to exercise unfettered discretionary fund management.

However, the detailed trust management work, including the maintenance of trust records, preparation of accounts, routine correspondence with co-trustees and beneficiaries, custody of documents, securities, investment certificates and brokers' notes, was left entirely to a senior manager of the firm.

Over a period of more than three years, the manager forged trustees' signatures on building society withdrawal forms, involving four separate societies with whom substantial trust funds had been placed by trustees. The sums withdrawn were misappropriated by forged instructions to make transfers to other bank and building society accounts held by the manager personally.

The fraud was discovered when a partner in Phillipsons decided to conduct a spot check on trust files following complaints from beneficiaries that half-yearly summary statements, previously issued on a regular basis, had not been received.

Detailed investigation revealed that trust capital had been depleted by £815,000, which after lost investment income was included, resulted in a claim substantially greater. The sums lost had, in the main, been transferred abroad and full restitution by the manager, by then in prison, was extremely unlikely. The action against the building societies (for paying on forged signatures on withdrawal instructions) and the firm, for vicarious liability arising from the fraud of its employee, settled in full on a shared liability basis.

Lessons to be noted

- Cases of this nature highlight the need for vigilance by trustees of such funds and by trustees generally. There is no requirement for an annual independent audit of trust accounts, mainly because the vast majority of trusts are closely held family settlements.
- This case shows, however, the need for professional trustees to supervise the conduct of trust business and periodically to conduct detailed checks to ensure that
  - transactions and movements of funds can be reconciled against properly authorised instructions;
  - the records are accurate and up-to-date;
  - the trust funds according to the records agree with balances held in custodian accounts and other trustee investments.

L. Allegations of negligent valuation

When auditors are instructed to act as valuers under a company's Articles of Association, they are engaged because of the audit appointment rather than as experts in valuation. Cases arising under this heading have been dealt with in the previous chapter (see the section on 'Risks of undertaking work outside the scope of the auditor's expertise' on page 98).

Where, however, accountants are given a similar instruction but are not familiar with the circumstances of the business or the directors – a familiarity that the company's auditors would obviously possess – they must consider how comfortable they are with the instruction, given that they will be expected to act as expert valuers with the appropriate experience and knowledge. Therefore, this is an assignment in which rigorous independence and technical competence are paramount. If the prospective appointees have any reservations about their ability to act in such circumstances, possibly because they do not fully understand the nature of the company's activities, they should decline the appointment rather than face the potentiality of a negligence claim.

Even though the appointment is not made under the company's articles, the valuers would be expected to gain a familiarity with their terms, and with any shareholders' agreement that may exist.

Case L.1

A dispute concerning management and corporate policy arose between the two principal shareholders in this private company, which operated as an educational establishment for GCSE and A-level re-sits. The holder of 75 of the company's 100 shares of £1 then agreed to purchase the other shareholder's holding of 25 shares, at a value to be determined.

Although the company's articles included a clause whereby the auditor (acting as expert, not as arbitrator) could be engaged to determine the value of shares in the event of a dispute, this was not done because the auditor also acted as tax adviser for one of the parties personally, and was therefore felt not to be sufficiently independent.

The parties applied to the President of the Institute of Chartered Accountants in England & Wales to appoint an independent valuer to determine the value of the holding of 25 shares, and a partner in Dilks & Co was nominated for this purpose after confirming that he had never at any time had any contact with the company or its shareholders. He thereupon drafted a formal engagement letter and sent two copies to each of the solicitors acting for the shareholders, with the usual request that one copy should be signed and returned to him.

The partner's valuation of the holding was determined at £56,750 and immediately following notification thereof solicitors acting for the seller wrote to the other shareholder and to Dilks & Co claiming that the valuation was fundamentally flawed in that it allegedly failed to take into account the terms of a shareholders' agreement that had subsisted between the parties from the time the company was first formed. The letter stated that the valuation should be set aside as void and threatened legal action against both recipients.

Following notification to underwriters, an expert was appointed to investigate the allegations and to report on liability. The expert's report maintained that there was a good defence to the claim because Dilks & Co had reasonably assumed that the partner's appointment superseded the shareholders' agreement: had that agreement been effective there would have been no need for an independent valuation. Furthermore, the expert found that Dilks' valuation methods were consistent with those generally accepted for the purpose in question.

The claim was therefore resisted and the matter was eventually set down for trial, the Dilks partner having been named as Second Defendant. With only eight days to go to the trial date, a meeting was held with the First Defendant and his solicitor to discuss the possibility of making an offer to the claimant, purely for commercial reasons.

It was agreed at this meeting that an offer would be made to increase the purchase price of the 25% holding by a further £50,000, such sum to be inclusive of all costs incurred. The proposals were accepted by the claimant and settlement effected.

Lessons to be noted

- Accountants are often called upon to act as share valuers for members of private companies in dispute, and this case focuses on the dangers. These dangers are similar to those facing an auditor who is instructed to value a company's shares pursuant to its articles. The leading case on the subject of auditors acting as valuers is Arenson v Casson Beckman Rutley & Co (1975), which went to the House of Lords on the question of whether auditors are legally answerable to the parties for the valuation determined by them – a question answered by the Lords in the affirmative.
- In the case described above it would have been beneficial if the Dilks partner had clearly noted his assumptions regarding the status of the shareholders' agreement in his engagement letter, since that would have avoided subsequent dispute. If the assumptions had not been correct, the claimant would have had an opportunity to object in advance.
- Accountants are always invidiously placed when acting in such a capacity because, regardless of the value they arrive at, at least one of the parties is bound to be dissatisfied with it. Had there been a value to satisfy both parties there would have been no need for an

external accountant's involvement in the first place. It is therefore essential that all facts having a bearing on the valuation are made known to the valuer, and this requirement should be included in the engagement letter.

- It is, of course, preferable to issue a 'non-speaking' valuation, that is, without disclosure of working methods and the mechanics of the valuation exercise, because it is always possible for another 'expert' subsequently to dispute these given the highly subjective nature of the task. This is particularly true when valuing as an expert, rather than arbitrator, since an arbitrator enjoys a measure of quasi-judicial immunity from action. In the case in point, however, it seems that the appointment was as an independent technical expert in share valuations, and his terms may have required his methods to be disclosed to the parties – with unfortunate consequences, as we have seen.

M. The aftermath of disappointing acquisitions

Accountants frequently become involved in transactions by clients who are selling their business or buying another, and unless key precautions are taken they may find themselves in the firing line if the acquisition subsequently proves to be disappointing.

Elsewhere we have addressed the problems facing auditors of companies making acquisitions or who are themselves the subject of a takeover. In those circumstances the accounts that play a major part in pre-acquisition negotiations will assume a level of authentication based on the fact that they have been audited. This simply does not apply when the business acquired or disposed of is unincorporated and its accounts have not been audited.

In this section we deal with a variety of circumstances in which accountants have been subjected to adverse legal proceedings due to the part they played, and the level of responsibility imputed to their work, by virtue of their association with the financial statements in question or the activities of the undertaking being acquired, with which they were deemed to be familiar.

Case M.1

The claimant company acquired another smaller company, which manufactured kitchen units, for a cash consideration of £1.2 million. The acquisition documents had been prepared by the purchasing company's solicitors. The claimant company's accountants were asked to act for the company at the completion meeting.

After the purchase it was found that the acquired company was hopelessly insolvent, and proceedings were commenced against the former shareholders on grounds of misrepresentation. A parallel action was commenced against the accountants on the grounds that they had

- failed to detect that key documents, including audited accounts, were missing from the completion documentation;
- failed to check that the acquired company's assets existed and were worth the sums at which they were shown in the sale agreement;
- consented on the claimant's behalf to the deletion of certain warranty clauses in the agreement on which the claimant was therefore unable to rely subsequently;
- failed to discover the company's true financial position and inform the purchaser accordingly.

In defence, the accountants maintained that they had not been engaged by the claimant to act in the capacity implied in the Statement of Claim, although no letter of engagement (which might have assisted its defence) had at any time been issued. The accountants also stated that the purchasing company had acted with unbridled haste throughout the takeover negotiations and appeared totally unconcerned about any of the matters later complained of: its sole anxiety was to acquire the company.

The absence of any file information to support the accountants' position made it extremely difficult to establish a credible defence against the charge of failing to give timely and relevant advice to the purchasing company, and an offer of 75% of the sums claimed, plus costs, was made on underwriters' behalf, and accepted.

Lessons to be noted

- This case shows all too clearly the value of an engagement letter as a form of protection, particularly in relation to unusual or non-routine assignments. Because this was lacking it would have been difficult for the accountants to establish the bounds of the restricted capacity of their appointment had the case gone to trial.
- It also transpired that almost all of the accountancy partner's time on the assignment was spent in telephone conversations with the various parties and their advisers, but that it was not his practice

to make file notes of the import of these conversations, still less to follow them up with written confirmation of the matters discussed. This too meant that much of his evidence was reduced to unsupported hearsay, never a reliable basis for preparing for trial. In the circumstances it is hardly surprising that advice was given to settle on the most favourable terms that could be negotiated.

Case M.2

The target company to be acquired in this case was a successful advertising agency whose client base included a number of highly-prized companies, as a result of which the purchase price commanded a significant premium. The sole director and shareholder decided to sell the agency and instructed his accountant to prepare completion accounts based on the accounting records and information provided by the director. The accountant, who had for many years prepared annual financial statements from the agency's records, was entirely familiar with the nature of the business and its finances.

Since the proposed sale was scheduled to take place in the middle of an accounting period rather than at its conclusion, the accountant simply prepared a set of management accounts extracted from the records as they stood, without making any of the year-end adjustments that would normally be relevant. The management accounts did not include a balance sheet. The accountant's task was made more difficult by the vigorous secrecy imposed on his work, as none of the staff or clients were aware of the impending sale.

On his client's instructions the accounts were passed directly to the prospective purchaser. The accountant was aware of the purpose for which the accounts had been requisitioned, although he had not met the prospective purchaser or made any direct representations to her. The negotiations regarding warranties, disclosures and determination of the price to be paid were carried out between the prospective purchaser and the vendor, together with their army of legal and corporate finance representatives. The accountant was not involved in any of these issues.

The accountant was invited by the vendor to attend the completion meeting on his behalf, during which he was asked by the purchaser whether he was willing to warrant that the completion accounts that he had prepared on behalf of his client showed 'a true and fair view of the company's underlying trading position'. The accountant replied that the accounts were not audited, had been simply extracted from the underlying records and could not possibly be warranted.

The purchaser was, however, adamant that the absence of some form of warranty that the accounts could be relied upon for the purposes of the transaction would be an effective 'deal-breaker'.

Confirmation of the accuracy of the accounts was sought by the prospective purchaser on numerous occasions throughout the course of the long and difficult meeting that lasted well into the night, and on each occasion the accountant refused. However, faced with unbearable pressure from both his own client and the prospective purchaser, eventually, at 3am, it appears that his resolve crumbled and he agreed to confirm that, subject to the matters addressed in a disclosure letter, in his view the accounts were 'materially correct'.

Following completion the accountant billed his client for his fees, which had built up over the whole of the period of negotiation, and which the purchaser had previously agreed to underwrite. The purchaser, however, responded by claiming that the accounts were materially misstated and that she was not prepared to pay the outstanding fees. The amount of the accountant's fees was substantial and he sought recovery by instituting proceedings against the purchaser. This was duly met by a counterclaim to the effect that a duty of care had been established in favour of the purchaser and that the accountant had acted negligently in passing her accounts that proved, after the acquisition, to be wholly unreliable and misleading.

She commenced an action in the name of her company against the accountant in which she sought to recover the difference between the purchase consideration paid and the actual value of the company at the date of the transaction. In view of the implacable and entrenched positions adopted, litigation ensued. The Court ordered a split trial so that the question of liability should be addressed first, and the matter of damages (if any) being left to a subsequent trial.

At trial the Judge found against the accountant on liability. It was held in particular that the confirmation given by the accountant during the completion meeting constituted an acceptance of a duty of care. He also found that, notwithstanding the contents of the disclosure letter, the accounts were materially misleading.

However, at the second trial a year later the same Judge held that, irrespective of the question of liability, the true value of the acquired company's assets exceeded the purchase consideration paid and consequently the purchaser had in effect acquired a bargain! The issue of costs then dominated the proceedings, particularly since the accountant was also successful in the Court of Appeal, which reversed the 'duty of care' issue as determined at the first instance. The Appeal Court judges ruled that, in assenting at the fateful completion meeting to the proposition that the accounts were materially correct, the accountant was in fact addressing his remarks to his own client, who was then able to provide the purchaser with the warranty being sought. This ruling effectively demolished the argument on duty of care.

Lessons to be noted

- When the vendor instructed his accountant to send the management accounts directly to the prospective purchaser, the accountant should have been on notice that his position was vulnerable. Clearly he was aware of the context in which the purchaser wished to see the accounts and he should never have left the question of her reliance on those accounts up in the air.
- As a professional accountant a certain level of competence was deemed to have been exercised in the preparation of the accounts, but he should at the time of issuing them have made it plain that they were merely the product of entries taken from the underlying records, and were unadjusted, unaudited and unwarrantable for any purpose involving the transaction in prospect. This should have been supplemented with a request for any further instructions (via his own client) that the purchaser may wish to issue, such as a requirement for a balance sheet or for a full audit.
- The accountant attended the completion meeting without having taken any of the aforementioned precautions and found himself subject to immense pressure to 'certify' a set of uncertifiable management accounts. The pressure was as much from his own client (who obviously wished the deal to go through for his own personal financial reasons) as from the purchaser, who was not prepared to proceed without the warranty. He was therefore at a disadvantage from the outset.
- A further precaution would have been to have a colleague or member of his staff present with him at the meeting to take detailed notes of the proceedings, which would certainly have helped his case during the subsequent Court action.

Case M.3

The accountant involved in this case failed to observe the standard precaution of familiarising himself with a new client's business track record and level of business expertise. The client in question, Alfred Tomkins, had a lengthy history of business failure; the opposite, it could be said, of the Midas touch. Any business owned or managed by him was doomed from the moment of his first involvement. Perhaps unsurprisingly, in the light of his background, he also had a history of lawsuits against successive former accountants.

The instance in question involved the acquisition of a travel agency in a West London high street. The very first intimation to his accountant of the transaction was a request to prepare a profit projection for his bank based on the agency's historic accounts, accompanied by a brief report from the accountant. The accountant, knowing nothing of the business, merely amended the historic figures to reflect the impact of new categories of business that Mr Tomkins planned to introduce. The amended figures were based on Mr Tomkins' own observation, in his capacity as a potential purchaser of the business, of its activities over a three-month period during which he visited the premises most days.

The purchase went ahead and proved to be disastrous to Mr Tomkins. After six months he sold the business back to its former owner, for less than half the purchase consideration, under whose stewardship it continues to thrive.

Mr Tomkins issued a claim against his accountant alleging that he had failed to evaluate the commercial strengths and weaknesses of the purchase and to advise accordingly. The accountant responded by pointing out that virtually no discussion concerning the proposed transaction had taken place between them, and no advice had been sought.

In his defence the accountant relied upon Mr Tomkins' inability to adduce any solid documentary evidence, other than the profit projection prepared for the bank which, according to Tomkins, linked the accountant to the transaction in contemplation.

Regrettably there was no engagement letter – principally because, as the accountant argued, there was no engagement! More unfortunate, however, was the fact that the fee note that covered the meeting at which the profit projections were discussed began with the words

> To advising you in connection with the proposed purchase of a travel agent in Ealing Broadway.

The fact that his bespoke software began all fee notes with the words 'To advising you in connection with . . .' did not help the accountant's defence.

Mr Tomkins, having nothing better to do and with the benefit of legal aid, pursued the case doggedly. Much to the accountant's frustration, his insurers took a commercial view and settled the claim at 50% of the alleged losses plus costs.

Lessons to be noted

- No matter how small an instruction may appear, it is always important to issue an engagement letter for the client to sign. This should define the nature of the accountant's brief and the specific scope of the advice sought.
- Although the possibility of a subsequent dispute may appear to be slight, it is always essential to make clear file notes of telephone discussions and face-to-face meetings. Where appropriate these should be followed up with written confirmation of the matters discussed and any further instructions. In this case, much of the accountant's evidence was reduced to unsupported hearsay, never a reliable basis for defending serious professional allegations.
- Any report accompanying completion accounts or projections should avoid giving greater credibility to the accounts than is strictly warranted by the work actually performed. In this instance the accountant should have stated in his report that
  - the attached projections were based on information provided by the client, supposedly taken by him from the company's own books and records;
  - the adjustments to those figures were based on future trading plans explained by the client;
  - none of the foregoing had been subjected to any form of audit or due diligence process and that the likelihood of the projections being fulfilled was a matter on which the accountant could offer no opinion.
- With regard to narrative descriptions incorporated in fee notes, although it is sometimes tempting for accountants to resort to extravagant descriptions of the work undertaken in order to justify the weight of their charges, this is clearly two-edged. In this instance the accountant was using standard billing narratives that

unfortunately overstated the extent of his responsibility and served to compromise his defence.

- It is of interest to note that policy wordings adopted by professional indemnity insurers give them the right to take responsibility for claims management, including the right to settle a matter on pragmatic grounds despite the adamant view of the insured that the claimant's case would fail at trial. Some policies include a clause that entitles the insured to put the matter to an independent QC, but that involves time, trouble and costs, not to mention harming the relationship with insurers, and is therefore rarely invoked.

Case M.4

The claimants in this case were partners in a recruitment agency business in Bristol. In November 2002 they acquired for a total consideration of £166,000 the whole of the share capital of a smaller company carrying on a similar trade in Bath, the acquisition being based on trading accounts prepared by a firm of accountants, Tickle & Co (who were also the auditors of the acquired company), for the seven-month period to 30 September 2002. These accounts showed a profit of £40,200. At the same time audited accounts for the year ended 28 February 2002, showing a profit of £60,900, were produced to the claimants.

The claimants maintained that they relied on these two sets of accounts in deciding to acquire the company and in determining the purchase consideration. Subsequent to the acquisition, in February 2003, the acquired company experienced cash flow problems and the new directors were obliged to issue personal guarantees to secure an overdraft facility in order to carry on trading. By late April 2003 it was clear that the company could not continue to trade legally and the claimants repaid the overdraft, then standing at £87,000. Liquidation followed shortly thereafter and proceedings were commenced against the auditors.

It was alleged that had the claimants known the true position of the company they would not have acquired the shares and would certainly not have guaranteed its overdraft. The particularised claim alleged that the accounts prepared and (in the case of the February 2002 accounts) audited by Tickle & Co had materially overstated debtors by including assignments in progress as if already billed to clients. It was also alleged that certain current expenditures had been invalidly deferred to future periods.

Underwriters' solicitors reported that a defence could be based on the fact that the claimants were already familiar with the company's affairs prior to purchase and that insolvency occurred following acquisition.

Although Tickle & Co's files showed a lack of requisite professional care in preparing the accounts, the firm argued the following: negligence, if any, on its part was not causative of loss; the claimants were minded to purchase the company in any event; and hence the claimants had themselves largely to blame for any loss suffered.

To avoid the costs of proceeding to trial, however, a settlement between the parties at £94,000 was agreed, inclusive of interest and costs.

Lessons to be noted

- The sale of a client company is always a high-risk situation. Audited accounts and completion accounts are known at such times to be relied upon by third parties for a purpose that differs significantly from the more usual stewardship context and particular care should be exercised with this additional risk in mind.
- The audited accounts and supporting files should be subjected to rigorous review by a partner unconnected with the assignment to ensure that all necessary procedures have been performed and recorded, and that the accounts themselves are in every way plausible.
- Unaudited completion accounts should similarly be scrutinised independently and any accompanying report should avoid giving greater credibility to the accounts than is strictly warranted by the work actually performed. Judicious use of disclaimers is certainly advisable.

Case M.5

The claimant and his wife decided to use modest funds from a legacy to buy a business as an investment, and consulted accountants Strutt & Co in May 2002 with a specific proposition in mind. The business in question was operated by a family-owned limited company and comprised four DIY outlets in Blackburn, Preston, Bolton and St. Helens respectively. The most recent accounts of the company, showing a profit of £82,000 for the year to 31 January 2002, were passed to Strutt & Co for comment.

Strutt advised strongly against the purchase on the grounds that the claimants intended to play no active role and in any event had no experience of DIY retailing. Furthermore, their resources would not be sufficient to inject any working capital and the business would be heavily dependent on bank support, for which they would be expected to give personal guarantees. The overdraft per the accounts shown to Strutt & Co stood at £197,000. Although Strutt was adamant that the above advice was given, no attendance note was recorded and it lacked any documentary support.

The claimants went ahead despite this advice and acquired 80% of the company's ordinary shares in November 2002, leaving 20% as an 'incentive holding' with one of the existing shareholders, who undertook to serve as full-time managing director.

Strutt & Co was not consulted in any of these negotiations with the vendors, the purchase agreement being drafted by the claimants' solicitor. Shortly after the purchase, however, Strutt & Co was appointed auditors to the company, and the first accounts it prepared and audited revealed a loss for the year ended 31 January 2003 of £61,500.

The bank appointed a receiver in April 2003 and liquidation followed in May – exactly one year after the original consultation.

The claimants then sought advice from an independent firm of solicitors who commenced proceedings against

- the vendors for breach of warranties in the sale and purchase agreement in respect of turnover, gross margins and stock valuation at the date of sale; and
- the solicitor acting for the claimants in the transaction.

The latter's defence, however, maintained in mitigation that he had relied on the claimants' statement that Strutt & Co had 'been given, examined and approved' the January 2002 accounts of the company.

In October 2003, the claimants thereupon proceeded against Strutt & Co as third defendants in the action, claiming damages of £170,000, plus interest and costs. Although underwriters' solicitors reported that the claimants' quantum of loss could be sustained, it was unlikely that any negligence on the part of Strutt & Co could be established, especially because it was the accounts that the it had prepared and audited that first alerted the claimants to the seriousness of the company's true position.

Solicitors acting for the first and second defendants sought a settlement based on a contribution from Strutt's underwriters. In the interests of avoiding further costs in a complex four-way action, the relatively modest settlement terms were accepted.

Lessons to be noted

- This case demonstrates the lengths to which claimants will go in seeking redress from advisers in respect of losses suffered largely as a consequence of their own actions.
- It is always easy after the event and with the benefit of hindsight to point a finger at mistakes made by others, but that, after all, is one of the purposes of this book! Had the Strutt & Co partner given his explicit advice against proceeding with the purchase to the claimants in writing, involvement in the action might have been avoided altogether.
- He ought also to have returned the January 2002 accounts of the company to the claimants pointing out, again in writing, that on the basis of advice already tendered there was no need for the company's accounts to be considered further.
- The need for attendance notes and file notes of telephone calls concerning clients' affairs should now operate as an automatic reflex for staff as well as partners.

Case M.6

Ralph and Zeno (R&Z) had been auditors to Retain plc for many years, and then the latter was the subject of an unwelcome takeover offer from Detain plc.

Discussion eventually led to a Recommended Offer Document, which incorporated a profit forecast prepared by R&Z and supported by Retain's merchant bankers. Following the takeover, Detain plc was dissatisfied with the price it paid for the acquisition and claimed that the profit forecast was excessive in relation to the actual results of Retain plc, since published. This overstatement, it said, caused Detain to be misled and to pay substantially more for the shares than was appropriate. Proceedings were instituted against the directors and auditors of Retain plc, as well as its merchant bankers, for a sum in excess of £8 million.

Experts for the defendant firm reported that its work on the forecasts, in particular its procedures for ensuring that the management accounts used in preparing the forecasts were sufficiently reliable for the purpose, appeared to have been competently planned and performed.

During the course of acrimonious pre-trial pleadings and exchange of experts' reports, the Detain plc directors became less enthusiastic about their prospects of succeeding at trial, and they offered to reduce their claim to a total of £1.1 million, including costs, which the three defendants jointly agreed to accept.

Lessons to be noted

- Possible defences available to accountants and auditors facing claims in similar circumstances would include the following:
  - The form of wording used by the accountants in their report on the forecasts should include the standard caveat that the forecasts are the sole responsibility of the directors, and that the scope of the reporting accountants' work is necessarily restricted to the expression of an opinion on whether the forecast has been properly compiled on the basis of the directors' assumptions and presented on a basis consistent with the accounting policies normally adopted by the company.
  - The claimant company had not in fact relied on the forecast as the *primary* criterion for determining a price acceptable to the former shareholders.
  - The reporting accountants should be able to show that they had not, in fact, been negligent.
  - The reason for the shortfall in actual profit compared with the forecast was attributable wholly or in part to altered bases of accounting or management assumptions following the change of ownership. (This defence could be established only after disclosure of the claimant's documents.)
- No matter how defensively the accountants' report is worded, there can be no denying that one purpose to which the forecast can reasonably be put is the establishment of a fair market value for the company's shares. In this case the accountants played a major part in the actual preparation of the forecast, and were well aware of its purpose and probable reliance by a third party investor.

  Profit forecasts are inevitably based on (i) assumptions about the future and (ii) historic management information currently available, and so it is essential that the reasonableness of the first, and the accuracy of the second, are very carefully considered by reporting accountants. Assumptions about the future include the extent to which debts will prove to be good, liabilities will materialise and depreciation provisions will prove to be adequate. The management accounts must be based on the company's usual accounting policies, and the degree of accuracy achieved in the past against actual results must be taken into account.

- The attitude of the Courts in cases of this nature is always difficult to pre-judge. There can be little doubt about proximity (duty of care) because the very context of accountants' work on profit forecasts is one in which investment decisions are implicit. For this reason the usual scope warnings declared in accountants' reports may afford less protection than the form of wording used suggests. Reliance on management information is unavoidable, but accountants are expected to have reviewed this with due circumspection, in terms of both assumptions and accuracy.

  The Courts will, of course, also be aware of the temptation to blame subsequent disappointments on alleged reliance on failed forecasts, and claimants will always have a difficult task in establishing not only negligence, but also a causal relationship between alleged losses and alleged negligence.

Case M.7

Redland & Co acted as tax adviser to the owner of an art gallery. Prior to the sale of the gallery, an unincorporated business, the owner was asked by the potential buyer to provide specific warranties, inter alia, as follows:

- turnover figures were accurate in the last three years for which accounts had been finalised for tax purposes;
- turnover in the most recent year (for which the accounts were not yet finalised) was within 10% of the turnover for the previous period;
- all overheads for the latest period were within 10% of the sums shown in the previous year's accounts;
- gross profit before overheads was not less than 40% of turnover in each of the three most recent years;
- in the four months prior to the sale of business, both overheads and turnover were within 10% of their equivalent amounts in the preceding year.

The owner gave the warranties and the sale proceeded. Within ten months of the sale the buyer of the gallery brought proceedings against its former owner, claiming to have suffered substantial loss due to warranty breaches. The former owner in turn, just as the case was coming to trial three years later, joined Redland & Co in the action, claiming indemnity in respect of any sums he would be found liable to pay to the claimant.

Although Redland & Co's defence was based primarily on the assertion that the scope of its appointment did not include an involvement in the sale particulars or advice on the warranties sought, it became clear to the underwriters' legal advisers that the role of the Redland's partner involved had in fact extended beyond that of acting purely as tax adviser. The sale particulars, for example, carried Redland & Co's name and address, from which they were sent to interested parties. It furthermore transpired that the partner had been shown by fax the specific warranties prepared by his client as required by the purchaser, but had neither investigated their veracity nor demurred from their content despite having the accounts to which they related in front of him at the time. Furthermore, even a rudimentary comparison would have highlighted important disparities between the accounts and the figures sent by fax.

Subsequent investigation showed that the vendor of the gallery had withdrawn substantial amounts of cash as 'reimbursements' of business expenses paid personally. Redland & Co had been instructed, however, to apportion these between 'business' and 'private' items, the latter possibly being contrived to keep business costs down to the levels warranted. These entries were recorded after the Redland partner had become aware that his client was being sued for a breach of warranties, and yet he made no detailed enquiries into the validity of the entries he was being asked to make.

During negotiations prior to trial, the former client made threats of disclosure of Redland & Co's alleged involvement in tax fraud. This spurious attempt to coerce Redland into a disadvantageous settlement was wisely resisted, and was never raised again.

Settlement was eventually reached – literally at the door of the Court – whereby

- the former gallery owner paid £480,000 to the claimant in full satisfaction of its claim against all parties inclusive of costs; and
- Redland's insurers made a contribution of £80,000 to the first defendants in satisfaction of their claim, parties bearing their own costs.

Lessons to be noted

- This was a complex case involving three litigants:
  - the purchasers of the gallery;
  - the gallery's former owner (Redland's client);
  - Redland & Co.

  Each party had appointed its own legal advisers and professional experts, acting intermittently for several years, and it is perhaps salutary (if not surprising) that the total defence costs of the gallery's former owner and Redland & Co alone amounted to some £220,000 – substantially more than the settlement figure in the action against the accountant!
- The Redland partner, although appointed nominally as tax adviser, failed to appreciate the extent to which the accounts of his unincorporated client, prepared specifically for tax purposes, could be relied upon for the purpose of assisting a third party potential purchaser in reaching an investment decision.
- Although the Redland partner did explain to the agent of the purchaser the nature of adjustments required to render the accounts more useful for the buyer's purposes, it is unfortunate that he did not
  - recommend that the buyer appoint an independent accountant to report on the gallery business and its accounts; and
  - issue explicit disclaimers of responsibility to all the parties regarding the usefulness of accounts prepared for tax purposes as a basis for reaching an investment decision
- The partner in Redland & Co was to some extent the author of his own misfortune even after becoming involved in the disposal process. Having been sent the warranted figures for turnover and overhead expenses he failed to compare them with the accounts on which they were purported to be based. Had he noted the disparities he would have been in a position to warn his client not to warrant unrealistic amounts and once again to disclaim in writing to his client any responsibility for the consequences of so doing.
- Redland & Co's defence was hampered by the lack of file evidence regarding the substance of meetings and telephone discussions. The partner often had to resort to memory of events occurring over three years earlier, and the memory of a partner and an assistant. Had the case gone to trial, such unsupported reliance would

undoubtedly have been exploited by counsel for the first defendants – particularly if the clients had documentary evidence of issues being contested, such as Redland & Co's personal initiatives in supporting its client's warranties.

- The final point to remember – and it applies to the majority of claims – is that indemnity insurance can never compensate for the traumatic effect of fighting a claim over an extended period. Smaller firms have scant resources available for this purpose; the lost management time and the consequential neglect of other clients – let alone the psychological disturbance implicit in such adverse circumstances – is often far more damaging than the claim in its monetary form.

4.4 SUMMARY OF KEY LESSONS

- Chartered accountants lend credibility to financial statements by the mere association of their name with those statements. They should take all reasonable measures to protect themselves against a liability to a third party including the use of appropriately worded disclaimers.
- Accountants' bills that simply read 'professional services rendered' are always a recipe for disagreement and dispute.
- A high proportion of claims notifications received under all claims headings arise from internal administrative failures rather than negligent professional work or advice.
- No matter how small an instruction may appear, it is important to issue an engagement letter for the client to sign. This should define the nature of the accountant's brief and the specific scope of the advice sought.
- Accountants should be wary of overplaying their part in seeking to achieve their clients' objectives.
- Accountants should note the formal guidance issued by the major accountancy bodies on the subject of confirming details of clients' income or assets to third party lenders.
- Accountancy firms should have a clear policy on client communications covering partners, staff and consultants.
- Professional practices should also lay down limits of authority for partners and staff and impose some form of internal monitoring system to ensure that the firm's operational standards are rigorously observed.

5

Tax Related Claims

5.1 INTRODUCTION

Tax related claims is by far the largest single category of claims when measured by the number of notifications to insurers under policy terms. This category is sub-divided between (i) negligent advice and (ii) failed administration, the latter making up some 40% of the total number of notifications received in most insurance years. It is impossible to generalise about claims in the area of tax advice, except to say that their rate of incidence has declined following HMRC's clamping down on tax mitigation 'schemes' involving a series of artificial steps and offshore transactions.

Administration failures continue at a worrying rate, however, and these claims typically include missed tax deadlines for elections, missed appeals deadlines, late submission of accounts and tax returns, failure to utilise tax losses by sensible tax planning, missed deadlines for group relief leaving investment income unrelieved, negligent omission of investment income from tax returns and so on.

Usually such deficiencies occur as a result of carelessness or poor organisation and the remedy is obvious – improve the quality of record-keeping and buy a diary! Every now and then, however, the underlying problem is more difficult to identify, let alone resolve. The starting point is often the discovery of drawers full of unanswered correspondence from HMRC in the office of a particular partner who, for one reason or another, has neglected his or her clients' tax affairs, sometimes for many years. The problem may come to light only on the apparently inexplicable disappearance of the partner concerned, usually for a temporary period of recuperation, but sometimes, regrettably, on a permanent basis.

The cause of such an unfortunate situation may have nothing whatever to do with the technicalities of the tax regime and everything to do with the culture of the firm. We have in the course of our professional work come across firms whose partners hold formal meetings only when a crisis arises, thus depriving themselves of an appropriate forum in which to share information, exchange ideas and provide mutual support.

Indeed the two partners of one particular firm communicated with one another for four years *only in writing*! In such circumstances it is hardly surprising that an individual's inability to cope with whatever pressure he or she may be under can go undetected by those who purport to be the person's partners.

Acquiring another accountancy practice is patently a transaction in which the attendant risks are implicit, and this has particular relevance to the taxation category of claims. The increasingly competitive practising climate has spawned a large number of mergers and combinations of firms. When this occurs the interests of the parties involved are invariably opposed: retiring partners and vendors of practices are keen to close down their risks and rule off the books. Purchasers, in turn, are reluctant to assume liability for pre-acquisition mistakes made by their predecessors in business. In such circumstances the advice of specialist brokers is required to deal with the insurance arrangements that are most appropriate to the circumstances.

For those retiring or otherwise departing the practice, professional insurance regulations require partners to use their best endeavours to purchase at least two years of retroactive run-off cover to allow for the emergence of past liabilities. It is, however, recommended that four or five years such cover is purchased for greater security and peace of mind. Due to underwriters' experience of such post-cessation claims, however, the premiums will tend to be higher than expected, and where retired partners rely on their former firm to maintain the policy they should seek evidence annually that adequate cover is in fact in place.

Those at greatest risk are, of course, the continuing partners, or those who are members of a firm that has purchased another practice. They may find that their own insurers are reluctant to underwrite cover for past liability under their existing policy, or are prepared to do so only in return for a substantially increased premium, often with policy restrictions. In the event of a claim the firm will find that renewal terms become exceedingly onerous, or may be declined altogether.

The purchasers should therefore strive to ensure that the vendors assume liability contractually for all claims relating to an acquired practice, and that the vendors purchase, and annually renew for six successive years, separate professional liability (PI) insurance at a sufficient level to cover any such claims.

In essence, the golden rule to be followed whenever possible is simply not to take on the liabilities of others. Where this is unavoidable for some reason, however, the assumption of such risk is best done by way of separate insurance, at least for the early post-merger years.

5.2 PROVISION OF INCORRECT OR INADEQUATE ADVICE

The tax statutes have now reached dimensions and complexity such that even specialists dispensing tax advice regard this area as a potential minefield in which every element in recommendations to clients needs to be checked and double-checked. The scope for error is prodigious, particularly when the circumstances of the client may have altered without the accountant necessarily being aware of this change.

Sometimes an accountant is asked to make recommendations that 'will save me tax' and in the absence of clearly defined parameters the accountant may well make recommendations that seem appropriate enough at that time but which, following a change in circumstances or in the legislation, prove to be ineffective at best and detrimental at worst.

Increasingly, general practitioners are finding that they need to turn to specialist colleagues on technical matters and legal interpretations rather than rely on their own experience, which always runs the risk of being out of date. Exceeding the scope of one's own expertise is a theme that runs throughout this book and it is a special hazard in the field of tax advice.

A. Failure properly to investigate a client's circumstances

It is always dangerous to make assumptions about clients' circumstances without checking the facts, particularly when more than one jurisdiction applies.

Case A.1

In this case the taxpayer was a non-UK domiciliary who worked for an international bank based in the United States. After transferring to the bank's London branch, the taxpayer should have been assessed to UK tax under what was Case II in respect of UK duties and under Case III (the remittance basis) in respect of his duties overseas. His accountant prepared his tax returns on the assumption that he was being paid abroad, when in fact all his earnings were paid by the London branch of the bank. On the basis of the returns received, HMRC issued a PAYE refund that the taxpayer was subsequently required to repay to HMRC with interest. He took action against the accountant, alleging that he should have alerted him to the potential benefits of payment offshore in respect of his non-UK duties.

Lessons to be noted

- There are obvious dangers for accountants in providing tax advice to a client with whose circumstances they may be unfamiliar, without undertaking research to ensure that they have the full picture concerning that client's financial situation and sources of income. It can be all too easy to advise on a particular issue in a vacuum, without properly considering other relevant factors that may impact on the overall position.
- Accountants should never make assumptions concerning their clients' financial arrangements. It is essential that a clear understanding of all the relevant facts is gained before advice is proffered.

B. Danger of not keeping abreast of changing circumstances

This case illustrates the dangers of using generic terminology when drafting engagement letters. Phrases such as 'advising you generally with regard to your business and tax affairs' should be avoided altogether given that their coverage may easily be deemed to be all-embracing even when the areas of actual involvement are far narrower. This situation can be lethal when coupled with a change in the client's business circumstances of which the accountant is unaware, but concerning which it would have been appropriate to make enquiries.

Case B.1

In 1992 Mr Blain set up in practice as a sole practitioner after leaving a four-partner firm from which, with his former partners' consent, he took a modest core of clients, mainly individual traders and small companies. The practice was successful and, to cope with expansion, two unqualified staff were recruited and one was given responsibility for looking after clients' routine tax affairs.

In 1999 a formal complaint was made to Mr Blain's professional body by a client concerning, inter alia, delays in dealing expeditiously with tax matters, in respect of which Mr Blain signed a Consent Order admitting the complaint, and was reprimanded and fined £2,000. In accordance with policy terms his underwriters were notified.

Some six months later the same client, a driving school instructor, achieved a turnover that significantly exceeded the VAT threshold, but registration was overlooked, for which omission HMRC imposed a penalty of £21,000. The client sought recompense from Mr Blain and proceedings for recovery were issued.

Since Mr Blain's letter of engagement assumed a 'responsibility for your business, financial and tax affairs generally', it was clear that no credible defence could be assembled and a settlement was effected at the amount claimed.

A short while later Mr Blain received a claim from another client whose affairs had been managed by his recently recruited tax assistant. The client and his wife held joint majority shareholdings in three companies, which were classified as associated companies for the purpose of determining the small companies' rate of corporation tax.

The assistant had neglected to inform the client of the anti-avoidance rule that requires the standard small company profits threshold to be divided by the number of associated companies – in this instance three. Two of the companies, despite the downward adjustment of the threshold, were nevertheless able to take advantage of the lower corporation tax rate. The third company's profits, however, exceeded the limit and were therefore liable to corporation tax at the full rate. HMRC assessed the additional tax liability at £42,500.

The claimant maintained that, had he been acquainted with the correct position earlier, it would have been possible for him to arrange the manner in which the companies were linked so that no full rate tax would have become payable.

HMRC accepted an offer of £39,000 in settlement.

Lessons to be noted

- This case demonstrates the problems faced by many small practices in keeping abreast of technical changes and developments while also maintaining a watching brief over the impact of such changes on their clients' affairs and advising/acting before it is too late. Monitoring clients' turnover and profit levels on an anticipatory basis, as was necessary in the circumstances described, is an example of what is needed on a continuing basis for clients generally.

- Engaging staff with the appropriate skills to cope with client needs is obviously essential, but so is the need to supervise their work and ensure that they have systems in place to alert them to the hazards implicit in today's complex tax legislation regime.

C. Failure to define responsibility following an engagement

Accountants are called upon to perform a number of activities that do not fit in to the normal run of professional work. Consequently standard engagement letters are simply inappropriate and should not be issued without being tailored to the exact terms of the client's needs. This is an important discipline in its own right, because only when attempting to draft instructions that meet the client's precise requirements is it realised how many vague areas need to be clarified before work commences.

The engagement letter, duly signed by the parties, is the evidence that the Court will turn to when making any decision on what was contractually agreed. This is obviously of critical importance when the nature of the work does not fall into any statutory or otherwise regulated activity.

Case C.1

The defendant firm had acted as accountants and tax advisers to an unincorporated client who owned a dry cleaning business and various other commercial interests, including three small limited companies. The client's cleaning business expanded rapidly, and branches in four towns were opened in one year, 2003. A partner in the defendant firm, who had also maintained the accounting records of the entities, suggested that an in-house accountant should be employed, and conducted the interviews of applicants personally, culminating in the appointment of a qualified accountant in 2004.

In early 2007 the accountant employee resigned and accepted a job elsewhere. It was then discovered by the defendant firm that the in-house accountant had failed to deal with the client's tax affairs in a satisfactory manner. In particular, he had not submitted business or company accounts in time and had failed to appeal against estimated assessments. He had also failed to disclose overdrawn directors' current accounts in the companies' books, either to HMRC or in published accounts. A number of relief claims had also not been made by their due dates.

The partner responsible accepted that these were duties that, prior to 2004, he would have been expected to perform, but assumed that the in-house accountant would take responsibility thereafter, as allegedly explained to him during the original interviews. It seems, however, that the appointee did not in fact understand how to conduct the client's tax affairs, nor did he appreciate the law (either fiscal or company) governing loans to directors.

The partner then attempted, unsuccessfully, to secure a lenient approach by HMRC, and High Court proceedings against him were thereupon commenced, a sum of £316,000 being claimed, representing penalties and additional tax. At this point the partner concerned, who was due to retire, suffered a nervous collapse and was unable to assist further in defending the claim.

The firm's position was additionally weakened by the fact that no revised engagement letter had been issued following the internal accountant's appointment, and there was no documentary support for the responsibilities allegedly agreed at interviews.

In the circumstances, the insurers' legal advisers strongly recommended a negotiated settlement, and this was finally agreed at £226,000, including the claimant's costs.

Lessons to be noted

- It is by no means unusual for accountants to be asked to assist clients with selecting staff for accounting functions. This was, however, a new appointment with the intention that the successful applicant should take over many of the responsibilities previously conducted by the defendant firm. The appropriate professional conduct in such circumstances is to
  - agree the detailed job specification with the client in advance;
  - ensure that the client is present at final interviews and that the actual selection is made by the client – albeit based on the adviser's recommendation;
  - advise the client to confirm the detailed terms of the new appointment in writing without delay, subject to receipt of satisfactory references, which should always be taken up;

- assist the new appointee as necessary in the early weeks of the appointment, ensuring that the client is fully aware of such assistance;
- issue a new engagement letter to the client, requesting written confirmation by return, setting out the requirements of the revised professional relationship;
- stick to the basis agreed until such time as the client seeks any variation – which should then similarly be agreed in writing.

  It would appear from the details supplied that none of the foregoing procedures and precautions were followed by the defendant firm with, one regrets to add, predictably disastrous consequences.

- It is clear that the partner in the defendant firm was under considerable pressure of work and he completely failed to ensure that the basic administrative tax work and company secretarial responsibilities were being fulfilled by the in-house accountant. Not surprisingly, an examination of the audit files for the three companies for the years 2004 to 2007 inclusive showed total reliance on the work of the internal accountant, whose supporting accounts schedules were the sole contents of the 'audit files' in question.

Case C.2

The accountant in this case, Mr Donald Hampton, was the auditor of a substantial heating and ventilation consultancy. In 1999 he introduced a golf club acquaintance, who had recently been made redundant, to the client as a possible employee. The company did not, however, put him on their payroll but engaged him instead as a troubleshooting subcontractor under a loose arrangement whereby he would accept ad hoc assignments in the UK and abroad for clients of the heating and ventilation consultancy, by whom he would be paid a basic retainer and a commission based on fees generated by him. These sums were paid to him gross, although he was not permitted to accept work from any other employer.

No formal contract, whether 'of service' or 'for services', was issued, although a letter dated 18 August 2004, setting out his terms, warned that 'you should make ample provision for your own tax liabilities, in respect of which we recommend you obtain independent advice, and for which we accept no responsibility whatsoever'. The employee thereupon invited Mr Hampton to act for him personally with regard to his accounting, VAT and taxation affairs generally, and Mr Hampton accepted the appointment but issued no engagement letter.

In 2006 the employee was invited to accept full-time employment with an engineering company in Northampton, a client of his consultancy employer, who agreed to release him for this purpose. The employee informed Mr Hampton that he would no longer require his services as an accountant. As his new employer, the engineering company made enquiries as to his previous tax arrangements and, on discovering that their new employee had paid little or no tax for some four years, recommended that he bring his tax affairs up to date without further delay. This led in turn to an HMRC investigation, culminating in an agreed settlement in May 2007 of £278,550 including interest and penalties.

In June 2007 Mr Hampton received a claim from the former employee alleging negligence in failing to introduce the claimant to more than one prospective employer, incorrect initial advice regarding the terms of the claimant's employment, failure to advise properly on the tax consequences of working for only one employer, and failure to keep his tax affairs up to date and keep him fully informed as to his tax position on a timely basis.

Although Mr Hampton believed that he had a good defence against the allegation of negligent conduct of the claimant's tax affairs, in particular his alleged failure to advise on tax relating to matters for which he had never been engaged, legal advice suggested that it would be unwise to allow the claim to proceed to trial. Counsel was, however, confident that the quantum was excessive and recommended a payment into Court. This was done and, after negotiation, the matter was settled at an amount considerably below the original claim.

Lessons to be noted

- The device of making a payment into Court is often used when the claimant's quantum is so unrealistic as to impede any sensible settlement negotiations. Its effect is to put the claimant on notice that he will be responsible for the whole of the defendant's costs incurred after the payment into Court if any eventual award is less than the sum paid in. The judge will, of course, be unaware that such a payment into Court has been made. This device invariably serves to concentrate the minds of the parties on the risks of proceeding to trial, thus helping to narrow the gap between what the claimant will accept and the defendant (or insurers) will pay. It certainly had such an effect in this case, facilitating a settlement.

- The accountant's failure to issue an engagement letter undoubtedly damaged his ability to establish a defence. Such letters should be sent following all appointments, and the client's signed acknowledgement of acceptance obtained. Had this case gone to trial it would have been difficult to rebut charges of failure to advise on tax mitigation without evidence of the exact nature of the original brief.
- The hazards of the claimant's employment from a tax point of view, notably the apparent incompatibility between (i) being paid gross and (ii) being prohibited from accepting work from other employers, should have been obvious to the accountant, and yet no evidence of formal advice or warnings existed on his files. It is probable that HMRC would have claimed the tax from the employer on the grossed-up payments to the claimant had it failed to recover payment from him directly.
- Undoubtedly there were 'makeweight' elements in the claim that could successfully have been rebutted had the parties continued along the litigation path. But the story shows that any serious chinks in a defendant's armour will usually set insurers and their advisers thinking about settlement rather than trial.

D. Consequences of giving casual advice that proves to be inappropriate

This is a general section covering several instances in which accountants have given advice that simply does not accord with the realities of clients' circumstances. These cases include: failure to recognise the tax consequences of a transfer of assets between a company and its shareholders; proper recognition of what constitutes 'earned' income; and incorrect advice on capital gains tax (CGT) avoidance and on value added tax (VAT) ratings on building materials. The lesson throughout is that advice given casually, without adequately exploring circumstances and the applicable law, is a recipe for adverse litigation.

Case D.1

The claimant company, Reed Ltd, a building subcontractor providing irrigation and water supply services for new housing developments, had engaged the same accountant for 19 years. The company's accountant also acted for Mr Reed, its proprietor, personally and was well-acquainted with the business and Mr Reed's own financial circumstances.

In anticipation of his future retirement from active work, Mr Reed acquired the freehold of shop premises in a West London high street. He proceeded to install improved services and redecorated the premises throughout, following which he let the property to a shopkeeper on a 15-year lease with three-yearly reviews.

Mr Reed had intended to acquire the property in his own name, but lacked the necessary funds. He therefore sought the advice of his accountant who recommended that Reed Ltd should instead purchase the property because it had a substantial sum in the bank.

Shortly before Mr Reed's retirement the accountant advised him to transfer the freehold from his company to himself personally. HMRC queried the value at which the transfer was effected, and the accountant replied that the original cost was used for this purpose in order to give effect to Mr Reed's original intention that he personally should own the property outright. This was not accepted by HMRC, who raised assessments for CGT arising on the transfer, as well as demanding interest and penalties because of late declarations.

In breach of the terms of his professional indemnity policy, the accountant conceded that his advice had been incorrect, both when the shop premises were acquired and subsequently. When Mr Reed initiated proceedings against him for recovery of the tax and penalties he had unnecessarily suffered, the accountant's underwriters therefore considered whether the prior admission of negligence had compromised their ability to defend the claim. Fortunately for the accountant, so patently had he mishandled the tax aspects of Mr Reed's transactions that no defence could realistically have been established anyway. Indemnity was therefore granted despite his admission. It is ironic that had he been a little less negligent his admission may have cost him his insurance cover!

The claim issued by Mr Reed set out in detail the defects in the accountant's advice. Reed Ltd could have provided Mr Reed with the necessary funds by way of dividend which, despite higher rate income tax and the Advanced Corporation Tax then applicable, would have been more tax effective than the method actually used to purchase the property. Alternatively Mr Reed could, without difficulty, have raised the purchase price independently of the company and obtained tax relief on the interest. He would also have been entitled to retirement relief following a subsequent sale.

The abortive attempt to transfer the property from the company to Mr Reed at cost price generated lengthy correspondence with HMRC, in turn causing delays in the payment of tax due, and thus incurring penalties. A significant proportion of the total fees paid to the accountant regarding these matters, for which no value was received, was included as a separate head of claim.

Negotiation with Mr Reed's solicitors failed to reduce the claim significantly, and settlement was reached at the full amount of tax that might have been avoided had the appropriate advice been received, as well as penalties and costs.

Lessons to be noted

- Confusion regarding ownership of the assets of a closely held company and those of its proprietors is a perennial source of tax disaster, and represents an area in which the greatest caution over planning should be exercised. Once property assets are locked into a company there is the risk of double taxation arising, first when the assets are sold and then when the proceeds are subsequently distributed to shareholders. The important point in this instance was to avoid the company acquiring the shop in the first place. From then on it was downhill all the way, and misguided attempts simply to transfer it out at cost served only to make matters worse.
- On recognising the serious consequences for his client of having tendered poor advice, the accountant should have notified the circumstances to his PI brokers or commercial insurers rather than make an admission to the client. All PI policy terms state that admissions of mistakes without the insurer's prior consent can lead to indemnity being denied altogether if the insurer's position has been prejudiced thereby.
- It is not possible for an accountant accurately to anticipate what a claim might include. It may vary considerably from what the accountant has admitted to, and yet the admission itself could compromise the insurer's position by making a complete and credible defence especially difficult to establish.

Case D.2

A partner in Venning & Co had acted as personal tax adviser to Mr and Mrs Loveday for over 20 years. They were good friends and met socially on a regular basis. Mr Loveday was the director and principal shareholder in a retail jewellery company for whom Venning & Co acted as auditor. Mrs Loveday had no office and did not participate in the company's activities.

Venning & Co included Mrs Loveday's income in Mr Loveday's tax return because in the view of the partner at Venning it could not properly be classified as 'earned'. At the relevant time, Venning & Co was owed professional fees in excess of £22,000 by the jewellery company, and these had been outstanding for seven months because Mr Loveday disputed the size of the bills in relation to the work performed.

The relationship deteriorated and Mr Loveday, the claimant, contended that Mrs Loveday contributed secretarial, administrative and public relations services to the company from home, and hence that separate earnings elections should have been filed with HMRC. Legal proceedings were issued against Venning & Co, and the Statement of Claim alleged negligence and breach of contract in that the necessary elections had not been validly made; reimbursement of additional tax liabilities, damages and interest of £46,500 was sought.

Venning & Co's expert accountant considered that they were vulnerable because HMRC had accepted without question subsequently submitted separate earnings elections for Mrs Loveday, and Venning & Co could not therefore rely on the contention that Mrs Loveday could not justify the sums paid to her as an earned salary.

Venning & Co and Mr Loveday met privately without the knowledge of Venning & Co's underwriters and agreed a compromised set-off under which the outstanding fees would be met in full and £20,000 would be paid to Mr & Mrs Loveday in final settlement of the tax-related claim, each side bearing its own costs. However, by this time Mr Loveday had retired as a director of the company and lacked the authority to agree to settle Venning & Co's disputed fee notes. The respective actions had therefore to be continued separately.

Again without the involvement of the underwriters' solicitors, the parties met privately and agreed to 'drop hands' on the whole issue, each side settling its own costs. This effectively deprived the underwriters of their legal right to recover a proportion of costs from the party who agreed to drop the action, namely Mr Loveday. Recovery against Venning & Co was therefore sought in the amount of £17,000, which was negotiated down to £12,000 with the brokers' assistance, the underwriters having achieved an overall saving by not having to settle a claim against which there was no defence.

Lessons to be noted

- This case again demonstrates that friendship is no barrier to litigation, particularly when the claimant is aware that the accountant is covered by insurance. The insurance factor often has the effect of depersonalising litigation to the extent that normal professional relationships are easily resumed or even continued uninterrupted. This is one of the untoward, from the insurers' standpoint, by-products of compulsory insurance for the whole profession.
- Although the Venning partner's unilateral efforts to reach settlement worked out satisfactorily in this instance, his conduct was in flagrant breach of policy terms and conditions. This is a dangerous path to tread and, in the event that unauthorised negotiations serve to compromise the insurer's position, there is the risk that indemnity under the policy can be denied altogether.
- Venning & Co's fee notes referred merely to 'professional services during the quarter ended. . .' without explanatory narrative. Although the parties had a longstanding relationship, it did not avoid the acrimony that stems all too easily from charging fees that the clients do not expect. Billing software is highly sophisticated and, in the case of one-off assignments particularly, it is always advisable to explain the basis of charge and the hours worked in sufficient detail to avoid the sort of query that can easily put the accountant on the defensive in a potentially adversarial context.

Case D.3

In this case, the accountant, a part-time sole practitioner in semi-retirement, advised his client that CGT on the sale of his fish farming business could be avoided altogether if he lived abroad for three years, leaving before 5 April after selling his house in the UK, staying overseas for the whole of the first year and returning to the UK for not more than 90 days in each of the two following years.

Although the business had not as yet been sold at the date of departure, the client followed the accountant's advice, but continued to manage the business from Portugal until it was sold a year later. It subsequently transpired that the advice was defective, the ongoing management of the business while abroad being caught by s12 CGT Act 1979, and the liability to CGT therefore remained.

High Court proceedings were commenced and the claimant incurred further losses (in addition to the CGT liability of £192,000) attributable to

- the forced sale of his residence to meet the 5 April deadline;
- the sale in haste of the fish farm to ensure that it happened in the following fiscal year;
- the expenses of moving to Portugal;
- the inability to invest the proceeds of the sale to maximum advantage, as might otherwise have been possible.

Solicitors for the underwriters advised that liability was unavoidable and they were instructed to concentrate on reducing the quantum. With the underwriters' permission, the claimant's solicitors were advised that the limit of the accountant's indemnity was £150,000 and that any settlement in excess of that figure would have to be met by him personally.

In consideration of the accountant's position, including the fact that he would have to sell his home to meet his personal liability, settlement was agreed at the indemnity limit of £150,000, subject only to the self-insured excess of £4,000.

Lessons to be noted

- The accountant was very fortunate indeed in wringing the concessionary settlement from a claimant clearly entitled to a good deal more. Such magnanimity cannot be relied upon generally. The claim demonstrates that incorrect advice can have seemingly disproportionate consequences and gives the lie to the notion that the small practices never suffer large claims.
- Disclosure by the accountant of his insurance details, such as the limit of cover, to a potential claimant could be regarded as a breach of policy terms, which is why in this case the underwriter's prior permission was needed. It is not difficult to see, conversely, that in some circumstances such information could of itself tempt a claimant to inflate the quantum of a claim.

- Sole practitioners are increasingly joining discussion groups and consortia in which technical issues can be double-checked before advising clients. Had the accountant in this case taken advantage of such a resource he might have avoided the unfortunate claim altogether.

Case D.4

A partner in Crackle & Co was asked by a client whether input VAT on building materials needed for conversion work on his property could be reclaimed. The partner asked an HMRC officer, while seeing him on an unrelated matter, whether input VAT on building materials was reclaimable, but failed to mention that the query related to a conversion rather than to a new building. The officer simply replied that 'do-it-yourself' builders could reclaim VAT on materials purchased, and the client was advised accordingly.

The client then bought the necessary materials and employed a firm of builders to do the work. The subsequent claim for a VAT refund was rejected on the ground that the legislation provides for refunds only when 'do-it-yourself' house builders have built a complete new dwelling, no refunds being given in respect of conversions.

The client brought a claim against Crackle & Co for the irrecoverable VAT, arising from incorrect advice, stating that he would not have proceeded as he did had he known the true position.

The claim was met in full by underwriters following legal advice that the firm had no defence because:

- the partner at Crackle & Co admitted that he did not know that conversions, as opposed to complete new dwellings, did not qualify for VAT recovery; and
- the client maintained that he would have arranged for the building firm to supply the materials, in which case no VAT would have been charged to him because supplies of this kind from a builder were zero-rated at that time.

Lessons to be noted

- This claim amply illustrates the hazards of giving advice more casually than circumstances require. The precise position should have been checked against the legislation directly, if necessary confirming interpretation with an expert. The description conveyed to the HMRC officer was lacking in detail. Much of the communication appears to have been conducted verbally – always a hazardous basis for marshalling a defence after the event.

- Crackle & Co's admission of lack of knowledge of the legislation indicates that they would not in any event have been aware of which specific aspects of the arrangement might have been critical for determining the recoverability of the input VAT incurred.

E. Absence of advice may be negligent

Clients expect their accountants to be proactive when it comes to the provision of advice following new case law or changes in legislation. Simply to do nothing may leave clients significantly exposed when advice previously given, sensible at the time, no longer applies and the consequences may indeed be detrimental. It will not satisfy the needs of a sound defence to say that all clients were sent the firm's bulletin on fiscal changes. That is far too general. It may alert some sophisticated clients to seek answers to specific questions, but other clients may find out too late that their existing arrangements result in higher tax liabilities. Advice must be given positively in a manner that is tailored to individual circumstances.

Case E.1

The practitioner's client, Ronald Amery, ran a number of small unincorporated businesses, including a newsagent, a television repair shop, an off-licence and a hairdressing salon. The services provided by the practitioner, Clarke Knightley, included preparing annual accounts, providing tax advice as necessary and finalising the client's tax liabilities from year to year based on information supplied. No audits were required or conducted.

Mr Amery had a large family. He ran the TV repair enterprise in partnership with his wife and a son, and the hairdressing salon in partnership with his wife and a daughter. Both businesses had turnovers below the then operative VAT threshold. The other businesses, all VAT-registered, were operated under the proprietorship of the husband and wife.

Following a family dispute in 1992, the daughter resigned and the hairdressing partnership was effectively dissolved. The salon then continued to be run by Mr and Mrs Amery. For VAT purposes it should from that point have been treated as amalgamated with the other VAT-registered businesses under husband and wife proprietorship, but no steps were taken to inform HMRC of the change and VAT was not accounted for. Registration of the business for VAT purposes did not take place until mid-1995 following a VAT inspection covering all the client's businesses.

A claim against Mr Knightley was received two months after his dismissal as the Amerys' accountant. The claim alleged that timely advice would have enabled the client to arrange his partnership affairs so as to avoid the obligation of having to register the salon for VAT, and also to avoid the default interest and modest penalties subsequently levied by HMRC.

After taking account of recoverable input tax allowed by HMRC as a concession, the total claim for loss and damage amounted to £38,500. Mr Knightley admitted that he was aware of the partnership changes in 1992 but that due to pressure of work he had overlooked the VAT implications and had failed to tender the appropriate advice at the time. He added that he had found Mr Amery perennially fee-resistant and difficult to deal with, and was disinclined to devote time to his affairs when full fee recovery was unlikely.

In the circumstances, the insurers instructed solicitors to negotiate a settlement on the best terms possible, and their offer of £35,000 costs inclusive was eventually accepted by solicitors acting for Mr Amery.

Lessons to be noted

- 'Pressure of work' is increasingly heard in litigation involving sole practitioners. Although it is a fact of life that accountants in sole practice often have to work a 70-hour week to keep abreast of clients' affairs, let alone keep up to date on the law and professional developments, regrettably this cuts no ice when negligence is alleged against them following an oversight.
- This particular case involves few issues at the technical level that do not fall within the competence of most accountants. Instead, it demonstrates the fact that negligence can occur just as easily by omission as by commission. The advice that should have been

given was not specifically sought, but should have been triggered by changes in the client's circumstances of which the accountant was aware.

- This is particularly true in the fiscal realm. Clients are rarely aware of the tax implications of their actions, and expect, sometimes unreasonably, their accountants to step forward with the appropriate warnings before it is too late. The validity of this attitude depends, of course, on the accountant being aware of the client's intentions at the relevant time.
- In one famous 1980s Australian case, a wealthy Italian immigrant disposed of a large tract of forested land as a wedding gift to his daughter. The disposal occurred within the period designated for the purposes of incurring liability for short-term gains tax and a substantial sum became payable. His accountant had no foreknowledge of the intended disposal and yet the Court held that the accountant should, at the time of the purchase, have warned his client that under no circumstances should he dispose of the property until at least 12 months had elapsed, particularly as the client was known to have no knowledge of Australian tax law. The judge said that failure to give advice at the right time 'was just as heinous' as giving negligent advice (Sacca v Adam, 1983, South Australian Supreme Court).

F. Danger of giving advice that falls outside one's expertise

This is an all too common situation where an accountant acts for an individual or entity from the inception of its operation. Gradually, over a number of years, the business expands and its financial and tax affairs become increasingly complex. Eventually something happens – the business is restructured, or a transaction outside the normal course of trade is undertaken – the tax consequences of which require a level of technical expertise that is beyond the accountant's competence.

Case F.1

This case concerns an accountant whose client was the majority shareholder in a holding company with seven subsidiaries, each of which operated an off-licence liquor store. After almost 20 years in business the shareholder decided to sell to a third party the trade, licences and assets belonging to each of the subsidiaries. The proceeds of sale of the assets, each of which were qualifying assets for business rollover relief purposes, aggregated some £4.5 million.

The accountant advised the shareholder that business rollover relief would be available in respect of the reinvestment of the proceeds of the assets sales so long as the proceeds were reinvested in qualifying business assets. However, because he was himself unaware of the rule, he failed to advise that the definition of qualifying business assets for this purpose was restricted and did not at that time include shares in a limited company.

The client subsequently invested £2.5 million of the proceeds in shares in a limited company. When HMRC refused to recognise this reinvestment as qualifying for business asset rollover relief, the client sued the accountant not only for the tax assessed on the gain from the sale of the original investment, but also, on the basis that he would not have purchased the shares had he been properly advised, for recovery of the trading losses incurred by the company in which he had reinvested. The case eventually settled at approximately 75% of the amount claimed plus costs.

Lessons to be noted

- The accountant proffered advice to his client based on his own inadequate research and his wish to appear to be on the ball. The advice subsequently proved to be incorrect and the client sued for recovery of the additional tax, penalties and interest paid and the other indirect losses that he incurred as a consequence of acting on the advice he received. The lesson in such a situation is simple. Accountants must never stray beyond the limits of their own technical knowledge merely to avoid losing face with clients.
- The relevant tax provisions must be researched thoroughly before advice is provided, particularly on complex or unfamiliar issues. The circumstances and the intended advice should always be discussed with another appropriately qualified professional.
- If the issues are too complex for an accountant to handle, he or she should be prepared to suggest to the client that advice be sought from a specialist on the matter concerned.

Case F.2

A partner in Dobbins & Co had acted for the claimant group of companies in the hotel and leisure centre industry since 1979. In 2005 the group decided to set up a new division offering wholesale catering supplies to schools, canteens and government departments.

They sought Dobbins & Co's assistance on how to set up the new division and were advised by letter that the simplest approach would be to incorporate the catering services division as an independent VAT-registered company, and that 'there would be no significant tax disadvantages' in so doing. In the event, however, despite certain corporation tax savings due to group relief, the recommended structure caused the client to incur heavy VAT payments that could have been avoided.

It appears that the newly incorporated company made exempt supplies that exceeded 10% of its turnover, and this inhibited its ability to recover the full amount of input tax suffered. Furthermore, from their audits of successive years' accounts, Dobbins & Co were aware that substantial intra-group management charges were levied on which VAT was payable. Due to the subsidiary's exempt supplies it was not possible for the full amount of VAT received on management charges levied on the parent company to be set off against its input VAT.

The Statement of Claim calculated that the monetary value of the catering company's exempt outputs would at all material times have fallen well within the *de minimis* level as calculated by reference to the combined group turnover, if it had been established as a division rather than incorporated as a separate limited company. It alleged that as a consequence of the advice, avoidable VAT was suffered in the amount of £189,000 until a remedial restructuring was effected.

Independent experts stated that a complete defence would be difficult to establish and, after negotiating through the claimant's solicitors regarding corporation tax savings plus interest and possible contributory negligence in failing to remedy the position earlier, a full and final settlement, including claimants costs, was reached in the sum of £148,000.

Lessons to be noted

- This is, regrettably, one of many cases that illustrates the dangers of advising on commercial structures without fully exploring the potential VAT implications of what is being proposed.

- Practising accountants acting for clients in a variety of advisory contexts must face up to the hazards of an increasingly complex legislative environment, particularly in the fiscal realm (despite the Chancellor's annual attempts at simplification!).
- Larger practices often enjoy the advantages of establishing in-house specialist departments with high level technical expertise, but smaller firms, as in this case, should recognise the natural limitations of information to hand, and should not venture to advise 'cold' without themselves checking their proposed advice with recognised experts. In the event of a claim they and their insurers would, of course, have recourse against those experts.

5.3 FAILED PRACTICE ADMINISTRATION

G. Failure of accountant to keep records of client contact

Standards of practice administration can all too easily be allowed to slip when familiarity compromises professionalism. Informality in dealing with clients who may have become personal friends over the years may well lead to the provision of advice being unrecorded. In such circumstances the risks of misunderstanding and incorrect implementation are obvious and a Court will never be impressed by oral argument when a documentary background should have been the order of the day.

Case G.1

The accountant in this case acted as de facto finance manager for a client who operated a number of restaurants in North Wales and North West England. They were in daily contact, always by telephone or face-to-face, no written correspondence ever being generated. The client was an astute businessman who had bought and sold numerous restaurants for over 30 years. On one particular occasion he sold a restaurant in Chester but neglected to reinvest the gain in qualifying business assets within the relevant time period so as to be able to claim rollover relief. He blamed his accountant for the oversight, claiming that he did not receive the appropriate advice.

The accountant's defence was that they had discussed the necessity for reinvestment on a number of occasions and, in any event, the client was fully aware of the relevant tax provisions. Unfortunately, however, the accountant had no documentary evidence to support his defence. The case settled at almost the full amount of the claim.

Lessons to be noted

- This is an old chestnut that recurs time and time again, particularly in tax related cases. When an accountant is in almost daily contact with his client, providing advice on a variety of issues either by telephone or face-to-face, it is undoubtedly difficult to ensure that each piece of advice is noted and recorded on file. After all, as one defendant commented, 'there was no point in writing to my client – he never reads letters!'.
- It is precisely these circumstances, however, that lead to all manner of arguments concerning who said what to whom and whether or not certain advice was provided at the relevant time. Engagement letters are usually of no assistance whatsoever for this purpose because they are general in nature and so much advice is necessarily provided to clients 'off the cuff'.
- Even if an accountant is not in the habit of corresponding with a particular client, he or she should always make a written note on file of any discussions or advice given orally.

Case G.2

The client owned all the shares in a flourishing extrusion plastics company that specialised in making garden hosing and industrial tubing. He also owned three loss-making investment property companies, each owning a single property, all of them being financed by interest-free loans from the plastics company, both for initial purchase and for subsequent refurbishment.

In response to his client's perennial request for 'proactive' tax advice, the accountant recommended that the property companies should be transferred into the ownership of the plastics company by means of a share-for-share exchange. This would achieve three tax-saving objectives:

- Once the plastics company owned the shares in the property companies the properties themselves could be transferred to the plastics company and the property companies could be made dormant. The

small company corporation tax band would not then need to be spread over four companies.
- Costs of maintaining the properties would reduce the highly profitable plastics company's tax bill.
- Tax assessed on the plastics company on notional interest receivable on the interest-free loans to the property companies would disappear.

The client, who was a very experienced businessman, accepted the accountant's advice and the share transactions took place.

Four years later, due to heavy competition, the plastics company failed and went into administrative receivership. The receivers sold the assets, including the properties, to pay off the creditors, and the client's shareholding became worthless.

Legal proceedings were commenced against the accountant, it being alleged that, at the time the advice was given, he negligently failed to make it clear to his client that

- in the event of the plastics company's future failure, the properties would be lost to him and would form part of the assets available to the receivers;
- the share transfers, once transacted, were effectively irreversible because the tax consequences of attempting to reverse them were potentially disastrous.

The case was referred to mediation and after prolonged and bitter negotiations a low-level settlement was reached – much to the satisfaction of the accountant's insurers.

Lessons to be noted

- Accountants should never make assumptions regarding a client's understanding of complex accounting or tax issues. It is essential that the full implications are set out in writing.
- At the time of making the original tax-saving recommendations, the plastics company was flourishing. The possibility that adverse economic conditions and increased competition from the Far East might cause it to flounder was simply not in contemplation, either by the accountant or by the client. Yet the unthinkable was precisely what happened.
- The accountant and his client were close friends. Their families met socially and they were partners in the regular Sunday morning

friendly 4-ball at the golf club. Yet when the client's financial fortunes waned the relationship became a secondary factor, particularly as the perception of deep-pocket insurance invariably depersonalises legal disputes. In this case the financially depleted client was simply seeking a scapegoat to compensate him for his misfortune and, despite the obvious weaknesses in his claim, he was able to obtain legal and expert accountancy advice that buttressed his suspect allegations. The obvious lesson is that a close relationship with a client, particularly when acting in a tax advisory capacity, should never supersede the need for formally documented engagement terms and the other features of a professional relationship.

H. Failure of internal systems within practice administration

The following three cases are examples of human error at the most basic level – often forgetfulness – resulting in liabilities for income tax that clients would not have suffered if a system of deadline controls had been enforced within the office. Sometimes the administrative hiatus results from accountants carrying an excessive workload, working late night after night regardless of the toll on their mental faculties and ultimately their ability to keep abreast with the demands of running a tax advisory practice.

Case H.1

The client, Mr Phil Pearce, ran a highly successful skills training business for which his accountant, Mr Melvyn Mitchell, had acted since its inception 14 years earlier. In order to reduce Mr Pearce's total tax bill, Mr Mitchell recommended that Mr Pearce's wife be introduced as a partner in the business so that her allowances and lower rate tax bands could be fully utilised.

Mr Pearce readily assented to Mr Mitchell's suggestion and instructed him to draw up a suitable partnership agreement. Mr Mitchell also prepared the appropriate form of tax election to ensure that the business be assessed on a preceding year continuing basis. The election was duly signed by the Mr and Mrs Pearce and returned to Mr Mitchell for submission to HMRC. Although Mr Pearce was adamant that the signed election was posted, Mr Mitchell had no record of its receipt in his office. He had by then proceeded to prepare year-end tax accounts and check his calculations of tax saved, but forgot to chase his client for the election and hence neglected to submit it to HMRC within the two-year time limit.

Despite lengthy discussions on the question of the late election, HMRC refused to accept it out of time. Mr Pearce had no alternative but to accept that a larger tax liability would result as a consequence of the cessation caused by his wife's admission to partnership. Furthermore the timing of the change could not have been worse, the business having enjoyed its most profitable year to date per accounts already submitted to HMRC. Tax on these profits was assessed by the inspector on a cessation basis.

Proceedings were immediately commenced against Mr Mitchell by Mr Pearce in the amount of £240,000 representing the estimate of additional tax and interest he had suffered as a result of Mr Mitchell's failure to submit the election in time. As liability was difficult to contest, underwriters instructed their solicitors to settle the matter on the basis of the sums claimed in order to avoid incurring further costs.

Lessons to be noted

- This is a classic example of the 'human error' syndrome to which all of us are subject, despite the march of technology and the safeguards generated thereby. In its most basic terms, the accountant concerned simply forgot to get the election to HMRC. His advice was sound; he prepared the agreement; he drew up the election and sent it to the client for the necessary signatures to be added; but not having received it back from the client, and having become involved in other matters, the essential follow-up escaped his attention.
- The fact that the signed election did not arrive back at his office would not have availed him in his defence since, as the professional party in the relationship, it fell to him to do the necessary chasing and, if required, obtain a duplicate election, duly signed.
- It is essential for every practice to adopt such internal systems as will minimise the risks of the type of oversight described in this case, such as the physical logging of actions required against recorded deadlines, or the use of software systems.

Case H.2

The claimant company owned three freehold industrial and warehousing premises on Tyneside at which it and two subsidiaries manufactured canvas sports bags, hammocks, tarpaulins and sails. In 2005 the demand for its products declined and by the end of the year it had ceased to trade, leaving only the management of the premises and the receipt of rents as its business activities. In 2006 it had no significant VAT outputs and its VAT group registration was deemed to be inappropriate.

The company's accountant, who had some two years earlier been appointed to act as group auditor and adviser, arranged in July 2006 for the VAT registration to be cancelled by writing to HMRC to that effect. However, he later overlooked the cancellation he had himself effected and proceeded to submit late VAT returns for the year ended December 2006, and further advised the company to charge VAT on its rental income in future in order to offset the VAT it suffered on its various inputs, such as professional charges.

Due to the accountant's neglect, however, no VAT returns were in fact submitted in 2007. In March 2007, the company's financial controller expressed concern for the consequences of this failure and sent the accountant a blank cheque payable to HMRC for completion in the appropriate sum, based on records in the accountant's possession, and for onward transmission to HMRC. The accountant calculated that the VAT now payable exceeded £100,000, which would have thrown the account into overdraft and for which no facility existed, despite the accountant having previously undertaken to arrange one. The cheque was placed in the accountant's desk drawer and no action was taken by him.

In mid-2008 HMRC officers visited the accountant and collected the whole of the company's papers and records, and at the same time the accountant handed over the cheque, now completed in the amount of £118,000 based on his estimate of VAT liability. Four weeks later criminal charges were instituted against the accountant under the relevant VAT legislation, in that he, with intent to deceive, produced an invoice for rent that was materially false in including VAT and a VAT registration number in the name of a company that was not in fact so registered.

The accountant notified his insurers who appointed specialist loss adjusters to handle his application for costs of his legal defence and for the consequences of the civil action that would inevitably follow.

To complicate matters still further the accountant was forced at this time to file for his own bankruptcy due to his failure and inability to pay the VAT in relation to his own practice, and a Possession Order was taken out on his private residence. The loss adjusters, on enquiring further into the accountant's practice affairs, identified seven similar instances of potential claims from clients whose tax and VAT affairs had been allowed to fall into serious arrears.

Due to the complexities of both civil and criminal actions pending, and the gross improbability of the accountant being able to contribute his self-insured policy excess, underwriters were advised to reach a composite settlement with HMRC regarding outstanding VAT and penalties, and the accountant's trustee in bankruptcy.

With the assistance of the loss adjusters, a financial package was eventually settled in which amounts due to HMRC and company's solicitors were agreed, the underwriters being prepared to waive the payment of the policy excess.

Lessons to be noted

- Fortunately the catalogue of disasters here relayed occurs relatively rarely. When it strikes, however, it can play havoc with clients' interests, not to mention those of third parties and insurers. Accountants uniquely occupy a position of immense trust in relation to clients' affairs and the status of the profession as a whole is undermined whenever things go so badly wrong and suffering is caused. It was partly to minimise the risk of loss and damage of this type that the scheme of compulsory insurance was first established some years ago.
- So blatant were the mistakes described in this claim that there is no need for any comment at the technical level. It is more to the point to note that the accountant's workload became unmanageable and that he failed, in time, to heed the danger signs. It seems that he badly neglected his own affairs, billed irregularly and rarely chased outstanding fees. His own financial position worsened and personal bankruptcy was the all-too-predicable outcome.
- Criminal proceedings, if issued, will take priority over any civil actions in contemplation, and findings in the criminal case will have an obvious bearing on the likely outcome of a civil case heard at a later date. Any finding of culpability in the criminal court will usually destroy any reasonable prospect of subsequently establishing

a credible defence to a civil suit. This case also serves to warn practitioners of the hazards for themselves under the criminal code when acting for and on behalf of clients in a variety of contexts.

- The story also demonstrates the sound sense of arrangements whereby 'alternates' are appointed by sole practitioners as a safeguard against any situation resulting in them becoming unable to run the practice. Such arrangements are, of course, obligatory if the firm is authorised to conduct investment business, but merely recommended in other cases. The accountant stated that he had always intended to come to such an agreement with a locally-based colleague but, as with so many of his other practice matters, he never got around to doing anything about it.
- A further advantage of appointing an alternate is that such a relationship facilitates the sharing of practice problems, including technical questions, achieving their easier resolution through discussions held on a regular basis out of office hours.

Case H.3

From 1986 to 2005 Caramel & Co acted as accountants and tax advisers to a lady running a successful florist's business in a suburban high street in London. She also ran a market garden that supplied her shop and other customers with flowers, organic vegetables and decorative items such as gourds.

In early 2000 Caramel & Co advised her to introduce her husband as a partner because he had no independent income at that time and tax savings could be achieved by such a move. The advice was taken and the husband became a partner in the florist business, the wife continuing as the sole proprietor of the organic gardening business.

The accountants prepared year-end accounts for the garden business and, although no formal instructions were given or an engagement letter issued, the client assumed that they would do the same for the new partnership. The first two years' accounts were in fact prepared, but never submitted to HMRC. Accounts for 2002 to 2004 were not prepared, although the relevant books, papers and vouchers had as a matter of routine been supplied by the wife in a large box, delivered to the premises of Caramel & Co. Estimated partnership profits were, however, included by Caramel & Co on the couple's tax returns with 'details to be supplied' entered. Yet this was never done for any of the years in question.

In 2005 Caramel & Co advised their clients to form a limited company to acquire the two businesses, which would then discontinue trading. The partner concerned explained that the rules for assessing opening and closing years of a business would apply and would result in overall tax savings. The advice was accepted, the wife and husband becoming directors and shareholders in the company.

In early 2005 HMRC raised heavy estimated assessments on the partnership, backdated to its inception in 2000. The partner in Caramel & Co entered Notices of Appeal and recommended that his clients make a substantial payment on account to avoid further interest being incurred. He then prepared and submitted the partnership accounts for all outstanding years.

It became clear to the clients that their tax liabilities would be substantially greater than they had been led to believe, and they thereupon appointed other accountants. Shortly thereafter they instructed solicitors to issue a claim against Caramel & Co alleging negligence causing them to suffer additional tax, interest, penalties and accountant's costs in unravelling their tax affairs. Additional damages relating to anxiety and ill health were also included in the substantial claim of £245,000.

Loss adjusters appointed by insurers reported that little or no defence was available to Caramel & Co, whose partner was unable to offer any substantive explanation for the severe delays in preparing and submitting accounts for the partnership, other than 'pressure of work'.

A substantial settlement embracing all heads of claim was reached, excluding the interest element, the claimants having had the use of the money.

Lessons to be noted

- There is little that is not self-evident in the details of this case. This is a sorry, but regrettably common, tale of what happens when a practitioner's execution lags behind his or her advice. Once a backlog of work begins to accumulate it can rapidly get out of hand, culminating in crisis. The quality of advice tendered was not addressed and it was not clear from the case file, but having given the advice Caramel & Co should have followed it up with accounts and computations prepared on a timely basis, especially as the clients had delivered the records and vouchers to its office at the end of each of the years in question.

I. Know your partners. . .

As the trend for practices of all sizes to merge continues, accountants need to be mindful of the hazards of combining forces with colleagues on whom insufficient due diligence has been exercised. Aside from reputational damage, professional indemnity insurance arrangements can all too easily be placed in jeopardy if partners in the combined practice are held to be jointly and severally liable for mistakes made by predecessor firms with whom they have merged. This is an area in which pre-merger advice from a specialist broker is indispensible.

Case I.1

The partner who had acted for the claimant was no longer a member of the firm, having been excluded from membership of the Institute following disciplinary action. Four years after his cessation as a partner a claim was brought by a former client against the practice, which had since been sold to another firm.

The claim alleged that, as a result of negligent advice given by the ex-partner, the client sold her shares in her hotel company and used the proceeds to buy another company operating as a travel agency. She alleged that she was advised that the transaction would qualify for CGT holdover relief, whereas in fact the purchase of shares in the travel agency company did not constitute qualifying assets for CGT holdover purposes. As a consequence CGT in the amount of £194,000 became properly assessable.

The Statement of Claim particularised the nature of the negligence, stating that the tax could have been deferred if a sale of assets rather than shares had been advised. It further alleged that the ex-partner's prevarication and delay in dealing with the matter resulted in substantial interest charges and penalties, totalling £87,000, being levied by HMRC.

Although the accountancy practice had since been sold, the purchase had been on the basis that the acquiring practice would not be responsible for claims arising from pre-acquisition mistakes and that the former partners would therefore maintain their own past liability cover. The two former partners had held their position only nominally at the relevant time, both being salaried partners, and neither had any knowledge of their ex-partner's practice affairs or any involvement in the management of the firm. They maintained that the claim should therefore more properly be directed at the estate of the ex-partner, who had since died.

Solicitors appointed by underwriters sought to defend the action by reference to time limitation, but it was not clear whether the additional period allowed under the Latent Damage Act 1986 might avail the claimant. In view of this uncertainty, which would have been a matter for determination at a preliminary hearing, and the lack of any substantive defence to the main allegation, insurers authorised their solicitors to seek a settlement on the most favourable terms negotiable. This was achieved at a total of £185,000 including costs borne to date by the Legal Aid Board on behalf of the claimant.

Lessons to be noted

- Apart from highlighting the potential complexity of the legislation on CGT holdover relief and the advisability of seeking prior HMRC clearance or, at least, expert tax advice, this case contains a number of lessons, perhaps the most important of which is 'know your partners'.
- Many smaller firms are based primarily on the advantages of sharing overheads, the individual partners effectively running their own practices according to their own style of management. No overall control or accountability structure exists and in some instances it is only the costs rather than profits that are shared. This is a dangerous practice philosophy for all concerned and is at variance with both the external perception and partnership law, under which all partners, salaried or otherwise, that are named as such are jointly and severally liable for the full amount of the firm's liabilities, however these may arise.
- Underwriters now seek more information on such questions as the frequency and formality of partners' meetings; technical briefing and interchange of problems and experience; monitoring of staff and partner Continuing Professional Development (CPD); and conduct of internal peer reviews by independent partners on the completed assignment files of their colleagues.
- The problems that arose in this case were exacerbated by the ex-partner's failure to address in a timely manner the difficulties arising from the shares sale and subsequent purchase. When a possible error is first recognized, it is immediately notifiable to insurers as a policy condition, and the subsequent conduct of the matter, including negotiations with HMRC on the client's behalf, can then take place with the insurer's knowledge and support, including

requisitioning expert advice on the risk of penalties arising from further delay.

- It is normal and sensible for an acquiring firm to exclude responsibility for the past liabilities of the acquired practice, and the de facto cessation of the former practice must, under Institute rules, be accompanied by a minimum of two years' retrospective insurance cover to deal with any past claims that might surface post-merger. Five years' cover is the recommended period, given the delay that commonly occurs prior to claims coming to light.

Case I.2

Cropper & Co was the result of a merger between two two-partner firms. The claimants were two brothers who jointly owned a company, Entrepot Limited, that ran a restaurant in Northampton, and were clients of one of the pre-merger practices who acted as tax advisers. Shortly after the merger, the company's and the brothers' tax returns for the preceding six years were scrutinised by HMRC, following which they were required to pay additional tax, interest and penalties on the grounds that

- income of the restaurant had not been fully included in the company's annual accounts;
- certain costs had been inflated and non-allowable expenditure had been incorrectly classified in the accounts;
- there were repeated delays in submitting tax returns and accounts to HMRC;
- the brothers' other income had been excluded from their tax returns.

A claim against Cropper & Co was issued by Entrepot, but a search showed that it had been struck off the companies' register earlier in that year. The defendants' solicitor applied to strike out the action because the company was no longer in existence. This move failed, however, since the company was duly reinstated under the relevant provisions of the Companies Act 1985.

Experts appointed by Cropper's insurers concluded that the firm had indeed failed to deal expeditiously with the company's and the brothers' tax affairs, and had also made several errors in the accounts and returns resulting in too little tax being paid. Underwriters settled the action for an amount that included costs, additional tax and penalties for late submission of accounts and returns.

Lessons to be noted

- The merged practice was obliged to take responsibility for the claim because it related to the acts and omissions of their 'predecessors in business' prior to the merger.
- With hindsight it would have been preferable if the merger agreement had required each of the two previous firms to purchase and maintain run-off cover in respect of any pre-merger mistakes – especially since three similar, although smaller, claims surfaced shortly thereafter, all of which resulted in adverse settlements against the merged firm.

Case I.3

It was discovered by partners in Ackroyd & Hither, only after the retirement of one of them, that nine years' accounts of a client were submitted to HMRC by the now retired partner in one batch in August 2006. This prompted HMRC to undertake an in-depth review of the client's affairs, following which excess tax, interest and penalties of over £300,000 were levied. This resulted in a claim against the firm for recovery of all sums above the tax that would have been payable had the accounts been submitted on time.

It was apparent that the partner concerned was suffering from severe mental anxiety, which had a serious effect on his work. Although there was some contributory negligence on the client's part, in failing to supply stock figures for the purpose of finalising the accounts on time, there was little doubt that the claim would have succeeded had it gone to trial. It was settled at the sum claimed, together with those made by other clients of the retired partner faced by a similar situation.

Lessons to be noted

- Although it is clear that the client was dilatory in submitting accounts to Ackroyds on time, the partner concerned clearly had a responsibility for communicating the potential problems that would arise if the delays got out of hand. There was no evidence of warnings of this nature having been issued.

- The circumstances described (including the mental anxiety syndrome) are more widespread than is generally appreciated; all firms who have not already done so should institute administrative procedures that avoid total dependence on individual partners or tax department staff for meeting critical tax deadlines. Such procedures should (with the aid of appropriate software) operate automatically for all tax clients and hence act as a general alarm system for the firm as a whole, alerting all partners to delays in any one quarter.
- Such a system should apply not only to routine tax matters, but also equally to specific client circumstances arising periodically, such as deadlines for elections.

J. . . .and your employees!

Failure to supervise apparently reliable employees can lead to the discovery, too late, that their management of the affairs of clients with whose care they have been charged has been catastrophic, resulting in inexcusable delays and having to deal with the consequences of inaccurate accounts and tax returns.

Every practice has its quota of hard-working, diligent and loyal employees who have been doing much the same sort of work over many years – be it the calculation of PAYE for the monthly payroll, preparation of trust accounts, completion of VAT or personal tax returns, accounting for ground rents receivable or simply completing postings to the nominal ledger of a client unsophisticated in accounting matters. It is always tempting to let them get on with it without interference or supervision.

Although this passive reliance works well most of the time, there are occasions when the trusted employee has his or her own agenda or becomes careless through the sheer tedium of repetitive work. In such circumstances it will avail the firm nothing to say in defence that it relied on a tried and tested employee. There is no one in a firm whose work should not be peer-reviewed periodically.

Case J.1

An experienced but unqualified accountant had been engaged by Fowler & Co, the defendant firm, to prepare accounts, undertake audit work and assist with clients' tax matters. As he gained the trust of the partners his work became largely unsupervised and he signed letters on the firm's notepaper.

In October 1999 a partner was advised by one of his farming clients that HMRC were investigating his affairs, whereupon the partner examined the accounting and tax files and correspondence and discussed these with the unqualified assistant, who had been working on them. It soon became clear that the client's taxable profits had been materially understated for at least two years, at £629 and £468 instead of £65,200 and £73,550 respectively, as properly adjusted. The misstatements had been contrived by using false farm stock figures, capital allowances for equipment never purchased and bogus expenditures.

The partner immediately advised HMRC, withdrew the false accounts and lodged the corrected ones. The assistant was dismissed after admitting to similar occurrences with several other clients. His motivation was never fully explained, and it was never established whether he had received back-handers from clients for his activities, nor the extent of any connivance on the part of the clients affected.

When HMRC became aware of the possible extent of the assistant's activities they raised penalties against all assessments known to be based on false accounts. By mid-2000 writs were received from solicitors acting for three (now former) clients claiming damages in respect of the firm's negligence in failing to keep them informed of their liabilities for unpaid taxes. The quantum of these claims included the costs of having their tax affairs sorted out by other accountants, and substantial penalties imposed by HMRC.

Following disclosure to HMRC, Fowler & Co had drafted replies to formal back duty questionnaires that effectively precluded the firm from subsequently claiming in their defence that the clients concerned had colluded in the tax evasion exercise. Expert accountants examined the files and reported that the claims would be very difficult to defend and that proceeding to trial could cause Fowler & Co great embarrassment.

Costly settlements totalling £255,500 were achieved to cover all three instances after prolonged negotiations.

Lessons to be noted

- Areas of reserved professional work, notably financial services and auditing, require 'fit and proper' enquiries to be made and recorded in respect of all staff. Similarly, supervision and control over the work of all staff feature systematically in the regulatory process. Taxation work and advice remains an unregulated area in the UK (unlike France) and can be undertaken without any formal qualification.

- From the practitioner's point of view, however, this case makes it abundantly clear that the work of senior staff engaged in *all* professional activities must be properly monitored and controlled if vicarious liability for their mistakes is to be avoided. In the case in point the assistant concerned had not provided references from previous employers, and none were sought. It is suspected that he had been 'helping' clients to reduce their tax liabilities in similar fashion during previous employments. Indeed, he is probably still active in this field!
- Partners are deemed to 'know their clients'. They should have been alerted by accounts showing unrealistic profit levels. The partners in Fowler & Co were far too trusting; the assistant was technically competent, and had a pleasant and plausible personality. When he was working on clients' affairs there were never any complaints – for reasons only too painfully clear after the event.

Case J.2

An unqualified employee, Crispin Notts, of Bayfield & Watch was responsible for preparing the accounts and dealing with the tax affairs of over 200 clients, mainly small farmers. A complaint from a client while Mr Notts was on holiday was investigated by a partner, who was appalled at what he found when examining the files. The other partners were called in and extended their investigations further. They found that files were in total disarray and that accounts prepared by Mr Notts were grossly inaccurate, many having already been submitted to HMRC. Profits had been consistently understated, resulting in too little tax having been paid.

In the case of clients who had subsequently left the firm it was impossible to carry out corrective work. HMRC Enquiry Branch came on the scene and a prodigious number of back duty cases were commenced.

Clients faced with interest and penalties instituted proceedings against the firm, whose only defence, applicable in no more than a few cases, was that clients had colluded with Mr Notts to defraud HMRC. The firm's right of indemnity against Crispin Notts was considered to be unproductive.

Mr Notts' motives were unclear. He liked to be known in the area as being 'good at minimising tax liabilities'; indeed, several clients remained with him following his dismissal from the firm. One client is known to have provided him with two free suits each year.

This unwholesome situation became a nightmare for the partners. The underwriter's initial reserve was tentatively placed at £500,000 although it is acknowledged that more than £1,000,000 may still have to be paid.

Lessons to be noted

- One previously known act of dishonesty by the clerk should have been sufficient to alert the partners to problems of this type and constituted 'notifiable circumstances' under the policy working, which if strictly applied would have justified the underwriters' refusal to give indemnity altogether.
- It is obvious that the firm's internal procedures for monitoring and supervising the work of its junior members were woefully inadequate. Although it is tempting to leave routine tax affairs to members of the tax department staff on low charge-out rates, they should never be left to their own devices entirely. Mr Notts' work should periodically have been reviewed by a partner or senior manager, if only for the purposes of his own annual or semi-annual appraisal.
- The provision of gifts in return for saving tax demonstrates that Mr Notts was far from independent in his dealings with the tax affairs of his farming clients. It must be assumed that every one of those clients had been allocated a partner of the firm as the point of contact for communications, fee notes and advice. The partners so named were culpable of allowing Mr Notts to develop these cosy relationships unhindered by any internal constraints.

5.4 SUMMARY OF KEY LESSONS

- Accountants should never make assumptions concerning their clients' financial arrangements. It is essential that a clear understanding of all relevant facts is gained before advice is proffered.
- Accountants must never stray beyond the limits of their own technical knowledge merely to avoid losing face with their clients.

- Engaging staff with the appropriate skills to cope with client needs is essential as is the need to supervise their work and ensure that systems are in place to alert them to hazards implicit in today's complex tax legislation regime.
- Confusion regarding ownership of the assets of a closely held company and those of its proprietor is a perennial source of tax disaster and represents an area in which the greatest caution over planning should be exercised.
- Even if an accountant is not in the habit of corresponding with a particular client, he or she should always make a written note on file of any discussions or advice given orally.
- Accountants must remember that all PI policy terms state that admissions of mistake without the insurer's prior consent could lead to indemnity being denied if the insurer's position has been prejudiced thereby.
- Similarly, in the event that unauthorised negotiations serve to compromise the insurer's position, there is the risk that indemnity under the policy can be denied.
- Disclosure by an accountant of insurance details, such as the limit of cover, to a potential claimant is a fundamental breach of policy terms that may result in indemnity being denied.

6
The Disciplinary Framework

6.1 INTRODUCTION

In this chapter we outline a number of disciplinary cases whose circumstances do not fall naturally into the subject matter of earlier chapters. There are, for example, instances of audit failure that have been dealt with in Chapters 3 and 4 that finished up in the disciplinary arena. Consequently this chapter should not be regarded as an exhaustive catalogue of potential disciplinary offences.

6.2 STRUCTURE AND PROCEDURES

Disciplinary proceedings arise in two ways:

- Formal complaints from third parties, fellow members of the Institute or clients/former clients.
- From information in the public domain such as an adverse finding against a member in a criminal action. Bye-laws require members, as a professional duty, to bring a complaint against a fellow member in cases where that member's conduct is likely to bring the profession of accountancy into disrepute.

In the first instance, complaints are dealt with by the Professional Standards Office and, assuming they are to be taken seriously, they are normally passed to the Investigations Committee and a Case Officer conducts the investigation process.

High profile public-interest cases, such as those involving listed companies, may be referred directly to the Accountancy and Actuarial Discipline Board (AADB), which brings disciplinary complaints against accounting and auditing firms in high-profile cases.

In the vast majority of instances the Case Officer investigates the complaint by visiting the member/firm and conducting correspondence, both sides being copied in. The Case Officer will complete his or her work with one of the following recommendations to the Investigations Committee:

- There is no case to answer and no further action should be taken.
- The member should be issued with a formal caution but no further action should be taken.
- A Consent Order should be offered to the member. This is equivalent to a 'slap on the wrist' whereby the member/firm accepts that there has been a lapse in standards of a relatively minor nature resulting in a formal reprimand. This nevertheless becomes a matter of public record and if, as is often the case, the member suspects that the complaint is a precursor to a formal claim, the firm will naturally be reluctant to accept a Consent Order if it believes it has a defence.
- The matter should be referred to the Disciplinary Committee for a formal hearing before a three-member Tribunal (two members and one lay person) at which the member is entitled to be legally represented and at which the Investigations Committee may engage a barrister from the criminal bar to present its case against the member. Although relatively informal in terms of procedure, this is analogous to proceedings in Court and will result in a finding, usually pronounced by the Chairman of the Tribunal on the same day, on each of the charges brought.

In the event of either of the first two findings above, the complainant has the right to have the matter referred to the Institute's independent Reviewer of Complaints. The Reviewer will either concur with the finding or refer the matter back to the Investigations Committee for reconsideration, together with his or her reasons.

In the event of an adverse finding on any of the charges the member has the right to take the matter to the Appeal Committee, whose Chair is invariably a leading QC.

The Disciplinary Tribunal may make adverse findings of varying degrees of severity including a reprimand, severe reprimand, suspension of membership for a specified period (subject to reapplication) and lifetime exclusion. The latter will usually follow a finding of guilty on serious charges in the criminal courts. A member's bankruptcy (as opposed to an Individual Voluntary Arrangement) automatically leads to exclusion.

Details of all adverse findings from Consent Orders through to exclusion become a matter of public record and are included on the website of the Institute's magazine *Accountancy* (if not in the hard copy itself) and are sent to local newspapers and District Societies.

6.3 COSTS

Any adverse finding by the Disciplinary Committee or the Appeal Committee will involve costs as well as a fine. A fine following a severe reprimand can typically fall in the £10,000 to £25,000 range, and costs in such cases are typically between £2,500 and £15,000, although there have been notable cases in which vastly higher amounts have been imposed.

Although fines are not recoverable under PI policies, most policies will cover defence costs at Disciplinary and Appeal Committee Hearings. This is subject to the usual requirement, of course, that insurers have been duly notified and been kept fully informed, and have given formal prior written consent to the instruction of solicitors, counsel and experts of their choice.

Given the correlation between complaints and subsequent claims, insurers recognise the importance of defeating complaints from third parties, often lacking in merit, and being brought plainly in anticipation of a contemplated legal battle, at the outset. For this reason policy coverage will normally include such defence costs, although this does not feature in the Institute's agreed minimum policy wording.

In cases where the member is wholly successful at the Disciplinary or Appeal Committee level in defeating the allegations brought by the Investigations Committee, the Tribunal may award costs against the Institute and in favour of the member.

A. Conflicts of interest

It is astonishing how blind accountants and auditors can be to circumstances that any intelligent third party would immediately recognise as being rife with conflict. No matter how emphatically it is proclaimed that 'independence is a state of mind and my position is unassailable', the factual circumstances, if they indicate potential for conflict, will always prevail. Accountants overlook the reality of perception; independence must not only be present but also must be *seen* to be so.

Perhaps it is the naive belief that they are able to handle both ends of the assignment far more competently than anyone else, or the need of their egos to involve themselves in every aspect of the job, that leads to acceptance of a role that is bound to end so acrimoniously that a formal complaint becomes inevitable.

Case A.1

The Institute of Chartered Accountants brought a disciplinary action against an individual partner, Kevin Miskin, in a medium-sized firm on the grounds that he had reported on the proposed purchase of 100% of the shares in Lastrana Limited by the pension fund of Servicare Limited, when his firm was currently acting as auditors of Lastrana (which was a loss-making subsidiary of Servicare), the pension fund and Servicare.

The complaint against Mr Miskin was that he should not have undertaken the assignment because it constituted a serious conflict of interest due to the auditing roles of his own firm.

In his defence Mr Miskin explained that he had recognised that acceptance of the assignment to advise on the acquisition of Lastrana Limited constituted a potential conflict of interest and for this reason he consulted his firm's technical committee. It was their conclusion, after due deliberation, that there was no irremediable conflict as regards the firm. Mr Miskin claimed that he was well aware of the need for his report to be accurate, unbiased and prepared with diligence so that the directors of Servicare and the trustees of its pension fund could be seen to have acted properly.

The critical factor in the allegation of conflict lay in the fact that Servicare benefited by the significant amount of cash it received from its own pension fund as consideration for the sale of Lastrana to the pension fund. As auditor Mr Miskin would have been well aware of Servicare's dependence on the cash injection. Furthermore, Mr Miskin's firm would have been unable to provide Servicare with a clean audit opinion but for the cash received on the sale. The circular nature of this crucial dependency was evident in the fact that the value to the pension fund of its investment in Lastrana would be severely diminished in the event of Servicare's financial failure because the latter was Lastrana's major customer for the sale of components. In essence, the survival of the group depended on clawing back money from the company's own pension fund.

Mr Miskin also cited the ethical rules of his professional body on corporate finance assignments in circumstances where the firm acts in a different capacity, notably as auditors. These rules do not explicitly prohibit the acceptance of such assignments 'provided that the member maintains objectivity and integrity throughout'. Mr Miskin's assignment was to report objectively on the proposed investment in Lastrana, which he maintained, he fulfilled without bias one way or the other.

Mr Miskin was unsuccessful in his defence. The tribunal concluded that the circumstances of the engagement were inherently prone to a situation of conflict such that the assignment to advise should have been undertaken by an accountant wholly unconnected with any of the companies involved.

Lessons to be noted

- Even though Mr Miskin's appointment was on behalf of the investing party, the pension fund, both Servicare and Lastrana effectively gave their tacit agreement to it. This, however, did not serve to ameliorate the situation.
- Abstract concepts such as independence, objectivity and integrity are never susceptible to factual proof, and yet they feature strongly in the day to day activity of accountants and auditors. This stands in contrast with, say, barristers, who are concerned solely with presenting their client's case in the most favourable possible light. Barristers act as advocates and are never tested on the level of personal belief in their client's case. Professional accountants are invariably judged in such matters by reference to *perception*, and in the circumstances outlined above it was inevitable that no protestations of objectivity or independence of mind would prevail.
- In circumstances of material doubt the only safe course is to avoid potential conflict by declining the relevant assignment.

B. Dangers of introducing clients to third party advisers

Clients are introduced to independent specialist advisers when, particularly in relation to investment and pension decisions, the expertise required is not held by anyone within the practice to a degree that will satisfy the stringent standards of current legislation. Regrettably, cases arise periodically when trust in such advisers or consultants proves to be seriously misplaced, which can lead to formal complaints against the partners in the main firm.

Case B.1

Two brothers, Alfred and Robert Ogilvy, were partners in this firm. Both were charged with the same disciplinary offence, which alleged that they had

- failed to control the activities of an unqualified associate, Ralph Ruffles, who acted as agent for companies selling insurance and pension products that the firm marketed to clients;
- failed to ascertain that Mr Ruffles had formed his own enterprise with a name virtually identical to that used by the Ogilvys for marketing their life and pension products.

Ruffles was unregistered and had no financial services authorisation, and was subsequently found to be defrauding the firm's clients and his own. The partners' failure to exercise an appropriate level of control therefore constituted conduct likely to bring the firm and the profession of accountancy into disrepute.

The Ogilvys' relationship with the agent was of many years' standing. When any of their clients required expert advice on insurance or pension products they were invariably referred to Mr Ruffles, and feedback from the clients concerned was always expressed in glowing terms.

Some time later, Mr Ruffles devised what appeared to be a tax effective investment product, which he marketed as the Equity Distribution Scheme (EDS). This provided returns that outperformed the market, and a number of Ogilvy clients were recommended by the partners to invest in it. It appeared to be successful and on the renewal date most clients reinvested for a new term. In view of the mutually satisfactory relationship that had developed between the partners and Mr Ruffles they were invited by him to act as managers for the wider dissemination of the EDS.

This would have been advantageous for Ruffles, because an association with the Ogilvy firm would have been a useful marketing ploy given the impression of respectability thereby endowed.

Although they turned him down, unbeknown to the partners, his marketing literature represented that the desired relationship existed. Following complaints against Mr Ruffles and the Ogilvys to the effect that the EDS failed to meet expectations, the Institute of Chartered Accountants commenced disciplinary proceedings against the Ogilvys.

By this time investigations on behalf of the financial services regulator brought to light far more serious irregularities and Mr Ruffles was indicted on charges that he had acted fraudulently in managing clients funds, effectively operating a pyramid structure that depended on the influx of new funds in order to meet promised returns to existing investors.

The case brought by the Institute against the Ogilvys was based on their failure to ensure that the Ruffles enterprise could not be confused by the public as being connected to their own firm. The matter went to a full Tribunal hearing at which evidence in mitigation succeeded in securing

- the lowest category of reprimand and financial penalty;
- agreement that the names of the parties should not be disclosed in the publication of findings.

Lessons to be noted

- The relationship of trust between Mr Ruffles and the partners, which existed over many years, clearly caused them to relax the level of vigilance over the details of their association. The firm's clients had consistently praised Mr Ruffles' expertise and the quality of his advice, and this led the Ogilvy brothers to pass to him many cases involving decisions on pension policies and related investment matters.
- Although understandable in the circumstances, this relationship did require monitoring in terms of the products that Mr Ruffles was promoting and the manner in which he represented his relationship to the firm in his marketing literature. Independent financial advisers are known generally to depend heavily on referrals and recommendations from accountancy practices but those practices have an obligation to their clients to keep the quality and integrity of advice given under annual review.

C. Dangers of not keeping up to date

There are many firms in which a small number of individuals with particular specialisms become recognised as the appropriate 'port of call' whenever assignments falling within their scope are undertaken. This typically applies to the accounts of solicitors, estate agents, architects, surveyors and, as in the following case, regulated financial services businesses. While matters proceed routinely all is well, but the firm must have procedures to ensure that the specialists maintain their expertise to keep pace with rule changes, legal decisions and other developments relevant to the client entities' affairs. This is the purpose of maintaining full records of Continuing Professional Development (CPD) attendances.

Case C.1

A complaint to the Institute was brought by the financial services regulatory authority against a medium-sized South London firm that they, as auditors of a regulated client company, had issued an audit report in an out-of-date format on the accounts of that company. The allegation included the complaint that the firm did not have in its possession a copy of the most recent applicable rule book.

Due to its size the company fell into the 'small company' category and its auditors regularly prepared its accounts in a format that relied on the exemptions currently available under the Companies Act, notwithstanding that those exemptions were not available to investment businesses.

The partners in the firm recognised the fact that the allegations were unanswerable and entered a plea of mitigation, based primarily on their reliance on an employee, a chartered accountant of 12 years standing, who was the firm's recognised expert on investment business audits and compliance issues. It was this employee who was responsible for the accounts preparation work, audit and the drafting of the audit opinion in successive years.

As often happens in such cases the reporting deadline was imminent when the relevant partner was asked to sign the audit report. Acting in haste he failed to notice that the format of the accounts and the wording of the audit report were inappropriate.

The Institute considered it unnecessary for the matter to proceed to a full hearing given the firm's acceptance of the allegations made against it. The firm maintained that its reliance on the employee in question had been fully justified given his considerable experience in dealing with the affairs of regulated entities and the fact that he had never previously let the firm down in the manner complained of. The Disciplinary Committee took all relevant factors into account and concluded that the complaint was well founded. However, the level of reprimand and the amount of the fine and costs reflected the firm's acceptance of the findings and its undertaking to install appropriate procedures to ensure that there would be no recurrence.

Lessons to be noted

- Even though the accounts and audit report complained of slipped through the supervisory net in this instance, the partner deemed to be the 'responsible individual' should have recognised that the format and wording of the audit opinion were incorrect, particularly as this had also happened in the two previous years.
- It is advisable to have an arrangement, either contractual or informal, under which advice from a professional colleague may be sought on the many aspects of practice management and technical issues affecting small and medium-sized firms as a matter of routine. It is the authors' own experience that consulting arrangements of this nature will often alert firms to situations that could unwittingly have led them into a disciplinary process had they not sought advice on a timely basis.

D. Non-executive directorships

Partners in accountancy firms are periodically invited to act as non-executive directors of client companies. In circumstances where the firm acts as auditor to the client company such an appointment would be prohibited under company law. In other circumstances, however, it may be advantageous for the client to have a qualified accountant as a senior non-executive director with the responsibility for overseeing the company's financial position on a more regular basis than is afforded by an annual audit.

The danger, however, is that company law makes no distinction between executive and non-executive directors in terms of their duties, responsibilities and, ultimately, liabilities. Being non-executive, such a director is usually at a disadvantage because he or she, working on a part-time basis, cannot be expected to be as familiar with the day-to-day affairs of the enterprise. While the financial position of the company remains strong the non-executive directors may have little to fear. In the case outlined below, however, serious problems arose when it was discovered that the financial position was very much weaker than the management accounts suggested.

Case D.1

The accountant concerned in this matter, a certain Selwyn Firkin, was the senior partner of his practice in the West Midlands. He was invited by Owen Peabody, the managing director and principal shareholder of a client company, Sparklers Limited, to join the board as non-executive chairman with responsibility for monitoring the results of monthly and quarterly management accounts and to report on these to the company's bankers. The company, a multi-branch, high street retail purveyor of fancy goods, souvenirs, pottery items, mirrors and other knick-knacks, produced its periodic management accounts on computer-generated spreadsheets under the control of its finance director.

A year after Mr Firkin's appointment he noted that the frequency of communications from the bank had increased and that the tone of this correspondence had become more anxious. The bank was clearly concerned over the level of outstanding borrowings and the adequacy of security, an important element of which was the very substantial volume of stock held in the various branches. Before the commencement of the Christmas season in 2004, the sales director mentioned to Mr Firkin that a very disappointing festive season was in prospect because of the lack of stock. Mr Firkin found this difficult to believe because the most recent management accounts showed stock levels valued at over £5 million, more than enough for the Christmas trade.

Mr Firkin was in a dilemma because he was about to go on holiday and feared that to report the matter to the bank could create panic, and in any event he was unsure whether to believe the sales director or the management figures. In the event, the seasonal trade was indeed disappointing, but it was never established whether a lack of stock was the main reason for this. Despite the disclosure of profitable trading in the management accounts, the cash position continued to worsen and, at Mr Firkin's instigation, the management director instructed a firm of insolvency practitioners to appraise the situation, a decision with which the bank concurred. Six months later the company was placed in administrative receivership from which it never emerged because its assets were disposed of on a piecemeal basis, the bank and other creditors sustaining a substantial deficiency.

Following investigations on behalf of the Treasury Solicitor, charges were brought against Mr Firkin under company directors' disqualification legislation. Both Firkin and his lawyers believed that he had acted honourably and had not breached his fiduciary duties to the company. However, the costs to him personally of a full trial, never without risk, would have exceeded £40,000 and absorbed a substantial amount of time and emotional energy. After full consideration of his plight he decided to accept a 'Carecraft' settlement under which he was banned from acting as a company director for a period of two years, the minimum disqualification period under prevailing practice. Carecraft is the UK equivalent of USA plea bargaining. It saves the costs of a full trial and represents a cost-effective resolution when it is not in the public interest to pursue charges all the way to a criminal trial.

Mr Firkin's decision was, of course, influenced by his own particular circumstances. He had young children about to commence private education and a successful practice to run. His pragmatic decision to accept the two-year disqualification period, although effectively amounting to an admission of culpability in some degree, allowed him to resume his professional life as a practising accountant.

Lessons to be noted

- Acting as a company director does not fall naturally within mainstream accountancy practice. Nevertheless, many partners in firms accept appointments of this nature for the following reasons:
  - to maintain relationships with important clients;
  - to ensure that the clients concerned operate in a well-structured and disciplined fashion, and hence that they are able to afford the firm's professional fees;
  - to increase the firm's income by the fees charged for this service.
- It is clear from this case that circumspection is warranted before accepting such an appointment – not only in terms of the financial viability of the client entity, but also the question of the willingness of the client company's management to accede to the implementation of the recommendations issued by the non-executive directors. In this particular case the managing director, Mr Peabody, welcomed the corporate adornment of having Mr Firkin on the board, but was consistently reluctant to implement his recommendations, particularly the installation of an integrated stock control system that, coupled with periodic physical stocktaking, would have facilitated the production of reliable management accounts.

If an accountant harbours any reservations concerning the integrity of senior management and its willingness to take compliance seriously, he should under no circumstances accept a directorship or continue an existing one.

- Once Mr Firkin's suspicions were aroused by the sales director's comment on stock levels he should not have kept his own counsel. He should have confronted Mr Peabody with the stated anomaly and immediately pursued his own enquiries to ascertain the truth of the matter, and then decide on what to tell the bank, and when. If it is not permitted under proceeds of crime or money-laundering legislation to raise suspicions with the managing director, it would be necessary to alert the appropriate authority as an initial step, following independent legal advice.
- At the time of accepting the Carecraft settlement, Mr Firkin did not consider the inescapable repercussions of so doing with regard to his professional body, and the consequences could have been fatal to his career as an accountant. In the event, the disciplinary committee accepted an independently commissioned expert's report as a plea in mitigation and Mr Firkin was issued with a formal reprimand and a requirement to bear the committee's costs. It was clear that the committee shared the view of the expert that Mr Firkin was caught in a fraught situation and had acted reasonably. The Committee's hands were tied, however, by the mere fact of his Carecraft admission. The true state of the company's stock levels was never fully investigated.

E. Complaints from official sources

When accountants act in unfamiliar territory that is nevertheless subject to a statutory framework, they should always familiarise themselves with the rules on what a client is or is not permitted to do in case they become implicated by acquiescing in that client's wrongful acts, as the following example clearly shows.

Case E.1

This case highlights the dangers of being unfamiliar with legal requirements governing unusual circumstances. The client in question, Rufus

Riley, had been made bankrupt and his affairs were in the hands of a qualified trustee responsible for supervising all his financial commitments and transactions. The accountant, Neil Nebish, was charged by his professional body with allegations of aiding and abetting breaches of the law on what activities unrehabilitated bankrupts are permitted to undertake, either in their own name or that of an entity of which they were formerly directors.

The accountant's firm acted as auditor of a company in which the bankrupt was a shareholder and the managing director. Following his bankruptcy his wife was installed as managing director and it is with her that the accountant should have dealt with regard to audit queries and other related matters, notably concerning the true nature of the company's activities and the dire state of its accounting records.

It became clear in the run-up to the audit that Mrs Riley was in no position to deal with Mr Nebish's queries. Indeed, she had little knowledge of the company's business and her appointment as director existed only in name. Mr Nebish also realised that recovery of fees relating to the audit and any consequential work that might arise therefrom would be problematic. Mr Nebish took a practical view and decided that he had better deal directly with Mr Riley, whose formal status in the company at that stage was as an employee.

Some months later the Department of Business, Enterprise and Regulatory Reform appointed an inspector to investigate the affairs of the Riley company, and he issued a formal complaint to Mr Nebish's professional body alleging that Mr Riley had committed acts in contravention of directors' disqualification legislation in that he was concerned in the promotion, formation or management of the company and in so doing was aided and abetted by Mr Nebish.

At the disciplinary hearing it was apparent that Mr Nebish was unaware of any impropriety when dealing with Mr Riley. He stated that at all material times he considered that his duty was owed to the Riley company of which his firm had been appointed auditors, and that this duty necessitated holding discussions with both Mr and Mrs Riley, the only other option being resignation which, in his view, would have been of no assistance to anyone.

Mr Nebish's pleas in mitigation influenced the disciplinary committee to the extent of allowing his name to remain unpublished and of imposing a relatively modest financial penalty to accompany the inevitable reprimand.

Lessons to be noted

- Whenever a complaint to a professional body emanates from an official source such as the Department of Business, Innovation and Skills, the Treasury Solicitor, the Official Receiver or a trade regulator such as the Civil Aviation Authority, the professional body's disciplinary machinery is bound to view the matter with the utmost seriousness. For this reason Mr Nebish should have been alerted to the extreme sensitivity of his relationship with a bankrupt director of a client company.
- If Mr Riley, either intentionally or unwittingly, breached the provisions of his bankruptcy order, that should have been a matter for him. Even though Mr Nebish would not be expected to be familiar with the precise terms of section 11 of the 1986 Disqualification Act, which prescribes the activities that an undischarged bankrupt may not undertake, either directly or indirectly, as a professional accountant he should have known that caution needed to be exercised on his part before having any contact with the bankrupt in question.
- Such caution was not evident in Mr Nebish's decision to put his queries to Mr Riley, a mere employee of the company, when it became apparent that talking to Mrs Riley was completely unproductive. If as a consequence it became impossible to manage the company's affairs other, suitably qualified, directors should have been engaged for this purpose and Mr Nebish was in a position to make such a recommendation.

F. How to respond to a formal complaint – the dangers

Accountants can experience a mixture of anger and fear when suddenly confronted by the rigours of officialdom in any of its forms, whether a professional disciplinary complaint or an early morning visit by the Special Branch and the forcible removal of the firm's computers. The latter is blessedly rare, but the former is an unwelcome experience shared by thousands of accountants.

The initial reaction of frustration and outrage needs, of course, to be moderated and advice should be taken in order to instil a cool and dispassionate sense of how best to deal with the issues, no matter how unjustly the accountants believe they have been treated.

Many disciplinary cases would be disposed of relatively efficiently and with minimal pain if only those targeted would learn how to co-operate with an investigation or enquiry without, of course, compromising their case.

Case F.1

An accountant should always undertake a degree of due diligence on the credentials of a new client. The accountant in this case, Tony Norman, was a sole practitioner who was asked by an individual previously unknown to him to check 15 insurance claims on behalf of cloth merchants, all to be submitted to a firm of loss adjusters, following a fire at the warehouse in which their goods were stored.

Without making due enquiries regarding the legitimacy of the claims, he undertook the exercise requested and examined the bundles of documents provided to him, consisting mainly of warehouse records of items admitted to storage and taken out, in each case showing the balance presumed to be in store on the date of the fire.

After correcting certain arithmetical errors, none of which were material, he submitted his report using the words 'I have compiled the attached claim from the documents supplied to me without carrying out an audit. I certify that the claim is in accordance with that documentation.' These reports, together with the related bundle of documentation, were then sent to the loss adjusters together with his fee note, which was duly paid.

Some months later Mr Norman was visited by the police and charged with being involved in a massive conspiracy involving the warehouse owner, all the tenants and most of their suppliers. It was alleged that none of the documents supplied to Mr Norman had been genuine. In doing his best to assist the police with their enquiries, he incurred the wrath of several of the conspirators who did not wish him to give evidence and he was thereupon subjected to threats and intimidation.

Although Mr Norman was never charged with any offence, the police clearly believed that he was tainted. They issued a formal complaint to his professional body alleging that he had merely signed his name on his certificates and pocketed his fees, but that there was no documentation that a competent accountant would have considered as supportive of the claims themselves. For good measure the police submitted the report of their own forensic accountant, which concluded that the police complaint was justified.

In the circumstances it is not surprising that the Investigations Committee of Mr Norman's professional body passed the matter to the Disciplinary Committee for a full hearing, which took place some two years after the police report was received. With the support of his insurers, Mr Norman engaged the services of a forensic accountant who was able to demonstrate to the satisfaction of the Tribunal that the papers supporting the police report, and that of its own expert, consisted of photocopies of only the top page of the relevant bundle thus disregarding the abundant supporting documentation that lay beneath each of those pages. Although this fact should have been apparent to any careful scrutineer, it was ignored by the police and their expert.

The Tribunal accepted Mr Norman's evidence and that of his expert in a case that, in the Tribunal's view, should never have been brought. The Tribunal's findings almost read like an apology for the torment and professional disapprobation that he had endured. This case was instrumental in the decision of his professional body to initiate a new discretionary rule whereby, in appropriate circumstances, the body would reimburse the costs of members who had successfully defended charges brought against them.

Lessons to be noted

- Although the outcome was entirely in Mr Norman's favour, it had nevertheless been necessary for him to bear a substantial deductible ('excess') under his professional indemnity policy. He had also to endure damage to his practice caused by the time taken up in defending himself against the allegations.
- The most important lessons are as follows:
  - Mr Norman should have retained copies of the documents that he had examined and which provided a colour-coded audit trail to the claim summaries. This would have enabled him to rebut any suggestion of wrongdoing at the outset.
  - On being informed by his professional body that he would be required to defend himself against a serious complaint, Mr Norman should have co-operated fully with the Case Officer,

rather than adopt a 'knee-jerk' rebuttal position of simply denying everything.

- Appreciating the seriousness of his position and its potential consequences, Mr Norman should have engaged the services of independent expert assistance at a much earlier stage.

6.4 SUMMARY OF KEY LESSONS

- Abstract concepts such as independence, objectivity and integrity are never subject to factual proof, and yet they feature strongly in the day-to-day activity of accountants and auditors. In circumstances of material doubt, the only safe course is to avoid potential conflict by declining the relevant assignment.
- Consulting arrangements with professional colleagues will often alert firms to situations that could unwittingly have led them into a disciplinary process had they not sought advice on a timely basis.
- Circumspection is warranted before accepting appointments that do not fall naturally within a mainstream accountancy practice.
- Whenever a complaint to a professional body emanates from an official source the professional body's disciplinary machinery is bound to view the matter with the utmost seriousness.
- Accountants who are required to defend themselves against serious complaint should co-operate fully with the Case Officer, and not adopt a 'knee-jerk' rebuttal position of simply denying everything.

Appendix
From the Archives

In the wake of every financial scandal there is a familiar hue and cry about inadequate regulation, governance and audit. Financial columnists annotate the particular lessons that distinguish this crime from all others that have preceded it – lessons that must be learnt with great urgency if the financial markets are not to be plunged into another ruinous abyss.

When we stand back however we see that individual distinguishing features are not germane to the big picture, which has an eerie sense of déjà vu every time we behold it. It matters not whether the instruments of fraud take the form of forged certificates, fake krugerrands, futures contracts for tulips or securitised sub-prime mortgages. The real fraud is the fact that widespread faith in such ephemera has taken on a life of its own only to be found, too late, to be based on fiction.

By way of epilogue we prove the point by reproducing verbatim two original articles by Emile Woolf published in *Accountancy* magazine over 30 years ago, describing two of the greatest deceptions of all time – not necessarily in monetary terms (although the sums involved were prodigious by any standards) but in the monumental audacity of the perpetrators and the scale of purblind gullibility of those ensnared.

The astonishing fact that emerges from reading material drafted so many decades ago – such as when reading in the following section about Tino de Angelis, his network of corporate vehicles and the unwittingly complicit institutions that made his fraudulent practices possible – is that it is all too easy to substitute names such as Bernard Madoff, Robert Maxwell, Jeff Skilling, Lehman Brothers, Bear Stearns, Enron, WorldCom or Parmalat. It matters not whether the operative medium for the fraud's perpetrators was phantom oil, phantom insurance policies or, as occurred in one of the cases in this book, phantom hire purchase contracts.

Auditors inevitably find themselves in the firing line, and it is apparent from the second article concerning the Equity Funding story that auditors can easily be sucked in to the machinations of fraud when they allow themselves to become too close to the client. This has been true since the very beginning of auditing, and it is a syndrome that always results in the same symptoms, such as taking at face value management's excuse that the evidence you are seeking 'is scattered throughout the building, but we will make a special effort to have it available for you by tomorrow morning'. Another symptom is to allow the client to explain the workings of systems and controls and accepting these explanations without checking their operation at first hand.

These lessons are littered throughout the cases described in this book, and it seems that auditors continue to struggle to verify transactions, assets and financial instruments that they simply do not understand. Companies masterminded by inventive crooks will always devise forms of seemingly authentic currency, whether field warehouse receipts or exotic derivatives, whose credibility lies solely in the fact that there are markets peopled by gullible traders ever ready to generate ephemeral profits that have no substance.

Back in the 17th century, coffee houses in the City of London were a favourite venue for the issue of public prospectuses describing profitable undertakings in remote corners of the globe, in terms more glowing than justified by the circumstances. One of the most famous of these was a prospectus to secure a large proportion of the national debt on the illusory fortunes of the South Sea company; another proclaimed its purpose to be 'the extraction of silver from lead'; and yet another sought to raise funds for a project whereby 'quicksilver would be transmuted into a malleable fine metal'.

One villain had the effrontery to offer a prospectus 'for a special purpose nobody to know what it is', and, unbelievably, he cleared no less than £2,000 in the course of a single morning in the coffee house before disappearing, never to be seen again. If after the words 'special purpose' we were to add 'vehicle' we would be straight into Enron territory and the off balance sheet instruments that are just as obscure as those of the coffee house vendors 400 years ago.

In those days, of course, concepts such as regulation, governance or even audit were non-existent and the very prospectus frauds referred to above were instrumental in spawning the regulatory environment under which the business world is now compelled to labour – but it seems that the proliferation of rules, standards and ethical strictures have made precious little difference to the predatory instincts of a certain breed of unscrupulous, self-seeking individuals who, with the shameful support of batteries of legal advisors, will use detailed rules designed as a safeguard as a shield against their own incrimination.

THE ASTONISHING STORY OF THE 'SALAD OIL SWINDLE'

The great US salad oil swindle was first brought to light publicly, by a strange coincidence, on Friday 22 November 1963: the day President Kennedy was assassinated. From the publicity angle, its full dimensions were overshadowed by that momentous event, but there is no doubt that its impact, which lasted several years, was comparable with the great Wall Street crash 35 years earlier.

An extravagant claim? The eventual losses were beyond precise computation, but must be placed conservatively at around $200m, spread over some 51 major banking and brokerage concerns in the USA and Europe, a number of which were bankrupted in the process. So analogous was the 1963 collapse to that of 1929 that one thing is clear: whatever lessons were learnt in the 20s and 30s were forgotten by the 60s.

It is this fascinating question of whether there is in fact any benefit in hindsight, whether lessons of this order are *ever* really learnt, that makes it worthwhile reconsidering the salad oil swindle from our present vantage point; we may then discover whether it is merely the appearances that alter from generation to generation – the essential and causal ingredients remaining unchanged.

Ingredients of what? Let me quote from the last few lines of Norman Miller's penetrating analysis of the case:

> Viewed in a broad context, Tino's success as a master swindler was another indictment of the ethics of a vast segment of business. He flourished only because bankers, brokers and businessmen thought his success was to their advantage. The reason they were convinced that Tino's deals were good can be stated in a word – greed.

At a time when our normally unshakeable faith in the ability of the system to transcend all political and economic setbacks is at an unusually low ebb; when standards of morality in public and business life are seen to be eroding in a seemingly inexorable slide; when disclosures of flagrant bribery at international government level are sanctimoniously wafted away as 'necessities of modern business conduct', it is clearly relevant to have another look at the incredible world of Tino De Angelis and the business circles in which he moved in such unencumbered style. The story is a narrator's dream – it speaks for itself.

Tino De Angelis was a thoroughly unimpressive figure. His height and his girth were of comparable dimensions, he wore black-rimmed spectacles on his bland moon face, and nothing in his crumpled attire suggested a position in life more edifying than that of a pizza cook. Yet from early on it was clear that his driving ambition would lead him to great exploits.

He was born in the Bronx in 1915 of immigrant Italian parents who arrived in the New World at the turn of the century. His first experiences of free enterprise in action took place in the meat business where, by sheer industry, he rose through the ranks to become manager of 200 employees at the age of 20. After three arduous years, now married with a young family, he commenced business on his own account, borrowing $2,000 to get started. Within a further three years his firm was cutting up 3,000 hogs a day, and making an annual profit of $300,000. The key to his success in the meat trade lay in his simple observation that it was more economic to slaughter in the Midwest and transport frozen meat, than to follow the traditional practice of shipping live animals to the East for slaughter.

But even in those early days, questions concerning his character arose. He avoided the draft during the war because he was a major pork supplier to the army, but subsequent credit reports alleged that his wartime success was based on black market sales; charges, however, were never brought. Another accusation concerned the export of substandard cooking fat to Yugoslavia, for which offence he was obliged to pay $100,000 in damages. Undaunted, he acquired control of the Adoph Gobel meat-packing company, whose shares were listed on the stock exchange, and began supplying smoked meat under the government-aided school lunch programme. Allegations of inferior products and short-deliveries poured in, and further damages of $100,000 were paid. This, in turn, was followed by SEC allegations of understated losses in Gobel's published accounts, and the company was put into SEC-managed bankruptcy. Then another Angelis company was accused of exporting inferior lard to Germany, and 'the usual' damages of $100,000 were paid. His rise to the top over the next six years was thus hardly lacking in warnings to all who did business with him.

With a newly formed company, Allied Crude Vegetable Oil Refining Corporation, and $\$\frac{1}{2}$m in capital, he took advantage of the US government's 'Food for Peace' programme, which was designed to subsidise the export of major crop surpluses, including edible oils, by private US companies. Allied operated from Bayonne in the New Jersey docklands, with a leased 'farm' of old petroleum tanks which Tino (plus 22 loyal cohorts from his Gobel company) proceeded to convert into suitable edible oil storage containers.

Business thrived from the start. Although Tino was competing with the Midwest giant oil crushers, his crude oil offer bids always beat the opposition, while his low refined oil selling prices, with uncanny precision, clinched the export order every time. So impressed were the large East Coast oil export companies that they bought all their refined oil from Allied, and also agreed to use his storage facilities at Bayonne. Tino was effectively eliminating their biggest opposition in the Midwest, and they agreed to lend him millions of dollars to finance further expansion. Eventually, even the Midwest crushers gave up and decided to join him, his buy and sell pricing defying all opposition; and they too took advantage of his conveniently situated storage facilities. No one could fathom how he made any money out of these deals, but it suited them not to dig too deeply. Their export business was thriving and they welcomed the interest he paid on their loans.

However, as seemed inevitable with Tino, there were alleged frauds. These included falsified shipping papers under the Food for Peace programme; $1.5m of personal income tax evasion; and fake inventories at Gobel. The first two were dealt with by out-of-court settlements, and the latter charge was dropped when the key prosecution witness mysteriously changed his mind about his evidence and suffered a prolonged bout of 'assisted' amnesia.

There were also allegations of underworld connections. *Cosa Nostra* hoodlums with colourful names like Leo (The Mouse) Rugendorf and John (Donkey Ears) Wolek were said to have direct connections with Tino's partner in one of his Chicago companies. The company was consequently refused a fat-processing licence by the Chicago police department.

Despite Tino's record and shady connections he was never short of business associates. Whenever allegations were raised, he would blame his 'enemies' in the Agriculture ministry, or the Spanish Catholic *Opus Dei* organisation. But as long as Tino was assuring the major export companies of large revenues, he could avoid direct dealings with all official government agencies anyway: the exporters obtained the Food for Peace contracts and Allied supplied the oil. While the profits rolled in, the respectable businessmen with whom he dealt were prepared to overlook: (a) his credit reports; (b) the fact that major banks refused to open an Allied account; (c) his considerable record of offences; and (d) the disinclination of several foreign countries to accept his oil due to its inferior quality and packaging. (Coolies in Madras, for instance, had refused to carry the leaking cartons of rancid oil.)

On his domestic front, Tino appreciated the importance of ensuring the loyalty and devotion of his key assistants. Some of the 22 'old faithfuls' held eminent positions at Allied, while others played no obvious role, except that Tino simply liked to have them around. But they all responded to his every wish without question – hardly a surprise considering each and every one of them was paid exactly $400 per week, and most drove Cadillacs paid for by the company; not to mention the fringe benefits which, to put it mildly, were liberal.

When it came to obtaining favours in any quarter, Tino behaved like an automated cash dispenser; during the first four months of 1963, 'petty cash' cheques totalled $458,000. A demonstration of his method took place during a visit to Bayonne of a Pakistani businessman who threatened to raise the roof over several drums of oil shipped to his country which turned out to contain seawater instead. Tino simply passed him a fat envelope whose contents amounted to several thousand dollars; the contented gentleman left, promising to buy from Allied again! To quote Tino himself on the incident: 'You know – it was a petty larceny way of having to do business in the world today in some places'.

The US government's programme of Food for Peace had the effect of perpetuating, through subsidy, domestic crop surpluses, and was one of the major keys to Tino's prosperity. The oil exporting companies would not readily accept the currencies of the underdeveloped importing nations, so the deals were underwritten by the government out of taxpayers' money. However, only authorised companies exported under the scheme and Allied was not one of them – but the bulk of the revenues finished up with Allied anyway, since it was the largest refined oil supplier to the exporters of 85% of the programme.

Several banks, too, were heavily involved in the cut-throat commodities business as lenders, with the goods invariably acting as collateral. Millions were loaned in this way, on the strength of certified 'warehouse receipts', an ancient and obviously sensible banking practice. With substantial sums habitually tied up in inventories until they are sold, a solution to the cash flow problem is to borrow by pledging the inventories. The banks universally insist, however, that warehouse receipts should be issued independently by a specialist storage company whose responsibility it is to safeguard the goods, and to issue the receipts to banks or others as security for their loans.

A variation of this practice is for the storage company to establish a 'field warehouse' on the property of the borrowing company. In practice, the field warehouse may simply be a section of the normal warehouse facility; in effect, the warehousing company merely places its own name on the particular storage area. It was also common practice for the warehousing company to 'co-opt' certain of the customer's employees onto its own payroll. As one field warehouse company's promotional booklet put it: 'Our desire is to avoid any disturbance of the routine operating procedure'.

The security defects in a system of such contrived independence are glaring. Since the warehousing company charges for the salaries of the guards it co-opts, their removal from the original payroll is purely notional. Warehouse receipt frauds, not surprisingly, were by no means unknown before Tino's crew entered the arena; yet the lending banks displayed an irresponsible degree of laxity in this direction. Anyone who at that time unsuccessfully approached a bank for a relatively small personal loan would have been staggered at the casual manner in which the same bank happily parted with millions of dollars on the strength of a piece of paper claiming that goods, which it had never seen, existed in a warehouse – so tempting was the bait of lucrative loan interest. It was precisely this blinkered unconcern that Tino so shrewdly observed, and then exploited.

Tino's big break came in 1957 when the chief executive of the field warehousing subsidiary of American Express, Donald Miller, was searching for a new and lucrative operation in which his loss-making company might engage. The American Express parent had set a \$0.5m profit target for each subsidiary activity but, despite a heavy sales drive by Miller, American Express Field Warehousing was still losing money. Then one of Tino's cousins called on Miller, turned on the charm and showed him round the impressive new Bayonne refining plant.

The results of Miller's enquiry into Allied's background would have deterred anyone less hungry for earnings. It was obvious to Miller that with Tino's record Allied had no direct access to normal credit facilities. But Tino had openly pointed out to him that bank money would find its way to Allied via the large and eminently respectable export companies, who were perfectly willing to lend on the strength of warehouse receipts, provided they were issued by a reputable warehousing company. They, in turn, would obtain bank loans covered by their oil in Tino's tanks, as certified by the irreproachable American Express stamp.

Could the bank decline? Hardly, considering the multi-million dollar business they were already doing in American Express travellers' cheques, all supported by deposits, of course. So Tino was the catalyst in a carefully structured arrangement which ensured that he was the chief beneficiary.

Although from time to time Miller had to deal with rumblings about the total ineffectiveness of the periodic inventory checks, as well as unauthorised movements of oil in his company's section of the tank farm, it was not until mid-1960 that the first real alarm bells sounded.

A mysterious telephone caller named Taylor, who claimed to be on the Allied night shift, warned Miller on several occasions that 'the biggest hoax ever pulled is being pulled on American Express because there is in fact water in the tanks, and we are counting it as oil'. The caller demanded $5,000 for more specific information, and although Miller made no promises he managed to obtain a few details. Taylor claimed, as an instance, that in the largest tank, number 6006, a metal chamber had been constructed, immediately beneath the sampling hole. *'Whenever we went to take inventory at that tank'* he confessed to Miller, *'we would be dropping the weight into this metal chamber which was filled with soybean oil, but the balance of the tank had water in it'*.

Miller immediately ordered a surprise inspection of the tank farm, which lasted a week. On the first day, a Saturday, the inspectors found water in the first five tanks they checked. When they returned after the weekend, however, nothing suspicious was found in the other 65 tanks. The sampling devices collected a cross section of each tank's contents, which were then sent for chemical analysis – unbelievably to Allied's own 'chief chemist'. Miller felt *'Allied ought to know what was in their own tanks'*, he later testified. The report on tank 6006 was 'inconclusive, since there were a number of sampling holes on top, and the inspectors were directed throughout the investigation by one of Tino's faithful lieutenants. The water in the first five tanks was officially attributed to 'broken steam pipes'.

Taylor's allegations were brushed aside as 'fantastic'. Yet, more than three years later, after Allied had gone bankrupt, inspectors opened up the main tap on tank 6006 – which was supposed to contain $3.575m worth of soybean oil – and seawater poured out for twelve days. The tank's floating roof sank lower and lower until the false chamber, welded to its underside and containing a few hundred pounds of soybean oil, came gently to rest on the bottom of the tank.

The obvious truth (for anyone who cared to look) was that Tino pledged warehouse receipts *ad lib* and retained just enough oil in his tanks to meet known physical demands – the same principle whereby banks retain in the till only the cash needed to cover anticipated calls. His tanks were interconnected by a complicated network of pipes; were rigged with false compartments and top-to-bottom 'sampling' tubes. He knew that he had little to fear from the casual American Express inspections.

In fact, he went still further and enlisted the services of the Harbor Tank Storage Company to run another field warehousing operation over a further 41 tanks in the Bayonne tank farm. So eager was Harbor Tank to oblige that they neglected to so much as check whether Allied had leasing rights over the tanks. Even a cursory check would have shown that of the 41 tanks in question, 23 were in fact already leased out to petroleum storage companies, seven were literally falling apart and unfit for use, one was non-existent, and only 10 were legitimate. The notional capacity of the Harbor Tank complex was a stock of 412 million pounds of oil – 393 million more than the actual contents which emerged from the 10 genuine tanks in 1963! Tino, as usual, arranged for a senior member of his '22 club' to 'assist' the Harbor Tank personnel who, on their own frank admission, 'knew nothing about the oil business'.

Of course, there was only a limited amount of oil to begin with at Bayonne, and so the main task was to convince the slack American Express checkers that the tanks were really full. In effect, one of Tino's henchmen would provide the 'numbers' required for each category of merchandise *in advance* of each Friday's official 'stocktaking' and on the Saturday the genuine stocks were checked by Allied's own staff. This enabled them to ensure they held sufficient quantities of oil to fulfil actual order requirements when they arose. One such typical 1961 accurate inventory disclosed 62 million pounds of oil – against outstanding warehouse receipts of 157 million pounds.

Allied staff had to become increasingly more resourceful, however, as the quantity of phantom oil on the records rose higher and higher. On one occasion in 1960 the warehouse staff were suddenly given four days' leave. When they returned several tanks, which they knew to be empty when they left, were brimful with seawater. Everyone knew about it; even the dockland taverns were buzzing with the information. Many of the staff were worried, and later admitted that they were looking for other jobs – but Tino's policy of paying twice as much as anyone else worked like a charm, just as he intended: they stayed on and kept their mouths shut.

Had Miller, at that time, read the statistical report published by the US Census Bureau, he would have observed that the oil supposedly stored at Bayonne, and supported by his company's warehouse receipts, *totalled twice as much as all the oil in the country*! So blind was Miller's trust in Tino that he even arranged the ultimate coup: a loan of $600,000 for Allied from his own parent company, American Express. The security? Need you ask? Tino provided them with one of their *own* phony warehouse receipts as collateral!

By the close of 1963 the warehouse receipts in issue represented close on 937 million pounds of oil (worth $87.5m); the actual quantities were below 100 million pounds. If a 10% 'liquidity' ratio was good enough for the big banks, it was good enough for Tino!

It was his pride that ultimately proved to be his downfall. He lost (through the intrigues of his old enemy, *Opus Dei* – he claimed) a large and valuable Spanish export order in the Autumn of 1961, against the execution of which Allied had bought heavily in the oil futures market – not surprising, since there was not enough genuine oil at Bayonne to fill even one-fifth of the 275 million pounds order. Not content to withdraw quietly, he held onto the oil futures, so sure was he of finding a foreign buyer to step in. The risks implicit were enormous: $18m would be needed if Allied had to take up the contract, while even a half-cent-per-pound drop in price at any time before delivery date would mean finding $1m within 24 hours in order to meet the commodity exchange margin requirements. To make matters even more risky the official export market reports were the most pessimistic in years. (Tino actually believed that even the market reports were deliberately fabricated by his 'secret enemies' and refused to give them any credence.)

Thus began a prolonged and sustained programme of futures buying, such as the commodity exchanges have never witnessed, either before or since. Not being an exchange member, Allied did its buying through as many different brokerage houses as would take on its business. This gave the impression (needed to push up the prices) that demand was coming from several sources, rather than a purely solo effect from Allied. Several brokers, such as Merrill Lynch, would not touch Allied because of Tino's criminal and bankruptcy record, but some three or four others succumbed to the temptation of the rich commission pickings provided by Allied's futures spree.

Despite the strenuous efforts of Tino's overseas sales team, no foreign Food for Peace orders came in to justify the heights to which the brokers, acting on his instructions, were driving the prices of soybean and cottonseed oil futures. He spoke confidently about heavy demand from Poland, Yugoslavia, Pakistan and Egypt: even though there was some substance in these stories, the precariousness of Tino's position should have been obvious: a company buys futures as a hedge against *firm* orders, not *hopes* for orders. The Chicago Board of Trade and the Commodity Exchange Authority investigated his position in the spring of 1963, and found that he had inadvertently but illegally traded with himself in an apparent effort to avoid taking delivery of future orders. Tino was suspended for 30 days for violating the 'fictitious trading' rules. But such was his momentum, so great were the commissions on his deals, and so weak were the rules against price-rigging by creating a 'corner' in the market, that Tino's buying surge continued unabated.

In May 1963 Tino persuaded one of the largest and most respectable firms of Wall Street brokers, Haupt & Co, to trade for him on the large New York Produce Exchange. Haupt was itself planning expansion and despite early misgivings, was ensnared by the tempting commissions.

Market reports became still gloomier with news of bumper foreign crops, but Tino was undeterred. Each time prices dropped Allied had to pay cash to cover the margins. Money was also needed to cover the losses of all the friends and associates whom Tino had persuaded to speculate on his behalf. Although he was issuing warehouse receipts at an alarming pace, still more money was needed. The tempo of the fraud took on new dimensions.

Tino arranged for an insider at the Bunge Corporation, one of the largest oil exporting companies, to hold back Allied's interest cheques, while recording the receipts as having been deposited. Given the size of the loans this saved a fortune in further interest charges. Further, Bunge often sold to Allied warehouse receipts which were registered with the commodity exchanges, since the latter insisted upon these to support the maturing futures contracts. Bunge would not accept payment for these registered receipts in the form of cheques drawn on Allied's own North Bergen Bank, but insisted on payment by cheque drawn on a major New York bank.

The normal practice was simply for North Bergen to advise its New York correspondent, Manufacturers Hanover Trust (MHT), to issue a 'cashier's cheque' to Bunge – transported by Allied messenger, of course. To suppress the MHT cheque would have been no use, since MHT charged North Bergen as soon as the cheque was issued, and North Bergen debited Allied. So Tino's insider at Bunge, once the pressure was on, would take the official MHT cheque (rarely less than denominations of \$1m) to the mens' lavatory, and pass it back to Allied's messenger in exchange for an ordinary Allied cheque, which would then lie indefinitely in the insider's desk drawer – the Bunge records showing that Allied had settled. The messenger would then return, as unused and not required, the MHT cheque to source – 15 minutes after it was first issued! When Allied went bankrupt, 26 such cheques were found in the insider's drawer.

Tino's mad buying had pushed prices so high that his actual chances of gaining export orders were all but extinguished anyway. Nor did anyone take the trouble to notice that he would hardly have needed all that oil if his tanks at Bayonne held what had been pledged by the American Express and Harbor Tank warehouse receipts. *On paper*, in late 1963, his holdings at Bayonne and in the futures market had mounted to 2 billion pounds – more than the total ever exported from the USA in a single year. The position was clearly desperate; the slightest drop in the price of oil futures, which were now under very strong pressure, would result in staggering losses. He had fallen into his own trap and was forced to keep up the senseless buying.

Meanwhile, Howard Clark, President of American Express, discovered that Donald Miller of his warehousing subsidiary had purchased 1,000 shares in Gobel, still listed on the stock exchange. Incensed with this breach of the group's 'conflict of interest' rules, and disturbed by comments surrounding the ineffectual nature of stock control at Bayonne, Clark ordered a thorough investigation by Haskins & Sells, the parent auditors, as a prelude to selling the subsidiary.

They caused no problems for Tino. Here is their report:

> 'We found that the plan of organisation provides for the usual segregation of functional responsibilities as between operating and accounting departments; the existing system of authority and record procedures provides reasonable accounting controls; sound accounting practices are being followed, and the quality of personnel appeared commensurate with assigned responsibilities. . . . In our opinion, on the basis of our review, the system of internal controls of American Express Warehousing is satisfactory'.

The prospect of the sale of the warehousing company, at the same time as his most urgent need for cash, caused Tino to throw all caution to the winds. He stole a pad of blank American Express warehouse receipts and proceeded to flood Wall Street with a deluge of fraudulent paper.

Haupt, the brokers, were so enchanted with the unprecedented commissions they were earning on the oil futures deals that they obligingly loaned Allied $2.5m, also on the strength of warehouse receipts, and agreed to forego the requirement for Allied to pay cash to cover margins. Haupt met the exchange margin requirements itself and borrowed from its own bankers in turn – once again using Tino's 'do-it-yourself' warehouse receipts as collateral cover.

The end had to come. In November 1963 the exchanges and government commodity agencies finally realised that no one wanted the oil at the astronomical prices to which Tino had driven it; and alarm began to spread among the brokerage houses when they realised (a) that they were all buying for Allied rather than for independent purchasers, and (b) that between them they held, *all on behalf of Allied,* 90% of all the contracts on the Exchange.

A Commodity Exchange Authority investigator marched in on Tino and demanded to inspect his records. The buying suddenly stopped; Tino's brokers stood on the exchange floor, awaiting his usual late afternoon buying instructions, but the telephone was silent. Prices plummeted, and by the following week Allied was in the hands of a bankruptcy trustee.

Haupt struggled to muster enough funds to cover its commitments, but failed, bankrupting all of its 15 partners overnight. Bunge presented the Allied cheques in desperation, but they bounced the same day. And everyone started scrambling for the oil.

The prolonged legal in-fighting and bitter wrangling that followed the collapse of Allied involved: the wide range of banks who found themselves holding worthless warehouse receipts; the brokerage houses who had covered Tino during the futures adventure; the export companies whose stocks of high grade oil turned out to be either non-existent or pledged to holders of warehouse receipts executed without authority; and, of course, American Express who, despite early protestations of full settlement in order to preserve the quality of its name, placed the warehousing subsidiary into bankruptcy and proceeded to play the game remarkably close to the legal rule book – especially when its insurers started reading out the small print on non-disclosure and misrepresentation of material facts.

But the acrimonious aftermath is really another story. Even Tino managed to avoid being brought to justice for almost two years, after which he was awarded 10 years for his pains. None of the subsequent scrambling helped to bring back the money. What Tino did with all those hundreds of millions of dollars was never fully accounted for, so ineffective, almost non-existent, were Allied's accounting records between 1960 and the collapse three years later. The bank's records simply showed that the money went out as fast as it came in – often through another company in the complex group which Tino had set up; or, equally often, via cheques drawn for cash.

What of the oil? *The Wall Street Journal* on 2 December 1963 reported the swindle, and stated that the missing salad oil would never be found for one simple reason: it did not exist.

What is one to make of this phenomenal story? What questions, let alone answers, does it prompt which are equally relevant today? Certain, almost incidental, morals may obviously be drawn: the management of the earnings hungry company will turn a blind eye and a deaf ear whenever its position is seriously threatened by unpalatable warning signs. It is true that without profits there is no business; but that does not justify making profits the only measure of a man's value to a company. Take Donald Miller, senior executive of the American Express warehousing subsidiary; he was measured by his company's revenue account, and this system 'breeds a pursuit of the dollar by any means, and thus may destroy ethics', to quote author Norman Miller. Tino always sensed, and fully exploited, this vulnerability of senior and middle management areas.

What about Allied's own auditors? They never featured at all. Allied was a private company with Tino as the main shareholder, and was not subject to SEC regulation. Unless one were looking for yet another scapegoat, it is obvious that any attempt at a meaningful enquiry by its auditors would have been a waste of time. Why should they, after all, have had less trust in independently certified commodity receipts carrying the American Express provenance, and based on procedures approved by *their* auditors, than, say, the Chase Manhattan, First National City, Bank of America, Schroders or Hill Samuel – all of whom were included in the 51 institutions which lost money when Tino's bubble burst?

Bunge attempted, at times, to ensure that its oil was safe: for instance, four tanks in the American Express section were earmarked for their exclusive use. Yet they encountered insuperable difficulties each time they attempted to verify actual contents. In the cold months contents would solidify, making normal sampling procedures impracticable; and when the contents were liquid it was only with the greatest difficulty that precise chemical analysis of the category, grade and quality of the particular edible oil could be determined – even by experts. These difficulties were compounded by two further factors: (a) it was a simple matter to open the interconnecting valves and oil would flow from one tank into another at a remote corner of the mazelike Bayonne farm, and

(b) it was impossible in Tino's set-up ever to feel sure of where staff allegiance lay. Tino was fast with the dollar – many dollars, in fact; and when enough people are involved, apparently outrageous practice all too easily becomes a way of life.

But the saga's real message is discovered only when one stands back from the scandalous mechanics of Tino's gorgeous charade and adopts a broad view. What one then sees is that Tino was not in the oil business at all. He was in the money business. The oil merely provided the notional backing. Bank money manifests in notes and coin, treasury bills, letters of credit, travellers cheques, money orders, etc – Tino's money took on a more straightforward and consistent appearance: American Express and Harbor Tank warehouse receipts. It was certainly not the absence of oil that ultimately defeated him; that part of the swindle was brilliant in both conception and execution, and was virtually self-perpetuating – as long as there was enough in store (a) to maintain the trust upon which each and every credit system ultimately rests, and (b) to meet such actual delivery commitments as arose in the course of trading.

It was the speculation in oil futures which proved to be his downfall. He was convinced that that too was a self-perpetuating cycle, as follows: he called the prices; the prices bolstered the value of his phantom inventories; the inventories provided the substance for the warehouse receipts; the warehouse receipts provided collateral for unlimited finance; the finance supported the oil futures deals; the deals determined the prices . . . isn't this where we came in? A myth supporting a myth supporting a. . . .

Putting it bluntly, Tino, with his Bronx background and blackened record, had ingeniously discovered a method of having the pillars of the commercial and financial establishment print money to order, for the sole benefit of himself and his loyal and trusted circle.

His system was beyond audit. Does the auditor of a bank verify the worth of the substance which the notes and bonds purport to represent? Does it matter, for cxample, that part of our money in circulation is financing the national debt, which will never be repaid? What should the auditors say about that? As long as the currency is trusted – nothing. On this basis Tino's currency could have carried on almost indefinitely, since the widespread faith in the establishment's paper was effectively conferred upon Tino.

Looked at in this way, even his theft of the blank pad of American Express warehouse receipts was less horrific than might at first appear: he merely borrowed the printing press for a while!

THE EQUITY FUNDING STORY

The 'crime of the century' took place during the 'sixties and 'seventies at Equity Funding, the USA financial services and life assurance group. Although the conception of the fraud required no computer, other than to provide immensity of scale, it was the first widely publicised case of computer crime, which demonstrated the manipulative possibilities of electronic data processing when it comes under the untrammelled control of the criminal mind, while also subject to totally ineffective audit.

The early '60s saw the initial growth of Equity Funding Corporation of America (EFCA), a financial services company with a modest capital of 100,000 shares issued to the public in 1963 at £6 per share. At first its trading followed a normal pattern of separately marketing life insurance and mutual fund shares, but its visionary founders soon saw an opportunity of making each dollar of income work twice.

To exploit the scheme, it was necessary for them to acquire their own insurance company, whereas previously they had simply acted as an agency, selling other companies' policies and mutual fund shares.

In 1966 EFCA formed its own mutual fund, and acquired another from Bernie Cornfeld's IOS (whose own collapse was almost as spectacular). They also acquired four insurance companies, including one which they renamed Equity Funding Life Insurance Company (EFLIC), and which they singled out as the prime vehicle for the dirty deeds which followed. Within days of the acquisition, the existing board and senior management were sacked and replaced by EFCA officers.

The Equity Funding concept was unique yet simple – and was marketed by exploiting that human failing whereby one desires more life cover than one can afford. This, of course, is just an extension of the necessary myth on which all life insurance is based; no one wants to die, yet the evidence suggests its inevitability; therefore the concept of life insurance (an obvious contradiction) provides some secondary consolation.

Of the four initial entrepreneurs of Equity Funding, only one, Stanley Goldblum, survived to carry their idea through to its ultimate consummation.

The idea was to offer mutual fund shares and life insurance in an attractive package to middle-income families. Each year the participant would acquire shares in the mutual fund, against the security of which he would borrow money from EFCA to pay the premiums on a life policy with EFLIC. The expectation (which sounded like a certainty when explained by the salesman) was that the income from the shares, together with their appreciation in value, would exceed the cost of the borrowing. Normally the 'programme' ran for a 10-year period, the participant paying cash in instalments for the mutual fund shares. EFCA paid the premiums and retained the shares as a security for premiums advanced. In essence, therefore, the participator's life insurance was funded by his equity in the mutual shares investment.

As each year's renewal premium and loan interest (at 6% to 10%) fell due, the loan was increased and the participant purchased additional shares to cover the amount of the loan increase. At the end of the 10-year period, the loan was repaid, either by the sale of a sufficient number of the shares, or by applying the surrender value of the life policy, or directly in cash, or by a combination of these methods. What is absolutely clear, of course, is that the success of the package depended upon a steady increase in the value of the mutual fund shares, which in turn required a generally rising stock market. Never stated at the time, however, was that the only certainty about the scheme was the two commissions received by the salesman!

Whatever happened to the shares, the loan had eventually to be repaid. Rather than a 'two-for-one' advantage, the buyer bought a potential 'two-for-one' disadvantage, and paid two commissions on the same dollars: once on the insurance and once on the mutual shares. Thus was formed the main platform of EFCA's success – a sales force which stood to gain twice as much as most others in the field. In 1964, the number of salesmen stood at around 500; by 1972, it had grown to more than 4,200, operating in 152 branch offices. It is therefore no surprise that throughout the '60s the growth of EFCA was swift and spectacular. This growth is clearly seen in the accompanying table.

Equity Funding's growth record ($m)

	1964	1968	1971
Total revenues	2.8	19.2	131.0
Net profits	0.4	7.8	19.0
Total assets	9.3	79.0	497.0

The December 1972 accounts, which were prepared but never published, showed a further 17% increase in net profits to $23m. The company's earnings per share had compounded on paper at an average annual rate since 1961 of 60.79% – which made it the fastest growing financial services organisation in the USA!

With the company's shares being publicly traded, its earnings became a matter of intense concern – especially among the salesmen and executives themselves, who were offered EFCA stock at attractive prices as 'production bonuses'. It was therefore in their interests that the market price of the company's stock should continue on the upward path which inevitably followed reports of increased earnings. But for Stanley Goldblum, Fred Levin, Sam Lowell and the inner circle of senior officers with vast holdings of EFCA stock, it was even more vital. Had EFCA stock maintained its price in 1973, for example, Levin's 4,000 bonus shares would have effectively doubled his $100,000 salary! Further, a healthy growth record was essential for the issue of new capital, and was also the first prerequisite for entry into the conglomerate game par excellence: merger by acquisition, on a simple stock-for-stock basis.

It was therefore clear that whatever the means of achieving it, the end had to be a continuous rise in reported earnings.

The underlying objective behind this vast deception was thus clear enough, and it united, with single-minded dedication and resourcefulness, the handful of men responsible for perpetrating it. What follows is a summary of their activities.

One of the main avenues selected for the fraud lay in the common practice of re-insurance. In 1969 EFLIC announced that all employees who requested it would be issued with free life cover for one year. The amounts insured were substantial, in some cases (depending on status) up to $50,000, and there was an option to continue the policy after the first year. As expected, of course, the majority of those who accepted the offer cancelled after the year of grace. In the meantime, however, the free insurance had been re-insured with other unsuspecting companies, EFLIC having received cash from them equal to 180% of the renewal premium; moreover, EFLIC had no salesmen's commission to pay. It was therefore a device for obtaining an immediate cash and earnings boost, leaving the re-insuring company with a virtually worthless asset.

But the conspirators did not let the matter rest there. When the December 1970 year-end accounts were being prepared, it became obvious to certain key employees that 'additional' business was being inserted. Whichever way the genuine figures were extrapolated – such as on the basis of monthly totals submitted from branches, or of salesmen's commissions earned – it was clear that the final accounts figure was more than double the most optimistic reckoning. By mid-November 1970, the face amount of actual life insurance produced in the year had reached $375m (the 1969 accounts had reported $370m). Then the weekly management reports ceased, ostensibly for the year-end accounts preparation. Early in 1971, Pat Hopper, the senior executive responsible for sales, was amazed to learn from Fred Levin that EFLIC had written $826m in life insurance in 1970!

Nor did the published report itself make any sense to him: it declared that more than 31,000 mutual funding/life cover schemes were in existence, whereas Hopper had reported to Levin, for annual accounts purposes, that the total number of such files was 18,000 to 21,000. A year later the genuine funding files still totalled around 18,000 (ie surrenders and new business approximately cancelled each other out). Yet the 1971 annual report declared that there were 41,121 funding programmes operative.

Declaring fictitious business was one thing; producing the necessary back-up records was quite another. And this is where the computer came in. EFCA used an IBM 370/145 computer, which it ran in an open-shop service-bureau environment, serving about 100 EFCA subsidiaries and associates. The EFLIC actuarial department, responsible for producing the fake business, was treated as just another user.

There was a special code ('99') for bogus business, obviously unrecognisable to most staff (and certainly to the auditors), and the machine was programmed to skip these policies when running the monthly billings; this was essential, since none of the persons insured under these policies actually existed. In the open-house environment there was unrestricted access to the programs, the master files and the machine. It has been suggested in *Datamation* that what probably happened was that an EFLIC actuary or other DP user gained access to the live master file and regularly created a volume of 'test' data which would be blended with 'real' data, and would then become part of the scheduled input next time the master files were updated. As the contrived business became more sophisticated, EFLIC staff would run the same fake policies through three or four times; or a $10,000 policy could be rerun as $50,000, and so on. The permutations were virtually without limit.

In most cases these false records did not need to be supported by actual file documentation. However, whenever the auditors dutifully asked to see files containing the policy applications, medical histories, transmittal and settlement sheets and other papers, they were told that the files were scattered throughout the building and that they would be available the next day. This left enough time for the files to be ‘manufactured’ with every appearance of authenticity.

Occasionally the auditors sought independent outside confirmation directly from the insured. The EFLIC staff were always helpful in providing a ‘random’ selection of names and addresses from the master files. In fact, these were always those of co-operative employees who, having been briefed that the auditors were ‘running a computer test’, dutifully filled out the confirmations and returned them to the auditors – who were no doubt surprised at the high response rate!

Several computer staff became suspicious, but were strangely disinclined to report their feelings, fearing the consequences of biting the hand that fed them so well; the organisation was so fragmented that it was always tempting to regard one’s doubts as groundless and misguided. One manager, for example, noticed that there was a significant blank of 12,000 numbers in the policy number sequence on the master file. A few days later, running a test on some ‘real’ files, he was surprised to find that several of these carried unique numbers that fell into that space. Had he put two and two together he might have guessed, correctly, that the 12,000 blanks had been specially set aside for bogus entries.

The fake business was known internally by several euphemisms: ‘Stanley Goldblum’s Friends’, ‘The Chicago Telephone Directory’ and others. The number of fake policies created may be estimated conservatively at 11,000 in 1970; 45,000 in 1971; and, unbelievably, 64,000 in 1972 – twice as many as the genuine ones. And the EFLIC group was not content simply to ‘re-insure’ these policies once: many were re-insured as often as four times, with four different companies. A major assisting factor was, of course, the absence of any sales commissions – normally anything up to a full year’s premium.

Yet another convenient way of creating fictitious business was to keep genuine policies alive after they had been lapsed or surrendered. It was merely necessary to continue recording the premium payments. Thus a further source of suspicion, for anyone who was prepared to look, was the apparently declining percentage of lapsed policies each year – by 1972 lapses were virtually non-existent.

The naivety of the re-insurance companies was staggering. The fact is that not one of the companies which bought thousands of bogus policies from EFLIC lifted a finger to check whether these policies so much as existed. As far as they were concerned they were buying an entitlement to future premiums, and nothing else seemed to matter. As one re-insurance department head put it later: 'The insurance industry is like a club; you trust people'.

The question arises, of course, as to how the premiums were paid by EFLIC to the re-insurers in the second and subsequent years of a fake policy's existence. The answer is, in two ways: first, by generating and re-insuring still more fake new business, thus creating a totally phantom inverted pyramid, which would undoubtedly have toppled in ruins had it not been for the second ploy. This was to programme the 'deaths' of selected non-existent 'lives', thus (a) terminating the need to pay any more premiums on those policies, and (b) providing a welcome cash influx from the re-insurer which had acquired the risk, representing the capital death benefit insured. Providing the supporting death certificates proved no problem at all, for EFLIC ran its own printing shop!

When the monolithic edifice was dismantled in 1973, it became obvious that the fake business was by no means confined to EFLIC. The parent company, EFCA, adopted a number of devices to boost its assets position 'creatively', including the age-old method of simply forging securities. The chief printer was given specimen copies of blue chip share certificates, with instructions to reproduce them on metal plates and to run off a specified number. He was told: 'We're using them in a presentation by our investment department – they're working on new retirement programmes'. There were also specific instructions to destroy all the waste afterwards. Later, when the fraud was blazoned all over the newspapers, the printer described how he did his own sums: he listed the names of all the companies whose certificates he had created, and next to each name he entered the size of the print run. He looked up the stock prices in *The Los Angeles Times* and carried out the multiplication. He could hardly believe the result – it exceeded $100m!

This intense need to create bogus assets was an essential part of the acquisition game, whereby more profitable companies (with a higher earnings per share ratio) would be acquired by means of a straightforward share exchange. The basis agreed with the other shareholders would naturally rest on the apparent value of the EFCA stock issued in exchange; in effect, EFCA was steadily acquiring genuinely valuable scrip in return for its own worthless paper: the key to a financial fountain of youth.

The earnings and assets of the companies acquired (whose officers were invariably sacked and replaced by EFCA people) would then be parasitically transferred to EFCA by means of appropriate book entries and completely bogus charges. In the case of profitable life insurance subsidiaries, this had the incidental effect of robbing their participating stockholders of the profits to which they were entitled under their policies. The overall effect of these life-giving injections was, of course, to conceal the totally unprofitable state of the parent company.

No device was too far-fetched for Goldblum, Levin, the company's chief accountant Mike Sultan, its actuary Arthur Lewis or its treasurer Lloyd Edens. Even the time-lag between Los Angeles and the east coast was used to good effect: on one occasion a \$3m bank balance was 'shipped' from a New York subsidiary to EFCA in Los Angeles for three hours, so that at close of business on the year-end date it appeared in the records of both companies!

Fred Levin also dealt with the auditors when they decided to telephone Equity's branch managers all over the USA to confirm directly the amount of insurance/funding business on record. The calls were made from the audit room in Equity's offices, and the enquiries were based on a detailed schedule of insurance/funding programmes allegedly in existence at each branch.

The purpose of the exercise was sound enough: by this means the auditors would be able to reconcile the total business carried out by the group with the individual branch returns.

In the event, however, the test proved to be a farce: Fred Levin, having instructed the switchboard to alert him whenever the auditors used the telephone, had all the calls to outside branch managers diverted straight into his office. Depending upon where the branch in question was located, he carefully put on the appropriate voice and accent, and duly confirmed the amounts called over by the auditors.

Two errors of judgement therefore emerge – with hindsight, of course. Firstly, the calls should have been made from the auditor's own offices, thereby avoiding any possibility of internal tampering; secondly, the auditors should not have volunteered the information sought, thus merely requiring a straightforward 'yes/no' confirmation.

Although it would not have been foolproof (since Levin may have had a copy of the auditors' schedule in front of him at the time), the test would certainly have been more authentic if the auditors had required the 'manager' to provide detailed figures in response to their enquiries.

EFCA increased its borrowings by \$44m during 1971 and 1972 through public issues, yet cash flow continued to be a problem. Furthermore, the inter-company accounts became vastly out of balance; whenever EFLIC issued a new insurance/funding programme it would 'sell' this to its parent and show it as receivable in the intercompany account – yet EFCA never recorded liability and no cash ever passed.

By the end of 1971 the imbalance was $16m, which was then settled by a transfer from EFCA out of the proceeds of a public issue, thus clearing the account in EFLIC's books. However, the transfer was recorded differently in the books of EFCA. The bank advice on the transfer was intercepted by Mike Sultan, who altered it to show the $16m as a purchase of commercial bills, with a 'redemption date' shortly before the December 1971 year-end; the aim being to avoid attempts by the auditors to verify the fake investment. On this redemption date, the actual cash came back from EFLIC, who recorded it as a loan to EFCA. But in EFCA's books even $177,000 in fictitious interest on the 'commercial paper' was included in the 'redemption'. The non-discovery of the disparity was due to the fact that EFCA and EFLIC had different auditors; and as the bogus investment had 'matured' and the cash had been received, EFCA auditors made no attempt at independent confirmation. Throughout this intensive 'debit creation' exercise (whether for fake assets or cash received), the corresponding credit was always the same: earnings, earnings, earnings.

It was the aim of Goldblum and company that the highly profitable acquisition business would render it unnecessary to keep up the deception at this alarming level. In February 1973, in order to improve the cash flow, Goldblum launched a stringent cost-cutting exercise. Unfortunately (from his point of view), this resulted in the sudden dismissal of one of EFLIC's administrative officers, Ronald Secrist, who promptly 'blew the whistle' on the conspirators by talking to the Illinois state insurance officials and to Raymond Dirks, a securities analyst who specialised in insurance company stocks. At first the hearers were incredulous, and attributed the fantastic story to Secrist's bitterness at the peremptory manner of his dismissal. But Dirks persisted with probing enquiries, and the pieces gradually began to fit until no reasonable doubt remained about the fraud's grotesque dimensions.

Secrist had known a good deal, of course, and he was totally forthcoming in his declarations: the senior officers of the company were not merely complicit in the crime – they were its architects. Goldblum had not resorted to devices in bad years in order to 'plug a dyke' – he had built it.

Raymond Dirks was convinced that EFCA stock was worthless paper, and was determined to make the facts known. This naturally produced a flurry of trading in EFCA stock, coinciding with (a) Goldblum's persistent denials that there was any substance to the rumours; (b) the state insurance department's surprise audit as a result of Secrist's disclosures; and (c) the pre-publication preparation of the company's 1972 annual report.

But Goldblum could not halt the slide. The price of the eight million EFCA shares on the New York Stock Exchange fell from just under $30 per share at the beginning of March 1973 to $14 by the 27th. At the end of March the Securities & Exchange Commission (SEC) halted trading, and on 2 April the disaster was all over the newspapers. On 4 April the company was put into bankruptcy, facing claims of over $10bn in courts throughout the USA. The 10-year game was over.

The state investigators now worked in earnest to salvage the genuine assets of the group, unwittingly hampered by their offices being bugged – Goldblum and Levin listening to the tapes every night and thus being able to anticipate the next move. The investigators were in for some shocks. The EFLIC balance sheet dated 31 December 1972 (never published) included securities held at bank of $24m. On enquiry it transpired that the EFLIC account had been cleared out 10 months previously – there was nothing at the year-end; no cash, no stocks. The auditors had been sent a totally fraudulent confirmation at the year end, mailed by the conspirators (from the false bank address which they had given the auditors) after signing it 'Joseph S Phillips, second vice-president'. No such person had ever worked at the bank. Those banks which actually held EFCA balances virtually set these off against outstanding loans and overdrafts, despite the dubious legality of so doing. In the scramble for pieces, all constraints were thrown to the winds.

Lack of space prevents me from describing every post-exposure discovery in detail. No doubt what has been written so far suffices to indicate the lengths to which the ever-resourceful conspirators were prepared to go in order to maintain their pretence until they had acquired enough legitimate business to phase out the aberrations slowly, and bury the fraud forever. Their over-riding objective had been the maintenance of the price of the company's stock. With valuable shares, EFCA could exchange these for healthy companies; and high stock prices kept the salesmen happy since their remuneration included stock options. The one factor was totally dependent on the other; the fight to maintain the stock price was a fight for the life of the company. Before eventually handing over millions of dollars in cash and securities from his own personal strong box, Levin muttered pathetically: *'What hurts most is that in another year we would have been in the clear'*. By this stage, the collapse of the company's top management was total.

When all the fictitious layers were peeled away, EFCA emerged as relatively small, devoid of equity, and totally unprofitable. The money (missing cash, on its own, accounted for $80m) had gone in supporting substantial ongoing losses, occasioned not least by the vast and entirely disproportionate remuneration with which the conspirators enriched themselves.

After prolonged investigation by the state authorities, the SEC and the FBI, Goldblum and 18 others were criminally indicted on 105 counts. The arch-conspirators pleaded guilty, and all received prison sentences – eight years in Goldblum's case. Also imprisoned were two partners and one manager in Equity Funding's audit firm, Wolfson Weiner, which had been absorbed by Seidman & Seidman shortly before the collapse.

It is essential to draw the many strands together and consolidate the vital lessons which must be learnt, not least by auditors, if we are to make even minimal progress by improving the degree of vigilance over corporate activity which is so obviously needed.

The lessons for auditors

- Throughout the period of this growing fraud, the presence of auditors was regarded by the staff and officers of Equity as a mere formality, devoid of substance or significance. The two partners and manager of the small audit firm of Wolfson Weiner who were criminally indicted were in fact so close to Equity that one of them was personally listed in the company's internal telephone directory; a second had left the audit firm to join the accounting staff of Equity, but still 'supervised' the audit. The three indicated were regarded by Equity staff as effectively being on the payroll. Another Wolfson Weiner manager had left the firm to set up on his own account, but retained most of the conspirators as his personal clients. *The lesson: never allow familiarity between auditor and client to undermine the effectiveness of the audit function. Independence in name only makes a mockery of auditing. Even after the later Seidman-Wolfson merger, there was in fact no change in the audit staff involved.*
- Wolfson Weiner was taken over by Seidman & Seidman during 1972, and there is no evidence that Seidman suspected Wolfson Weiner of being complicit or acquiescent in the 'creative' accounting methods of its major client. Nor, unfortunately, is there any evidence of enquiry by them into the relationship between the

Equity officers and Equity auditors prior to the merger – let alone into the procedures adopted by the small firm, with its limited resources, when faced by the audit of a highly complex public conglomerate with a 'go-go' image. The evidence is rather that Seidmans succumbed to the old-fashioned lure of a high return. The fact that the merger has since been dissolved, and Wolfsons stand accused by their acquirers of deliberate deception, is small consolation for the heavy price of being remembered as 'the Equity Funding auditors', and also of being castigated by the SEC for the inadequacy of its procedures. *The lesson: we trust that it is obvious – enquire before you acquire!*

- When Dirks told Seidmans partner Robert Spencer everything he knew about the fraud and allowed him to Xerox all his notes, Spencer promptly took the extraordinary steps of telling Goldblum all that he had heard from Dirks, and handing over a complete set of these notes, which Goldblum duly circulated among his co-conspirators! The correct action, far from playing straight into the hands of the criminals, would have been to investigate the substance of the allegations and proceed immediately to the authorities with the findings, if positive. *The lesson: learn to distinguish when duty to one's client has been superseded by a duty to the public – especially where criminal acts are concerned. The auditor must take the initiative. After all, a criminal client is hardly likely to report one to a professional body for breach of confidence!*
- The auditors seem to have been led by the nose all the way. Some will inevitably suggest that they were trusting to the point of uselessness. The 'blood-hound/watchdog' – even sheepdog – argument hardly applied (unless the auditors are represented by the sheep)! They were content to go through the formalities of confirming assets independently, for example, but invariably allowed themselves to be 'assisted' by being given helpful lists of random file or policy numbers, thereby ensuring that the confirmations always ended up in the hands of the conspirators or their allies. Once the fraud investigation had actually commenced, Seidmans made a series of phone calls to alleged policyholders, and only six out of the 82 persons called turned out to be genuine. The inevitable question: why on earth were there no such phone calls in the course of the normal audit? *The lesson: when faced by technical difficulties*

in the course of verification, avoid the temptation of asking or allowing an obliging client to assist. It is essential to overcome the difficulties oneself if the audit programme is to carry any real significance.

- The disparity in intercompany balances between EFCA and EFLIC would never have been allowed to stand if both companies had had the same firm of auditors. This device of using different auditors only worked because each firm was content to verify the year-end balance (if any) in isolation, without considering either the nature of the voluminous transactions during the year, or the redemption and settlement dates that were so suspiciously close to the year-end dates. *The lesson: audit confirmations should always include direct contact with the other auditors on matters such as inter-company balances, and should require the submission and exchange of complete copies of all the book entries in the respective accounts during the period under review.*
- When the auditors were told that the files requested were not immediately available, they were always content to wait a day or two. *The lesson: standards of vigilance should have required them to insist on at least a handful of such files being traced immediately, regardless of any alleged inconvenience to staff. The auditors appear to have been altogether too accommodating – no doubt due to the circumstances described in the first point above.*
- Whenever the auditors decided to review the funded programmes control account, the computer would be made to duplicate a real programme a sufficient number of times so as to reach a total figure equal to the amount that the company was reporting for its funded programmes. The genuine programme bore five-digit numbers – repeated over and over again on the bogus tape. But the computer was programmed to print out only the last three digits. When the auditors asked to see the full five-digit codes they were told (and accepted) that this could not be done for mechanical reasons. Whenever the auditors attempted to confirm the bogus funded programmes direct with their 'owners', a series of three-digit numbers would be provided that resulted in the confirmations being sent to employees, their relatives or close friends, who having been advised in advance that the exercise was part of a computer 'test', would obligingly sign and return the confirmations to the auditors.

When the SEC asked the computer manager at Equity if he had spoken to the auditors, he replied that he had never even seen them. In the circumstances, what chance was there of them discovering, for instance, that there was no computer file of insurance policies that actually reconciled with the figure on the company's balance sheet? *The lesson: the client's computer expertise must be matched by that of the audit staff. The Equity auditors were attempting to audit 'round' the computer, when the complete absence of an audit trail ought to have made it obvious that the computer itself had to be used as a prime audit tool.*

The above lessons may appear to be too general, even facile – and yet the Equity auditors came nowhere near following them. The overriding lesson, of course, is that auditors dare not bury their heads in the books, hoping that everything outside of them is in order. They should audit the client – not merely the client's records or accounts. Just as a good doctor treats the whole patient, not just surface appearances or symptoms, so to the skilled auditor, it is the total picture which matters. Ray Dirks, understandably, is bitter about auditors:

> If the Equity Funding scandal proves anything, it is that auditors as safeguards are worthless. The 'independent' auditor may not be independent. Paid by the company being audited, he is worried about keeping the account. A frequently heard comment after the scandal became public was that 'routine auditing procedures aren't designed to detect fraud'. If routine auditing procedures cannot detect 64,000 phony insurance policies, $25m in counterfeit bonds and $100m in missing assets, what is the purpose of audits?

Dirks has, one must admit, a point.

The final indictment, however, is not merely of ineffectual auditors; state investigators hamstrung by their own regulations; credulous investors; salespeople and staff more concerned for the security and size of their pay than where it was coming from; or even the immoral and rapacious men who plotted the entire burlesque. The ultimate indictment lumps them all together – for the great shock of the Equity Funding scandal was the slackness of effort it exposed. Underwriters examined the company with care; banks analysed it intensively before lending it money; lawyers were paid vast fees to prepare each public prospectus; outside actuaries certified the insurance reserves; auditors passed the accounts without reservation. Every one of them failed – totally.

And the law? That proved to be an equally ineffectual safeguard. Every financial scandal prompts a cry for new legislation to prevent it happening again – and yet all the illegal manoeuvring that took place at Equity Funding has always been illegal: the need is certainly not for new laws. More than 1,000 people were on the Equity payroll, and yet only 22 were indicted. Many others suspected something was going on, even knew about it in some detail – yet it was their reluctance, based entirely on fear, to go to the authorities that highlights the impotence of just those authorities, despite all appearances of power and thoroughness.

Let the final word go to Ray Dirks, whose solo sleuthing in uncovering one of the most unwholesome spectres of this age uniquely qualifies him to sum it all up:

> When conscience is immobilised, public trust has disappeared. At that point, by default, institutions become omnipotent. May Equity Funding tell us, at a minimum, that there is work to be done not simply to police our commerce, but to redeem the efficacy of will.

Glossary

Analytical procedures These procedures are adopted by an auditor with the objective of assessing the plausibility of the financial statements as a whole. It requires an original and intelligent approach, and no single blueprint will fit all situations. Although analytical review normally requires comparisons to be made with equivalent amounts and ratios in the accounts of earlier years, and explanations found for unexpected variations, it will be necessary to broaden the test by taking account of external economic factors affecting the business such as currency fluctuations, significant changes in the raw material cost of components and factors affecting the markets that apply to the industry as a whole. Such features would be expected to be reflected in the entity's accounts and their absence would be surprising, triggering further enquiry on the part of the auditor.

Bank reconciliation This is an important internal control designed to ensure consistency between what is recorded in the company's cash book and its bank statements. The reconciliation process will adjust the balance in the cash book by adding all cheques paid but unpresented at the bank at the month end, and deducting charges made by the bank that appear on the bank statement but have not yet been recorded in the cash book. Deductions will also be made for lodgements recorded in the cash book but not yet reflected in the bank statement. Performing regular bank reconciliations is a rudimentary but indispensible internal control because it ensures that all transactions affecting the movement of cash have been accurately recorded.

Circularisation of debtors and creditors This is an audit procedure whereby direct confirmation of balances shown on the sales and purchase ledgers are sought and obtained directly from the third parties concerned. It is normal for the client entity to give the auditor permission to contact the suppliers and customers (or a sample of them) for the purpose of requesting such confirmation. This is a process that would, for example, serve to uncover fraudulent activities such as teeming and lading (see entry below).

Closely-held company A closely-held company has a small group of controlling shareholders. By contrast, a widely-held company has many shareholders. This is not to be confused with a 'close company', a term that applies under UK tax legislation to companies whose controlling parties number five or fewer individuals or other entities and which meet other criteria.

Companies under common control These are companies whose controlling interests are held by the same individual(s). Since there is no corporate ownership such companies will not form part of a 'group' for accounting purposes.

Control accounts As the name suggests these accounts act as a control over arithmetical accuracy in the personal ledgers described in this glossary. For example, the purchase ledger control account will be a complete reflection 'in total' of all the transactions recorded as credits in the ledger, and all payments recorded as debits so that the balance on the control account will be the same as the total of individual balances held in the personal accounts in the ledger itself.

Cut-off procedures Business does not grind to a halt at a company's year-end. Purchases and sales continue to be made and processed, production continues and goods move in and out of stores. At the crucial moment of close of business on the last day of the accounting period it is therefore necessary to apply a 'cut-off' that ensures consistency between

- transactions treated as sales;
- the corresponding debtor balance;
- the exclusion of items sold from the stock inventories, irrespective of their physical whereabouts at that moment.

Exactly the same principle applies to purchases, creditors and the inclusion of items purchased in stock, again regardless of whether they have in fact arrived at the warehouse.

Financial reporting and auditing standards Since the 1960s the professional accountancy bodies in the United Kingdom, Europe, the USA and several other jurisdictions have been developing reporting standards on the form, presentation and content of financial statements as an adjunct to the requirements of company law. In recent years these have taken on mandatory status and have application to all companies, although they will differ in terms of disclosure and technical complexity depending on whether the company is listed on a recognised stock exchange, involved in the financial services sector and, finally, by reference to defined size criteria. Requirements applicable in different jurisdictions are in the course of being 'converged' under the banner of International Financial Reporting Standards (IFRS), a process intended to be completed by 2012.

Auditing standards are currently being developed internationally, and these seek to codify the basic methodology that auditors must adopt in the course of their work.

Imprest system This is the part of the overall system of internal control that applies to the regularisation of payments made by petty cash. Such payments are usually relatively small in amount and relate to transactions that are traditionally completed in cash rather than cheque. The *imprest* is the amount held in petty cash from which such disbursements are made, and when the imprest has been exhausted it will be 'topped up' by means of a cash cheque drawn from the main bank account. The control relies on the fact that the amount sitting in petty cash at any time plus the total of expenditure as reflected in the petty cash record and supported by vouchers should equal the original imprest.

Internal control Businesses of any size will invariably install a system of internal control no matter how rudimentary. Regular opening of the post, banking of cheques on a daily basis, ensuring that the cash book can be reconciled with the bank statement and the maintenance of control accounts will all serve to enhance the reliability of the records as a basis for the preparation of management accounts and full annual financial statements. In the case of companies the design and implementation of internal control systems is the responsibility of the directors. In larger businesses responsibilities between members of staff will be divided in such a way that the work of each is automatically checked in the course of the work of others. The larger the entity, the greater the need for increased sophistication in internal control, which also serves as a safeguard against misstatement whether due to irregularity, fraud or error.

Ledgers

Nominal ledger This is the accounting record in which separate accounts are held for each heading of expenditure, income, assets and liabilities. Every transaction, either individually or in total, will be reflected in the appropriate account in the nominal ledger. At the end of the accounting period, income and expenditure accounts will be transferred to the profit and loss accounts, while assets and liabilities will be reflected in the balance sheet.

Sales ledger This is a personal ledger in which non-cash sales are recorded against the name of each customer. Each sales transaction is debited to the customer's account and remittances received credited. The total of all balances in the sales ledger (also known as the debtors ledger) will feature in the balance sheet as a current asset.

Purchase ledger This is the counterpart to the sales ledger. In contrast to the nominal ledger, the sales and purchase ledgers are personal ledgers. In the case of the purchase ledger a separate account is held for each of the entity's suppliers recording purchase transactions as credits and settlements as debits. The total of all balances in the purchase ledger at the year-end will be included in the balance sheet as trade creditors.

Materiality This is a subjective accounting measure that reflects the importance of a particular account balance in relation to the financial statements as a whole. Although materiality is always a matter of judgement, professional standard-setters have endeavoured over the years to prescribe general rules such as 10% of profit or 5% of turnover as yardsticks for the need to correct misstatements. It is always preferable to consider materiality from the point of view of the user of accounts. From this perspective an item would be material if its misstatement or omission would influence the decision of any legitimate user of those accounts, such as shareholders, lenders or prospective investors or creditors.

Post balance sheet events These events need to be considered in order to ascertain whether they are relevant to amounts included in the financial statements. *Adjusting events* are those that provide information on conditions existing at the balance sheet date although not known at the time. An example of an adjusting event is the receipt of a cheque from a customer to settle a material debt previously written off as bad. *Non-adjusting events* are those that do not impact on the accounts but may be of such size or significance (such as a major acquisition shortly after the balance sheet date) that truth and fairness require their disclosure by way of note. Audit work in reviewing the records for the ensuing period are referred to as *post balance sheet tests*.

Revenue recognition Income that is not represented by cash receipts at the period end may nevertheless be included in turnover if certain broad criteria are fulfilled such as the completion of all the material features of a transaction or the finalisation of a contract. Accounting regulators have always had difficulty in providing a reliable recognition formula because the criteria often involved subjective assessment on the probability that cash will ultimately be received. For example, it is not permitted to treat as revenue in the current period the future income flows that management anticipate from the development of a new product or service. Although this may be an obvious example there are many others more finely balanced and judgement will need to be exercised on the point after which revenue can be recognised in the financial statements.

Sampling theory Audit methodology employs sampling because it is physically impossible for an auditor to check every entry in the records and such lengthy and time consuming work would be unproductive in any event. Audit sampling is based on probability theory, which sets out the mathematical parameters within which a properly drawn sample may be relied upon to reflect the properties of the population under scrutiny as a whole. Where the auditor has tested a company's internal controls and found them to be conceptually sound and operating satisfactorily, the corresponding audit risk will be lower and the appropriate sample size will similarly be reduced. A sample may be considered valid provided that the selection of items within that sample reveals no 'errors' as defined in the sampling plan. If errors are found the sample size will need to be increased.

Substantive testing The audit process of authenticating transactions and balances as recorded in the company's books is known as substantive testing. An obvious element in such testing would be to vouch entries in the prime records such as cash book against supporting documentation that has been generated outside of the company's own system. A supplier's invoice would be an example of a document to support a payment recorded in the cash book.

Teeming and lading The origin of this strange term is lost in the mists of time. It refers to a particular type of fraud whereby the perpetrator covers up the theft of remittances from a particular debtor by crediting the debtors account with a remittance (or part thereof) received from another debtor. This process is continued and facilitates further thefts that the perpetrator will be careful to conceal in the same way. In relation to the total value of debtor balances, the sums stolen will normally be relatively small and by carefully 'plugging the dyke' in this way no debtor balance will be allowed to fall into such apparent arrears as to trigger the need for a bad debt provision or reference to a debt collection agency.

An example of teeming and lading is shown in the following illustration.

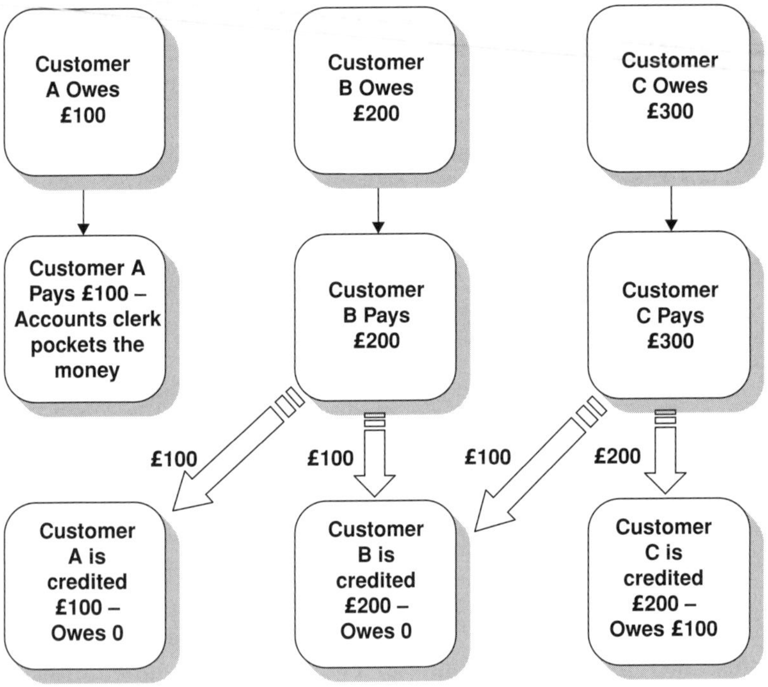

Index

Index compiled by Terry Halliday